MAKERS OF MODERN EUROPE

Edited by DONALD C. McKAY *in association with* DUMAS MALONE

CLEMENCEAU

LONDON : HUMPHREY MILFORD
OXFORD UNIVERSITY PRESS

Harris & Ewing

G Clemenceau

CLEMENCEAU

By

GEOFFREY BRUUN

CAMBRIDGE · MASSACHUSETTS
HARVARD UNIVERSITY PRESS
1943

PRINTED AT THE HARVARD UNIVERSITY PRINTING OFFICE
CAMBRIDGE, MASSACHUSETTS, U.S.A.

EDITOR'S PREFACE

FRANCE of the Third Republic passed through two great crises — 1918 and 1940. In the first she found a man who galvanized the nation to victory by the sheer power of his own will. In the second, France had no such man.

Few will be inclined to disagree with Mr. Bruun's verdict that Clemenceau was above all else a moral force, an embodiment of will and indomitable courage. He was other things — a realist in an age of large and windy words, an idealist, too, in his own way — but first of all he was a force disciplining his fellow countrymen into a great common effort when the slow paralysis of defeatism had already set in.

On the domestic front Clemenceau's career was one of many shades and vicissitudes. But in the foreign field it was monolithic: the German danger was a cold and unchanging obsession with him. For the rigidity of his fears Clemenceau was the subject of attacks, both before and after the first World War. The answer to his critics lies in the bitter vindication of 1940 — Clemenceau had become, says Mr. Bruun, "a Cassandra . . . dowered with a desperate foresight."

On a subject which lends itself to hyperbole, Mr. Bruun has written a book which is pondered and balanced — distinguished by economy of language, by cool and mature judgment, by a refreshing candor in the treatment of the Tiger's weaknesses. It is a book for our time, with dismaying parallels — none more so than the description of Clemenceau discovering in early October 1918 that the war would soon end, while he had still made no preparations for the peace.

The present volume is the third in the series of Makers of Modern Europe. The series has no intention of offering to the public once again the biographies of men which appear with almost monotonous regularity — Napoleon, Cavour, Gladstone, Marx. It proposes instead to present the lives of men for whom there is no adequate biography in English. At the same time these biographies will deal with men who left a significant impress on their age, men who may properly be considered as "Makers of Modern Europe."

DONALD C. MCKAY

WASHINGTON, D. C.,
September 6, 1943

AUTHOR'S PREFACE

THIS estimate of Clemenceau's place in history is not offered as a final or definitive biography. For such a study the time is not yet ripe, and important documentary material is still unavailable. Rather, this is offered as a pertinent appraisal of a European statesman whose significance has increased steadily in contemporary estimation since his death in 1929, and whose heroic devotion to the sterner democratic ideals has not yet been adequately honored in America or in Europe.

To thank individually the many friends and collaborators whose aid and encouragement enabled me to complete this assignment is not possible here. As the pages go to press each one revives some heart-warming recollection of assistance rendered, intelligently, graciously, unselfishly, by staff members in the libraries and archives of France and America, by colleagues who criticized various chapters in manuscript, by friends who made valuable suggestions and furnished illuminating references, and most of all by the editors whose tactful and tireless supervision eliminated many errors and improved many defective passages. For the sake of all these I wish I could have made the work better than it is; for the services of all these, the reader may be assured, the work is much better than it was.

GEOFFREY BRUUN

BROOKLYN, N. Y.,
September 10, 1943

CONTENTS

ILLUSTRATIONS

INTRODUCTION

IT WILL be several decades yet before historians find it easy to form a dispassionate estimate of the work of Georges Clemenceau. Possibly he is destined to remain one of those disputed characters, like Louis XI or Robespierre, about whose methods and motives there will always be conflicting schools of opinion. His temper was so arbitrary, the controversies into which he plunged were so critical and so exacerbating, that the ashes of the fires he fanned are still full of hot embers.

Clemenceau had already played a formative role in the political development of the Third French Republic before the First World War raised him to international fame and the fates which presided over the peace negotiations promoted him to be, in a very literal sense, one of the makers of modern Europe. Since then, the resurgence of Germany and the onset of the Second World War have induced a reëxamination of the Versailles settlement, and Clemenceau's fight for guarantees which might safeguard France no longer appears so vindictive or hysterical as some contemporaries considered it. When the history of the nineteenth century is viewed in longer perspective his penetrating comprehension of the forces shaping modern European civilization will be more deeply appreciated. He was a political philosopher as well as a politician, and his writings no less than his parliamentary and diplomatic labors will demand a judicious reappraisal as the picture of his age grows more complete.

For greatness as for genius there is no simple formula and perhaps it would be idle to argue here whether Clemenceau had a tincture of one or both. His outstanding quality was a ruthless realism which made him a touchstone of the genuine amid the shams, the sophists, and the mountebanks of a hypocritical age. His second noteworthy quality was courage. He dared to proclaim unpleasant truths and to fight for unpopular causes, rare attributes among men and rarer still among democratic statesmen. A third quality, which some might be disposed to deny him, was idealism. It was a crusty, harsh, and practical idealism; it proposed to accept man as he is, and to improve him, if improvement were possible, by sweat and tears. Above all, it proposed to treat him as a creature who could not be helped if he would not help himself. A propensity for myopic optimism, euphemistic promises, and Utopian formulas Clemenceau considered the major curse of humankind, and his indictment of most humanitarians, from Jean Jaurès to Woodrow Wilson, was that "their verbs were all in the future tense."

The significance of Clemenceau for his epoch will be found in this gift for astringent and realistic judgments. His mind mirrored realities; but because those realities were darker truths than most of his contemporaries cared to contemplate he seemed a sardonic Cassandra and his judgments appeared unwarrantedly black, like photographic negatives, correct in detail and proportion, but outlining familiar scenes and situations with the *chiaroscuro* starkly reversed. Time alone can test the veracity of a statesman's vision, and the years which have passed since Clemenceau retired in 1920 are too brief to establish his full significance. But his stature has continued to loom above the pigmies who succeeded him and many Frenchmen today must pray for a leader with the courage, the clarity, and the singleminded patriotism which inspired "the Tiger."

CLEMENCEAU

CHAPTER I

STUDENT AND VOYAGER
1841–1870

My people have always lived in the Vendée. And it is strange: I love the Vendéeans. They are decent people. . . . They have an ideal, and to defend it they have something stubborn, narrow and savage in them, which I like.[1]

GEORGES CLEMENCEAU was a son of the Vendée, and this fact affords more surely than anything else the clue to his tumultuous life. To the student of French history the name of this western *département* is forever charged with memories of bitter and uncompromising struggle. Here on the Biscayan coast, between Nantes and La Rochelle, some of the fiercest campaigns of the Wars of Religion were fought to a close. Here, after 1792, the hatreds kindled by the French Revolution burned themselves out in murderous sieges and reprisals. The natives of this region are tough, self-centered fighters, and when roused to conflict they defend their patrimony with a furious resolution as if obeying some dark imperious mandate of their blood.

This obstinate and egoistic strain in the Vendéean character owes much to the local environment. The province faces the Atlantic, turning its back upon the rest of France. Its farms and villages lie scattered and secretive, entrenched behind heavy thickets and wooded acres. Even the highways, sunken and masked in vegetation, appear almost impenetrable to a stranger. The land is made for lairs and ambuscades, for a people proud of their self-sufficiency, stubborn and independent. Beneath the ragged pastoral charm, beneath the ferns and woodbine and pink heather of the uplands, the plough that probes deeply enough soon discovers ribs of harsh unyielding rock.

A hundred years have wrought no great change in the straggling, low-roofed village of Mouilleron-en-Pareds where Georges Eugène Benjamin Clemenceau was born on September 28, 1841. Local tradition still retains some memories of a self-willed, precocious child, with sombre eyes, who

[1] Jean Martet, *Clemenceau* (New York: Longmans, 1930), p. 119.

walked those ways a century ago hungering after realities. To Georges as to many superior children childhood was a prison. He found the companionship of his brothers and sisters tedious, and soon experienced the indelible irony of discovering that most adults were equally stupid. Books offered him the readiest escape from the boredom of adolescence, and he read captiously and arrogantly, under a constant impulse to vindicate his conjectures. The bent of his thought was for harsh and mundane truths and his favorite literature was rationalistic, scientific, and secular.

All his youthful capacity for friendship and admiration focused itself upon his solemn father, who treated him as an equal, and responded gravely to his overtures from the depths of an intense but reserved nature. Dr. Paul-Benjamin Clemenceau was dominated by an austere sense of civic duty, and his son, accompanying him on his visits to the poor, learned to understand and respect this compulsion to serve the incapable. Under a more liberal government the doctor might well have become a distinguished public servant, but as a materialist in his philosophy, a republican in his politics, and an anti-clerical in his convictions, he remained out of favor with the functionaries who served Napoleon III. In 1858 his unconcealed opposition to the imperial régime led to his temporary arrest, until popular sentiment in the *département* induced the authorities to release instead of transporting him. This reprieve did nothing to placate the burning indignation of the sixteen-year-old Georges, who took an oath to avenge the injustice which his father had endured. But the elder Clemenceau rebuked his son's impetuosity. "If you wish to avenge me, work!" he chided with characteristic reserve.[2]

Georges had already decided to follow his father's profession. His quick mind mastered the medical courses without difficulty, first at the School of Medicine at Nantes, and after 1860 in Paris. But he found the duties of an interne and the rigors of research a dull discipline and preferred the political debates that raged in his favorite cafés. Even his dissertation, a dull enquiry *De la génération des éléments anatomiques*, transformed itself into a polemic in defense of materialistic monism, and he confessed as much in a candid preface. "I alone am responsible for the opinions which I express. I do not hold them because I have written this work. I have written this work because I hold them."[3] But despite the *a priori* character of his reasoning he had the satisfaction of seeing the thesis accepted by the

[2] Georges Suarez, *Clemenceau*, 2 vols. (Paris: Les Éditions de France, 1932), I, 31.
[3] Jean Martet, *Clemenceau* (New York), p. 311.

Faculty of Medicine of the University of Paris and received his diploma on May 30, 1865.

Meanwhile his political enthusiasms, which lay so much closer to his heart, had brought him to the attention of the police. He had arrived in Paris with a letter to the republican politician Étienne Arago, he joined the circle of admirers who paid court to Louis Auguste Blanqui in his prison cell, and in 1861 he threw in his lot with the group of radical journalists who edited *Travail.* This modest weekly described itself as a "Literary and Scientific Journal" and the first number contained some lugubrious verses entitled *Doute* by an unknown young poet named Émile Zola. Behind a façade of lofty abstract critiques the collaborators played a gleeful game of hide-and-seek with the censor, masking their political allusions in philosophical jargon. But to the young Clemenceau such restrained intellectual baiting appeared too tame. In February, 1862, he joined a couple of friends in the more exciting pastime of posting placards reminding the people of Paris of their lost liberties, and was promptly picked up by the police on a charge of inciting to riot. Two months in Mazas jail gave him a chance to meditate on the rewards of martyrdom and he emerged in a more bitter but more cautious mood. The gesture had been a typical act of sophomoric audacity, and during his three remaining years as a medical student he walked more circumspectly.

To celebrate the capture of his diploma in the spring of 1865 Georges and his father took a short holiday in England. A Paris publisher had agreed to bring out a second edition of the *Génération des éléments anatomiques* in exchange for a French translation of John Stuart Mill's essays on *Auguste Comte and Positivism.* Armed with the assignment, Clemenceau visited the venerable British philosopher and economist in London and received his assent to the project. The labor of translation so lightly assumed turned out to be a severe apprenticeship in English prose. Clemenceau had no real enthusiasm for abstract thinking and he abhorred long ineluctable sentences that "unrolled like carpets." His version, which carried over Mill's ideas with more force than subtlety, appeared in Paris three years later.

In the interval Clemenceau found other and pleasanter methods of mastering English. His interest had turned in this summer of 1865 towards the United States, where the final act of the great American tragedy had recently ended with the assassination of Lincoln. To visit the battlefields of the Civil War, analyze the problems of reconstruction, and study democracy at first hand offered more promise of adventure than settling down to a medical practice in Paris. His father, unselfish as ever, provided the means, and at the close of the year Georges Clemenceau disembarked in New York.

What had commenced as a visit lightly undertaken stretched to a four-year sojourn. The dynamic rhythm of American life stimulated Clemenceau's ambitions. He traveled as far south as Florida, visited Washington several times, and even meditated a journey to California. But New York remained his center of activity, and the bookshops, restaurants, and clubs of Greenwich Village his favorite resorts. As the months passed his father became impatient for his return and threatened to cancel his allowance. But New York society pleased Clemenceau, and his accomplishments served as his recommendation. His nimble wit, his horsemanship, his skill with sword and pistol, supplemented by an elaborate wardrobe from his Parisian tailor, fitted him to play the part of the romantic foreigner. There were receptions and hunting parties, and amiable ladies who acknowledged his charm, but his popularity could not blind him to the distrust which his American hosts felt for him as an outsider. Socially, his American adventure remained a comedy of manners that lacked sincerity and substance.

To supplement his income he undertook to compose letters on American affairs for the Paris *Temps* for which he ultimately received a stipend of 150 francs a month. These dispatches, with their clipped and positive style, marked him out as a born journalist. The ideas, it is true, were seldom original; he echoed the views of American leaders whom he came to admire, of Wendell Phillips, of Charles Sumner and Thaddeus Stevens, and he carried away many sage asides from talks with Horace Greeley, whom he met soon after his arrival. No democratic government had ever met a sterner test than the War between the States had imposed on Lincoln's administration; and Clemenceau followed with ardent hope the struggles of reconstruction. His faith, almost unlimited at the outset, pictured the emancipated negroes as worthy to take their place in time alongside the whites and compete with them on equal terms. Had not European serfs a few centuries earlier been equally backward and brutalized? But longer acquaintance with the "peculiar institution" darkened his optimism, and his final comments found his democratic and his scientific principles in conflict. The future of the blacks lay in their own hands: their character would be their destiny. "In this ruthless struggle for existence carried on by human society, those who are weaker physically, intellectually, or morally must in the end yield to the stronger. The law

The Bettmann Archive

Clemenceau at the age of ten, from a portrait reputedly painted by his father.

is hard, but there is no use rebelling."[4] The "law," which he had learned about since he wrote his doctoral thesis four years earlier, was Darwin's theory of natural selection.

To Clemenceau, with his ardent and combative temper, the scientific Calvinism implicit in the doctrine of survival of the fittest made a strong appeal. To be of the elect, who fight without thought of concession to the last ounce of energy and beyond, was already his secret ideal. It is astonishing in these letters how seldom and how reluctantly he acknowledged the virtue of compromise: a question is never settled, he reiterates, until it is settled right. All his ardor was reserved for the political conflicts, and as the great battle over reconstruction developed between Andrew Johnson and an obdurate Congress he portrayed with delight the unyielding pride of the chief protagonists. Charles Sumner he thought somewhat rigid and academic, but in Thaddeus Stevens he divined a twin spirit and his admiration was spontaneous and frank. The incredible tenacity with which Stevens clung to life and fought for his principles to his last breath incited Clemenceau to pen an eloquent obituary.

> Devoted heart and soul to the service of one ideal, the immediate abolition of slavery, he threw his whole self with no reserve and no personal after-thoughts into the cause he had chosen. . . . It must be admitted that Mr. Stevens stands out as a man of only one idea, but that does not matter a whit, since he had the glory of defending that idea when it was trodden in the dust, and the joy of contributing largely to its triumph. That should be enough accomplishment for one man, when the cause to which he has devoted his life and soul is that of justice.[5]

For the "Man in the White House," whose dogged opposition threatened for three years to negate the decision of the battlefield, Clemenceau felt a mixed sentiment. He did not doubt that Johnson was mistaken in standing against the forces of progress, but he came to believe the president sincere and respected his courage. As the tide of battle closed in on the White House and its lonely defender a note of admiration crept into his comments and he confessed that "Mr. Johnson believes in the power of daring." He thought the resolution to impeach the president would carry. "Mr. Johnson," he wrote, "like Medea, stands absolutely alone. He is his sole remaining friend. Unhappily, he does not suffice."[6] The power of Congress to depose a despotic executive, he continued, might well appear

[4] Georges Clemenceau, *American Reconstruction, 1865–1870, and the Impeachment of President Johnson*, ed. by Fernand Baldensperger (New York: Lincoln MacVeagh, 1928), p. 98.

[5] Clemenceau, *American Reconstruction*, pp. 225–226.

[6] *American Reconstruction*, p. 169.

surprising to citizens of "some other countries"; and radical readers of the *Temps,* who had pondered for fifteen years how to rid France of Napoleon III, could hardly fail to appreciate this implied contrast between the Second Empire and the United States. When the Senate failed to sustain the charges of impeachment the *dénouement* seemed to Clemenceau a lame and impotent conclusion.

The outstanding issue in Franco-American relations during these years, the attempt of Napoleon III to establish Maximilian on the throne of Mexico, Clemenceau chronicled without enthusiasm, interspersing his comments with allusions to the Fenian plots against Canada and the Indian wars in the west. Most circles of American opinion, he observed, accepted the news of Maximilian's execution in 1867 with no great pangs of conscience. The withdrawal of the French expeditionary force, which had left Maximilian defenseless, he passed over in silence, save for the sardonic comment that nobody remains loyal to a lost cause. The remark, like his loss of interest when the impeachment of Johnson failed, is revealing. Clemenceau loved a battle more than its outcome. Once a decision was in sight his interest shifted to other fields of fray.

This zest for conflict swept him into the rabid presidential campaign of 1868. The passion, the abuse and recrimination, which broke out in the press and often led to fist fights at the political rallies, was undignified, he confessed. But it was a sign of vitality, a form of catharsis which served to keep the body politic in a state of health. Secretly and inwardly he was more than a little perturbed by the chaotic manner in which this democracy went about the task of choosing a new president, and the only answer he found for such doubts was a stout affirmation of faith in the virtues of democracy and the hardihood of the American political system.

> The people of the United States (he reminded himself) have a peculiar faculty for adjusting themselves to circumstances and learning by experience, suddenly changing their course and thus nearly always disappointing prophets of disaster. The Americans will make mistakes but they will quickly find out how to remedy them. They will lose their way temporarily among the problems which beset them, trying out and abandoning unsatisfactory solutions, but in the end, when truth and justice have taken some kind of shape and revealed themselves to the eyes of the world, the people will seize upon them.[7]

What Clemenceau was seeking to identify and isolate, and seeking in vain, was the principle of harmony or unity which would constrain the divergent factions in the republic to cohere again once the majority had

[7] *American Reconstruction,* p. 40.

spoken. The schisms, the centrifugal forces in this riven democracy, were so strongly manifested in 1868 he asked himself what opposite drives could be counted upon to balance them. The problem was one which he had probed ardently in another field: his medical dissertation had been in its conception a search for the secret of growth which governed the development of a living organism and determined the harmonious functioning of its parts in relation to the whole. Now, analyzing the mechanism of a political organism, he found himself balked again in his effort to put his finger on the balance wheel, to identify the rectifying principle which would induce the discordant factors to adjust their rhythms and work together in political unity.

Such doubts and questions regarding the inward meaning and purpose of life and society had been answered in earlier times by faith in God as the creator and ruler of a universe which contained many mysteries too deep for human understanding. The fact that these enigmas still assailed Clemenceau so persistently at twenty-seven, and were to prove a lifelong heritage, marks him out indelibly as a son of the nineteenth century. He had embraced the dogmas of science and democracy as the twin gospels of his age, but he was too intelligent to believe their oracles had all the answers. Rationalism offered but a dusty comment on man's inmost hopes and aspirations, and the intellect alone could not harmonize the passions or even evolve a uniform system of philosophy. There remained always, in the individual as in society, the need for a subtler and sterner mode of integration than a constitutional document or a written code of morals could provide.

This integration, so elusive an ideal when sought intellectually, Clemenceau found for himself in the hammer blows of conflict. He plunged into each new fray with a sense of escape from indecision and fought each issue with the narrow, belligerent fury of a peasant defending his fields. His real convictions, he discovered, were in his blood rather than his brain; like a peasant he put his basic trust in character and energy and will. Abstract speculation and intangible ideals were the smoke of battle, not its substance. His strength did not lie in breadth of understanding nor profundity of thought but in this lonely and intrepid and unfailing zest for the fight. To Clemenceau ideas were weapons, thought was a form of action, action was life, and life was conflict.

The penalty of such intractable egoism is too often a sense of desolate and incommunicable singularity. The result is likely to be an inability to share life genuinely or generously with any constant companion. For such characters as Clemenceau's love and marriage is a nemesis which, accepted, divides their will and falsifies their convictions, or rejected, dedicates them afresh to their lonely belligerence. The young Clemenceau, cynical, headstrong, and singular, was not good matrimonial material. It is not remarkable that the marriage which he contracted during these American *Wanderjahre*, with a girl of different nationality, temperament, and ideals, should have ended after a few years in a permanent separation.

Despite the interest and research expended upon it, the romance of Georges Clemenceau and Mary Plummer remains, as perhaps such matters have a right to remain, private and obscure. They first became acquainted, apparently, in Stamford, Connecticut, where, after 1867, Clemenceau gave lessons in French and equitation at a girls' school. Mary Plummer was one of his pupils, and their engagement was announced in 1868. But Clemenceau's refusal to accept a religious ceremony, and other differences, perhaps, which are unchronicled, dissolved the engagement, and Clemenceau returned to France. A correspondence continued, however; the disagreements were finally harmonized; and Clemenceau once more embarked for America. His marriage to Mary Plummer, a civil ceremony, took place at the New York City Hall, June 23, 1869, and he sailed for France with his bride a few days later. Clemenceau was twenty-seven, his bride nineteen.[8]

Their first abode, naturally, was the ancestral farm in the Vendée. But after a few months they moved to Paris, where Clemenceau opened a practice as a doctor of medicine. Three children were born to them, Madeleine, Therèse and Michel, Madame Clemenceau spending part of her time with her husband, who was soon immersed in the political *mêlée* of the capital, and part with her parents-in-law. Growing differences of temperament divided them, and after seven years a separation was

[8] The certificate of marriage is on file at the Department of Health, Bureau of Vital Records and Statistics, New York City. It is filled out in somewhat perfunctory fashion and the information is not complete. Clemenceau's date of birth is not given, but his age at next birthday is cited as 27 (altered correctly to 28), his place of birth, Mouilleron-en-Pareds (Vendée), is filled in apparently in his own hand, the profession listed for him is physician and the place of residence Paris. Of his given names only one, George (*sic*) is mentioned. His father's name is listed simply at Benjamin, his mother's maiden name as Emma Gautreau. The bride's full name is given as Mary E. Plummer, age at next birthday 19 (corrected to 20), place of birth Springfield, Mass., place of residence, City of New York. Her father's name is given as William K., her mother's maiden name simply as Harriet A. Neither Clemenceau nor his wife signed the affidavit in the record book that the information given was correct, though they may, of course, have signed the copy of the certificate which they took away with them.

arranged. They were never reunited. But Clemenceau was too surely the son of his father, that reserved but deeply dutiful and affectionate man, for one to underestimate the scars which this separation left upon his heart. The failure of his marriage intensified the misanthropic elements of his nature, exiled him from the softening and circumscribing influences of domesticity, and left him free to employ all his phenomenal energy in politics and journalism. Had his marriage proved happier, and the details of family life commanded a larger share of his time and attention, he might never have evolved into "the Tiger," that ruthless and predatory recalcitrant of French politics, who formed so few permanent friendships, trusted so few collaborators, and justified his sobriquet by his preference for fighting alone.

CHAPTER II

MAYOR OF MONTMARTRE
1870–1871

It forced upon me a sound appreciation of the stupidity of public life to find myself between two parties, both of which desired my death.[1]

CLEMENCEAU

THE OUTBREAK of the Franco-Prussian War in the summer of 1870, and the violent changes which it unleashed in Paris, transformed Clemenceau from a doctor of medicine to a practicing politician. Like most of his circle of Parisian friends, journalists, radical students, deputies of the republican opposition, he viewed the war during its first six weeks with mingled feelings. Military affairs, it became clearer daily, were going badly for France, but French victories, to the republicans, would have been equally disturbing, for they would have served to regild, like a new dawn, the tarnished imperial régime of Napoleon III.

By September it was evident that the Second Empire was staggering to a fall, but the swiftness of the event took all Europe by surprise. On September 2, while Clemenceau and his friends were still concerting their plans for such an event, one hundred thirty miles away a white flag fluttered from the citadel at Sedan and Von Moltke dictated the terms under which 85,000 French troops laid down their arms. It was Saturday, the third, before the news of Sedan was released in Paris. Military censorship and ministerial evasion could no longer conceal the magnitude of the disaster: MacMahon's army had surrendered, Napoleon III was a prisoner of war, Bazaine and his forces were shut up in Metz.

In the squares of Paris groups of incredulous citizens gathered to read the announcements, lingered a moment, and then dispersed in stunned silence. But in the Legislative Chamber a hum of activity rose from the benches of the Left. The republican deputies, hitherto an ineffective minority, suddenly beheld the vision of power confronting them, like a

[1] Georges Clemenceau, *Le Silence de M. Clemenceau*, ed. by Jean Martet (Paris: A. Michel, 1929), p. 210.

riderless horse, theirs for the mounting. And in obscure corners of Montmartre and Belleville secret committees were organizing, students and radicals, journalists and jobbers, Blanquists and Internationalists, planning how best to seize and use the pliant hour which fate had suddenly offered them.

After a night of rumors Paris roused itself for a day of action. As if stirred by a single impulse the Sunday crowds marched through the clear September sunlight towards the Place de la Concorde. They were unarmed crowds, and unorganized, save for some detachments of National Guards, but they were united by universal indignation and they had come to voice a summary demand. The emperor must be dethroned, the imperial bunglers responsible for the ignominious defeats must be swept from office. While the Chambers hesitated, hunting precedents, a mob poured into the assembly hall, rendering deliberation impossible. Léon Gambetta gratified the visitors with a proclamation declaring the Napoleonic dynasty at an end, and then escaped to the Hôtel-de-Ville to organize a new government. By nightfall the leaders of the republican minority —Jules Favre, Léon Gambetta, Ernest Picard, Emmanuel Arago, and others—had divided among themselves the portfolios of the superseded ministry. Avid of power, they stepped recklessly into the void created by the wholesale repudiation of a régime, before popular agitators and socialist leaders could rally their supporters and press for equivalent recognition. The Second Empire was at an end. *Vive la République! Vive le Gouvernement de la Défense Nationale!*

Swept along with the crowds on September 4, Clemenceau cheered the downfall of a régime which he had hated since childhood. But his quick mind reached beyond the moment's tumult, his ambitious feet were already seeking the ladder of opportunity. At last he had friends in power with appointments to dispense, and his qualifications for office were self-evident. As a youth he had been jailed for attacking the imperial government; as a disciple of Blanqui he had sat at the master's feet when the latter held court in his cell at Sainte Pélagie; as a medical student he had ministered to the poor and earned their regard. Arthur Ranc, Clemenceau's mentor in the art of politics, had received a prompt summons from Gambetta to assist in organizing the new order. It is probable that Clemenceau accompanied Ranc to the Hôtel-de-Ville on September 5; certainly by the close of that day he had won his coveted appointment. A decree signed by Étienne Arago, the new Mayor of Paris, named him Mayor of the Eighteenth Arrondissement, and the following day his friend, Jean Lafont, with whom he then resided at 19, rue Capron, joined him as assistant.[2]

The assignment was no sinecure. The section of Montmartre, a working-class district, had long been a center of radical agitation. Its famous buttes, now crowned by the incredible Byzantine contours of Sacre Coeur, were then the Sinai of a new faith whence the proletarian oracle launched its thunders. Clemenceau's energies were taxed to exhaustion in the weeks that followed, rationing coal and oil among the destitute, organizing relief bureaus, heartening the timorous, equipping the National Guard. His poverty-ridden section was the first to face privation when the Prussians invested Paris three weeks later. It is a tribute to his administrative vigor and political acumen that he won the respect of his disrespectful constituents. They soon learned to recognize his stocky figure, the quick tread, the abrupt, imperious gestures, the lean, bearded face, the darting glance. At every hour of the day and night they encountered him in action, haranguing the dispirited, arbitrating disputes, prescribing for the sick, inspecting the ramparts, his mordant comments punctuated by the flashes of the Prussian guns beyond Pantin and Aubervilliers. Had all appointees of the new régime been his equals in talent and decision the story of the siege might have marched to a braver conclusion.

But the Government of National Defense failed in the one field in which it could not afford to fail: it failed as a government of defense. From their first day in power the republican ministers were condemned to maintain their ascendency by deception; to preach faith in victory when all of them, Gambetta perhaps excepted, believed the war already lost; to pretend that they had the authority to speak for France when constitutionally they could not claim to speak even for Paris; to affirm the power of the populace while excluding the populace from power. A plebiscite held in May, 1870, had demonstrated that genuine republican sentiment was confined to a few large towns, Paris in particular, and the elections of 1871 were to reaffirm this truth. Yet the *arrivistes* of September 4 dictated to the nation as masters, ignoring the fact that their emotional mandate was void unless it could be validated by victory. Had they reversed the drama of defeat France might have rallied to them. But their inflated proclamations, like the balloons they sent over the enemy lines, seemed

[2] Joseph Reinach, ed., *Dépêches, circulaires, décrets, proclamations, et discours de Léon Gambetta*, 2 vols. (Paris, 1886–91), I, 8. Clemenceau received his appointment direct from Étienne Arago. The order was first published in *Clemenceau peint par lui-même*, ed. by Jean Martet (Paris: A. Michel, 1929), pp. 164–165.

futile gestures in face of the relentless German successes. France lost confidence in Paris and Paris lost contact with France, for the political estrangement already separating the capital from the country was sealed by the military investment. Before September, 1870, Paris and France had spoken different political dialects. After four months of siege they were to speak different dialectics.

Despite their deftness in changing horses in the middle of a stream, the republican ministers found it impossible to organize a government or prosecute the war effectively. Gambetta escaped by balloon early in October to stimulate resistance in the provinces; but he left his colleagues in Paris paralyzed by their conflicting aims and hounded by defeat and disaffection. On October 31 they were forced to reveal that Bazaine had capitulated with 185,000 men at Metz, and that Thiers was seeking Bismarck to request an armistice. Once again the cauldron of popular indignation boiled over. A bewildered mob, crowding into the Hôtel-de-Ville with Gustave Flourens at their head, declared the government deposed. But the attempted *coup* miscarried and after a few hours saner counsels prevailed. To retrieve itself the Government of National Defense proposed a plebiscite for November 3, and the Parisians, sobered by the gravity of the crisis, confirmed its authority by a vote of 557,996 against 62,638.[3] Recognizing the implications of this popular mandate, the government pledged a war to the end.

A further election, held three days later, legalized the status of the mayors who had been appointed September 5. Clemenceau, who sympathized with the sentiment in his section, had proclaimed publicly on October 31 that an armistice would be an act of treason. Satisfied, the electors confirmed him in office by 9409 votes.[4] His hands were no longer so free, however, nor his rule undisputed. The faithful Lafont remained at his side, but as a makeweight the electors assigned him two extra adjutants of a more radical temper. Victor Jaclard, a labor organizer whose goal was a workers' republic, Clemenceau found it possible to respect. But Simon Dereure was dangerous. This ex-shoemaker, with the forehead of a scholar, black brows that veiled his eyes, and a cold, inscrutable smile, had higher ambitions than a post in the local *mairie*. As a leader in the International Association of Workers, and an accomplice in the bomb plot of 1870, he had been jailed by the imperial police, then set at liberty with other political prisoners on September 4. Instantly he set to work to

[3] Thomas March, *The History of the Paris Commune of 1871* (London, 1896), p. 52.

[4] *Clemenceau peint par lui-même*, p. 166.

organize a Committee of Vigilance in the Montmartre section. His abode at 17, rue de Clignancourt, became a center of underground agitation, where he shared the prestige of leadership with other revolutionaries of whom Paris was to hear more. Théophile Ferré came there daily, his lips pursed, his tiny *pince-nez* gleaming at the top of his long hooked nose. And Raoul Rigault was to be seen hurrying in and out, laden with lists of proscripts which he was compiling against the day of the people's vengeance. Clemenceau knew of Dereure's revolutionary activities, though officially he found it expedient to ignore them, and in company the two men watched each other warily, dissembling their distrust.

The Eighteenth Arrondissement had become a microcosm of Paris itself. In each of the twenty sections committees of vigilance came into existence after September 4, nominating delegates to a *Comité Central* which met at the headquarters of the International Association in the Place de la Corderie du Temple. Like Clemenceau in his *mairie*, the Ministry of National Defense wasted energy sparring against a relentless shadow government which waited to supplant it. To the people of Paris, in this winter of their discontent, the temptation grew stronger after each reverse to place the terrible weapon of their anger in the hands of these illegal and irresponsible committees. And as the tide of popular anger rose, the gendarmes, already compromised by their affiliation with the defunct empire, found their authority declining daily. Units of National Guards usurped the police functions in fifteen of the twenty arrondissements, and the government accepted the rebuff nervelessly, too uncertain of its power to reinforce its police agents when these dutiful officers of the law were insulted and disarmed by the sovereign people.

By January, when bread had grown scarce though wine remained plentiful, and horses that dropped in the street were carved to cutlets where they fell, the Central Committee came into the open. On the sixth, placards appeared on the walls stigmatizing the *Gouvernement de la Défaillance Nationale* for cowardice and incompetence and calling for the election of a Commune. Goaded to action, the government ordered a sortie for January 19; when it collapsed, General Trochu, military governor of Paris, was dismissed to cover the failure. But the disgust and anger of the populace could not be so easily appeased. On January 22 several companies of National Guards from the workers' sections attacked the Hôtel-de-Ville: they were beaten off by loyal Breton Mobiles with the loss of some twenty lives. Above those decrepit forms strewn about the Place de l'Hôtel-de-Ville the Parisians stared at one another as if awakening from an evil dream. This civil strife, added to the miseries of the siege, dismayed and sickened them. Yet their spirit remained unbroken. "In all these terrible circumstances no man talks either of surrender or of peace," the American envoy Washburne wrote on January 25.[5] He was mistaken. Jules Favre was talking of surrender at the Prussian headquarters, and Paris learned the terms three days later.

With this capitulation the legend of a popular betrayal took on the mask of truth. The political masters of Paris seemed less afraid of the Prussians than of their own armed workingmen. "A victory of Paris over the Prussian aggressors would have been a victory of the French workman over the French capitalist and his state parasites," Karl Marx promptly deduced with his inflexible logic.[6] At Tours the patriotic Gambetta repudiated the armistice and resigned in protest; but his coadjutors in Paris proceeded to hand over their forts and to disarm the regular garrisons at Bismarck's command. The National Guards, however, were permitted to keep their arms, to police the city, and to cherish the batteries of artillery which had been purchased for them by public subscription. The war was lost in truth now, but the Ministry of National Defense, a misrepresentative government to the last, continued to pretend that it planned a vigorous renewal of the conflict: the armistice was a temporary expedient to permit a general election. All the radical and republican organizations in Paris coöperated in the first week of February to elect a strong slate of candidates for the National Assembly. Their platform demanded "a republic, one and indivisible, democratic, social and universal" (whatever that might mean), and their nominees, led by Gambetta and including Clemenceau, were pledged to demand a war to the death.[7]

Paris in her bitter isolation might cling to a heroic pose, but in the provinces a more realistic mood prevailed. France lacked the will for further sacrifices. The assembly which convened at Bordeaux on February 12 concluded peace two weeks later, a peace that involved the surrender of Alsace and part of Lorraine and the assumption of a billion-dollar indemnity. The vote for acceptance was definitive enough, 547 to 107.[8] Obedient to their instructions, the delegates from Paris opposed the negotiations, and a majority of them resigned in protest. But Clemenceau

[5] Washburne to Fish, January 25, 1871. E. B. Washburne, *The Franco-German War and the Insurrection of the Commune* (Washington, D. C.: Government Printing Office, 1878), p. 134.

[6] Karl Marx, *The Civil War in France* (London: Martin Lawrence, 1933), p. 21.

[7] *Les Murailles politiques françaises*, 3 vols. (Paris, 1875), I, 867–868.

[8] *Annales de l'Assemblée nationale* (Paris, 1871), I, 125–126.

kept his seat in the assembly, ambitious to discover some formula of conciliation that might bridge the gulf so steadily widening between the soulless "capitulators" who spoke for France and the insensate populace of the humiliated capital.

It was a chimerical hope. The dominant *bloc* in the assembly, moderates, bourgeois, royalists, with Thiers at their head, neither understood nor sought to understand the quixotic mood and lacerated vanity of the Parisians. At long last France enjoyed an opportunity to rebuke its presumptuous capital and this "assembly of rurals" did not find the duty onerous. Ignoring the economic paralysis which still crippled all business life in the city the assembly rescinded the moratorium on notes and rents, stopped the wages of the National Guards, and chose Versailles for its subsequent sessions as a final rebuke to Parisian impudence. Wiser men than Clemenceau threw up their hands at this point and surrendered to what Favre was later to style conveniently "the ineluctable logic of events." But Clemenceau prized his little brief authority and the circumstances roused his stubborn spirit. Uniting his efforts with a handful of mayors and deputies — Tirard, Lockroy, Schoelcher, Langlois — who still labored for an intelligent solution, he returned to Paris in the role of mediator, filled with an over-sanguine self-confidence.

"Montmartre has the cannon: that is what fazes those b—— capitulators," exulted *Le Père Duchêne* in the middle of March.[9] Other radical journals, catching the spirit of '93, echoed this significant truth. Montmartre had the cannon, for the National Guards, still in possession of their arms, had hauled part of their prized artillery to the buttes for greater security. Clemenceau, back at his *mairie*, believed that he could persuade the citizen militia to relinquish the guns; so at least he assured General d'Aurelle de Paladines on March 12, and the general did not doubt his sincerity.[10] But when horses were sent to drag away the cannon it became evident that Clemenceau had exaggerated his powers of persuasion. His subordinate Dereure had warned the local Committee of Vigilance and the committee countermanded the proposal. The atmosphere in the Eighteenth Arrondissement was growing dangerously tense, how tense Clemenceau himself did not realize. His section no longer trusted him with its secrets, and the agents of the government, equally uncertain of his loyalty, duped him regarding their intentions. For Thiers had finally

[9] *Le Père Duchêne, Nos. 1–68* (Paris, an 79, [1871]), No. 4.

[10] Henri Améline, ed. *Dépositions des témoins de l'enquête parlementaire sur l'insurrection du 18 mars*, 3 vols. (Paris, 1872), II, 83.

lost patience. The assembly planned to open its first session at Versailles on March 20, and the "little man" wanted the *éclat* of greeting the deputies with the announcement that he had disarmed Paris. But there was another and more imperative motive. Business men whose aid he needed to liquidate the war indemnity insisted that financial negotiations could not prosper until he had crushed these wretched radicals: ". . . *si vous n'en finissez pas avec tous ces scélérats, si vous ne leur enlevez pas les canons.*"[11] To hasten the matter he decided to risk a surprise *coup*.

On March 18 Clemenceau was wakened at six o'clock in the morning by Simon Dereure, a grim messenger with grim news. Before dawn the Buttes of Montmartre had been occupied by government troops and the guns seized. Cursing the treachery of Thiers, Clemenceau dressed hurriedly, disconcerted by the hostility and suspicion in Dereure's eyes. A few minutes later he was climbing the buttes. At the summit he found General Lecomte in command of the military, and protested to him at the government's decision to use force without first warning the local authorities. Lecomte replied that he was merely obeying orders, and that as soon as the transport arrived he must drag away the cannon. Clemenceau advised him to waste no time. So far the populace had taken the *coup* calmly; there was apparently little thought of resistance; but it was still so early the section had scarcely awakened and the streets were almost deserted. Nearby, in the Rue des Rosiers, some prisoners had been rounded up by the soldiers and constabulary, among them a National Guardsman who was mortally wounded. Clemenceau returned to General Lecomte to request authority to move the injured man to a hospital, but permission was refused lest the sight of the victim excite the populace.

It was seven-thirty when Clemenceau returned to the *mairie*. Knots of indignant citizens had begun to gather in the streets, and some of them upbraided him vehemently as a renegade, an accomplice of the "capitulators." In the Mairie Square he found Dereure in conference with a score of the local leaders. The group fell silent at his approach and shortly dispersed, while he entered his office and began the day's business. But echoes of the awakening section soon broke in upon his labors. Bugles sounded in the distance, detachments of National Guards clattered across the square, and in the swelling ranks Clemenceau saw soldiers of the line fraternizing with the excited populace. By ten o'clock he gathered that the first act of the drama was ended. The cannon had been recaptured,

[11] Améline, *Dépositions*, II, 66–67.

half the government troops had gone over to the side of the people, and their officers were prisoners. An exultant multitude filled the square with shouts of *Vive la République*, pressed into the *mairie*, and unnerved Clemenceau by their contemptuous ostracism. His authority had vanished, his popularity withered in the chill of their suspicion. For a few moments his customary *sangfroid* failed him. Withdrawing to an inner room he bowed his head upon his arms and bitter tears of failure burned his eyelids. It was an excusable weakness and it passed quickly. Gathering the shreds of his dignity about him he stepped out again briskly to face the hostile inquisition of a hundred eyes.

For the moment their easy victory had made the demonstrators indulgent. Clemenceau persuaded the National Guards to intern some of their prisoners, members of the hated police and constabulary, in a nearby hall out of sight of the crowds. General Lecomte and his officers had already been confined in a dance pavilion in the Rue de Clignancourt, and Clemenceau saw to their needs and urged the guards to take every precaution for their safety should popular passions become more inflamed.

It was a vain admonition. About two in the afternoon a half-illegible dispatch arrived from some fictitious committee ordering that the captives be transferred to the Rue des Rosiers. In the midst of a swirling fog, as if Nature herself sought to blur the details of that ambiguous day, the eleven officers were marched up onto the buttes, followed by the imprecations of a gathering crowd. At No. 6, Rue des Rosiers, the captives were informed that they would be arraigned before a court, but the mob grew delirious at the continual delay. The arrival of another prisoner, General Clément Thomas, a former commander of the National Guard hated for his firm discipline, had raised the excitement to a new pitch. Thrusting aside all resistance, men and women hurled themselves upon the prisoners, tore Clément Thomas from the group, drove him staggering into the garden, and killed him with shots and blows. Certain that his own turn would come next, General Lecomte marched gravely out and stood against the wall, facing his executioners with a military salute. A ragged volley ended his life, but the enthusiasm of the assassins had been somewhat chilled by the superior dignity of a soldier's death. The remaining prisoners were spared.

Rumors of these critical developments first reached Clemenceau at the *mairie* (so he affirmed) about four-thirty. Mounting the buttes in breathless haste, he found an insensate mob surging through the Rue des Rosiers. "I observed then," he recounted in his record of the day, "that psychological spectacle known as blood lust. A wave of madness had engulfed the crowd. . . ." [12] Suspicious looks were flung at him, cries of "Down with the traitors" still broke forth at intervals, and when he learned that the generals were already dead he withdrew circumspectly. There can be no doubt that he would have been in considerable danger had he attempted to rebuke the demonstrators, but he preserved his composure and descended the buttes in safety.

The fate of the officers who had been spared, and of the gendarmes imprisoned near the *mairie*, weighed on his mind. Throwing official dignity to the winds, he decided to appeal to the Committee of Vigilance at their temporary headquarters in the Rue Clignancourt. Two of his fellow deputies, Lockroy and Langlois, had preceded him with the same end in view, and Langlois remembered the profound indignation with which Clemenceau announced the death of Lecomte and Clément Thomas. The members of the Committee, feeling themselves compromised by such excesses, promised to release the remaining prisoners secretly during the night, and Clemenceau returned to his *mairie* to watch over this humane but risky project. Langlois testified later that some fifty gendarmes who were set at liberty during the hours of darkness might well thank Clemenceau for their lives.[13]

Yet despite such favorable testimony Clemenceau's role in the day's tragedy, for which he was often attacked in later years, remains equivocal at best. To accuse him of complicity in the assassinations is absurd; no honest sifting of the evidence will bear out such a charge. Nevertheless, with full allowance made for his compromised authority, it must be admitted that he showed a disposition to temporize, to follow rather than to lead the course of events. His official acts appeared cautious and negative, his statements indefinite, his movements dilatory. Perhaps the shrewdest charge that can justly be lodged against him is that he remained prudent on a day of madness and this neutralized his effectiveness.

Nor should it be forgotten that more responsible officials than the Mayor of Montmartre watched in nerveless confusion while the tumult mounted. Thiers, who had come to the city to mark the effect of his *coup*, fled at three-thirty, after ordering a general withdrawal of all loyal forces. At the government headquarters, in the Ministry of Foreign Affairs, General Vinoy was popping in and out of his office like a cuckoo on a clock, distracted by the disappearance of the government troops,

[12] *Le Silence de M. Clemenceau*, pp. 297–298.

[13] Améline, *Dépositions*, II, 66–67.

which had melted away like snow in summer.[14] With darkness the exodus of responsible officials continued, while the revolutionary committees, alert and enterprising, hastened to seize every point of advantage. By dawn the shadow government was in control. The Central Committee, strengthened by delegates from the 200,000 National Guards, had become the *de facto* government of Paris, and the mayors of the twenty arrondissements were the only officials with legal status who remained in the rebellious city.

Now commenced that week of parleying which falls, like a farcical interlude, between the assassinations of March 18 and the fateful crescendo of the Commune. His energy restored, Clemenceau conferred with the other mayors, argued with delegates from the Central Committee, and sped to Versailles to defend Paris before a hostile assembly. "There is no longer any legal government in Paris," he reminded the deputies curtly on March 20, "save for some tottering municipal offices, and these may soon find it impossible to restrain the current which threatens to submerge them." The statement was no exaggeration as Clemenceau well knew, for the Committee of Vigilance had already seized his *mairie*, and warrants were out for his arrest.[15] But the assembly refused to be impressed, even when the moderate Tirard, mayor of the respectable Second Arrondissement, reiterated the warning. "We have done everything in our power," he pleaded. "Paris has been left to its own devices. The government has abandoned us now for two days — "

"That is not true!" Thiers interrupted, pricked by the thrust.

" — After attempting a *coup de force* which failed," jeered Clemenceau, rubbing salt into the wound.

"You call the execution of the laws a *coup de force*," Favre bristled indignantly. "What language is this?"[16]

It was an impasse. The urgent problem at the moment was to reëstablish a legal régime in Paris, but when Clemenceau demanded that the government authorize the election of a municipal council the assembly hesitated. Such a move, undertaken while the Central Committee dominated the city, might merely confirm its usurpation of power. Conditions in Paris were far from normal. Many of the wealthier citizens had left after the Prussians raised the siege, and some of these *émigrés*, crowding the antechambers of the assembly, painted lurid pictures of the reign of

[14] Edouard Lockroy, *La Commune et l'Assemblée* (Paris, 1871), p. 20.

[15] Georges Laronze, *Histoire de la Commune de 1871* (Paris: Payot, 1928), p. 60.

[16] *Annales de l'Assemblée nationale*, II, 4–6.

terror inaugurated by the illegal committees. The mayors of the twenty arrondissements, who would ordinarily have supervised an election, retained so little authority that, when they sent a delegation to the Central Committee on March 21, they were kept waiting an hour before they were even granted an audience. Yet there can be little doubt that a majority of the citizens still desired a peaceful and intelligent solution to the deadlock. Had this law-abiding majority, tradespeople, professional men, demobilized soldiers, loyal battalions of National Guards, found adequate leadership and encouragement they could have checked the encroachments of the Central Committee and its agents. The alternative, drawing nearer with each hour of abortive recrimination, was an appeal to arms.

As intermediaries between the Assembly and the Central Committee the mayors and deputies of Paris could see the shape of things to come. The vision paralyzed some while goading others to fight more desperately against the impending doom. "Don't go back to Paris," the sober Ducuing begged Clemenceau and Lockroy. "I feel in Paris a fatal current sucking you to destruction."[17] But the mediators would not confess defeat. "There was no 'fatal logic' to these events," Lockroy insisted afterwards. "The tragedy could have been averted, not once but a dozen times."[18] In the Assembly Clemenceau hurled this truth at the heads of his complacent auditors until his voice grew hoarse. Either the government must take a firm but conciliatory stand which would win over the sane majority of the Parisians, or it must accept the shocking alternative of a civil war. Without a responsible administration the capital was drifting perforce into the power of the Central Committee. Only a free election, approved by the Assembly, could retrieve it from the chaos which had reigned since the government abandoned the city. But Thiers had heard enough on that subject. "It is Paris which has abandoned us," he insisted primly, and the deadlock continued.[19]

The members of the Central Committee, anxious to legalize their position and test their support, had first announced an election for March 22. The mayors countered by a threat to declare such an election illegal and the Committee postponed it. When the Versailles government still hesitated to authorize a plebiscite the mayors lost face, and the Committee insisted that the election of a city council would take place March 26, with

[17] Améline, *Dépositions*, II, 48–49.
[18] Lockroy, *La Commune et l'Assemblée*, p. 6.
[19] *Annales de l'Assemblée nationale*, II, 5.

or without executive sanction. Yet the Committee honestly desired to avoid such an open breach, and pressed the mayors to approve this decision, promising that their *mairies* and records would be restored to them so that they could supervise the voting. The mayors were ready to compromise on April 3 or even March 30, but refused their approval for the 26th. Then, just twenty-four hours before the deadline, they "capitulated." In yielding to the Committee they also yielded to panic, which was spread among them by a rumor from Versailles. About midday on March 25 Clemenceau, Lockroy, and other deputies returned from the Assembly with a report that the Republic was in danger, that the monarchist majority meditated an Orléanist restoration. It was only a rumor but it alarmed the mayors, republicans in sentiment, and drove them leftward. All but two promptly seized their pens and signed the agreement with the Central Committee.

He who sups with the Devil needs a long spoon. The Central Committee, having gained its point, ignored further protests from the mayors and deputies, and rushed its placards through the press to signalize its victory. "The Central Committee of the National Guard, joined by the deputies of Paris, the mayors and their subordinates," invited the Parisians to the polls. Paris was satisfied that the rift between the authorities had been closed, and the proclamation of the mayors, which appeared later, failed to recover the ground they had lost. "The Deputies of Paris," they announced, "the Mayors and their adjuncts, reinstalled in the *mairies* of their arrondissements, and the members of the Central Committee," authorized an election in order to avoid civil war and maintain the Republic.[20] When the news reached Versailles late on that same Saturday the venerable Louis Blanc urged the Assembly to approve the action taken by the mayors, but the deputies preferred to wait and watch the outcome. By March 27 it was clear that Paris had chosen a Commune dominated by the more radical spirits, a council of eighty-six members ranging from advanced republicans to extreme revolutionaries. In the Assembly Louis Blanc's motion on behalf of the mayors was rejected almost unanimously, the Commune was denied moral or legal sanction, and Thiers announced that order would be restored in Paris as soon as possible.

As a mediator Clemenceau had reached the end of the road and he had the courage to recognize it. He wrote out his resignation as Mayor of the Eighteenth Arrondissement on March 27 and Lafont and Jaclard added

[20] March, *History of the Paris Commune*, p. 139.

their signatures.[21] To Versailles, the same day, he dispatched a note, cutting in its cold formality, to announce that he could no longer remain a member of the Assembly.[22] These definitive gestures proved again Clemenceau's clarity of vision; some of his colleagues were slower to react. Tirard, who had been elected to the Commune by his conservative section, resigned at the first meeting, but Arthur Ranc, Clemenceau's friend and mayor of the Ninth Arrondissement, sat until April 5, when fighting had already broken out between the National Guard and the Versailles troops.

The populace of Paris, betrayed, bewildered, seduced by socialist visions, had decided to fight, without understanding the odds or the ends involved. Half a century later the memory of that inexplicable tragedy still burned in Clemenceau's heart. "It was one of the stupidest, the most insane things in all history. No one really knew what the Commune was. Those people slew, committed arson, got themselves shot, sometimes with the greatest heroism. But they never understood what it was about."[23] Even the pure flame of patriotism was speedily obscured, for the leaders of the Commune offered to make terms with the Prussians, offered finally to surrender their forts to them, in return for recognition and aid. Indignation against the "capitulators," which had fanned the revolt, had been transmuted into hatred of the capitalists. "It was," Lenin later diagnosed, "this combination of contradictory tasks — patriotism and socialism — which constituted the fatal error of the French socialists."[24]

Active fighting between the National Guards and the Versaillais began on April 2. But even this did not deter a handful of the mediators — Clemenceau, Floquet, Ranc, Bonvallet — from making a final gesture at appeasement and clarification by organizing a Republican Union for the Rights of Paris. The government, however, ignored their overtures, and the Commune declared that further negotiations would be regarded as treason. The Union then endeavored to call a convention of delegates from all the cities of France, to open at Bordeaux on May 7. In order to attend, Clemenceau borrowed a passport from an American friend and passed the Versaillais sentries at Saint Denis by pretending that he spoke only English. The projected convention never met, and as he could not reënter Paris,

[21] Frédéric Damé, *La Résistance; les maires, les députés de Paris, et la comité central du 18 au 26 mars, avec pièces officielles et documents inédits* (Paris, 1871), p. 339.

[22] *Annales de l'Assemblée nationale*, II, 151.

[23] *Clemenceau peint par lui-même*, p. 47.

[24] Karl Marx, *The Civil War in France*, Appendix II, p. 79.

already besieged by the Versailles troops, he slipped away to his family home at L'Aubraie.

Though aware of his place of refuge, the government of Thiers made no attempt to arrest him. It showed no pity, however, toward the more radical leaders of the Montmartre section. Théophile Ferré and Raoul Rigault were shot, Simon Dereure, who escaped from France, was sentenced to death in his absence. The hill of Montmartre was stormed by the government forces on May 23, amid scenes of desperate carnage, and no quarter was given to those defenders captured with arms in their hands. For five more days the Versaillais fought their way through the burning city, while the Communards prolonged the hopeless struggle, shooting hostages, blowing up buildings, and firing churches in their desperation. By May 28 the shooting had died away, except for the activity of the government firing squads, and more than ten thousand dead testified to the thoroughness with which Thiers had restored order in Paris.

To Clemenceau in his retreat the report of these horrors came as the fulfillment of a vision which had haunted him for three months. To the end of his life he remembered the despair that had gripped him as he left Paris, knowing that the people who had been under his jurisdiction, the misguided fools whom he had cajoled and scolded and come to like, would soon shoot and be shot in their idiotic exaltation, and that he could do nothing further to avert their doom. The lessons which he learned during that dark winter of 1870–71 never faded from his mind: the deadly efficiency of the Prussian military machine, the irony of arguing with petty and obstinate men, the violence and instability of the populace, the need for firmness and decision in hours of crisis. His initiation into political affairs had been a severe and brutal test which he had passed with no great honor but without disgrace. "It forced upon me," he confessed long afterwards, "a sound appreciation of the stupidity of public life to find myself between two parties, both of which desired my death. Even that did not cure me. . . ."[25]

But this was the cynical judgment of old age. At thirty Clemenceau was still something of an idealist, an idealist who had seen his republican principles invoked in a disastrous hour, betrayed by timid and incompetent leaders, and perverted by an insensate mob. For the moment his reaction was one of black despondency, but the disillusionment which might have dulled a weaker spirit steeled and tempered him for further fighting. When he returned to the fray he was a more cunning and resourceful, a

[25] *Le Silence de M. Clemenceau,* p. 210.

more ruthless and implacable adversary. In a sense, the fifty years of political warfare that lay ahead of him was to be a long vendetta against the enemies he had identified in that first battle: against Thiers and Favre, against the monarchists, against the bloody-minded martinets on the general staff, against dogmatic priests, against socialist pretenders with impractical panaceas. And against the Prussians. Always, to his dying hour, against the Prussians.

CHAPTER III

MUNICIPAL COUNCILLOR
1871–1876

It is not making decisions that requires intelligence. There are heaps of people about who are making heaps of decisions — it's seeing them through.[1] CLEMENCEAU

REBELLIOUS PARIS, after the bloody suppression of the Commune, was placed upon a strict probation. The National Assembly continued to sit at Versailles, distrusting the mood of the humiliated capital, and the Parisians had to swallow their pride and take orders from this "assembly of yokels." Discipline, economy, and labor had become the order of the day for France as well as for Paris, and Thiers, named Chief of the Executive Power, symbolized the new government — middle class, unimaginative, and uninspiring, but pledged to liberate France from the German army of occupation and to promote a policy of cautious recovery.

To swing Paris into line with this national policy of stabilization and thrift it was essential to reconstruct the city administration and subordinate it to the authority of the Versailles régime. Clemenceau had proposed as early as March, 1871, that Paris be authorized to elect a municipal council of eighty members, the president of which would be mayor of the city. His project, submitted two days after the mob murder of the generals Lecomte and Thomas, never reached a vote, but it posed a problem the assembly could not long ignore. By a law of April 14, Paris received permission to elect a council of eighty members, four from each arrondissement, but the council remained subject to the Prefect of the Seine, who controlled the finances and exercised the real power of a mayor. As the police power remained in the hands of a Prefect of Police, likewise appointed by the national executive, it was evident that the city council would be little more than a secretarial and advisory body.[2] Though Bonapartism was at a discount since Sedan, the new masters of France

[1] Jean Martet, *Clemenceau* (London: Longmans, Green, 1930), p. 48.

[2] Pierre Bernheim, *Le Conseil municipal de Paris de 1789 à nos jours* (Paris: Les Presses modernes, 1937), p. 136.

were falling back on a Bonapartist principle: authority from above, confidence (it was hoped) from below.

In the elections of July, 1871, Clemenceau won a seat on this Municipal Council from the Clignancourt *quartier*. His six years of service at this post, even more than his six months of drastic initiation as Mayor of Montmartre, laid the real foundations of his political apprenticeship. There is little record of his activities; his role, like that of the council, remained subordinate and unimpressive. The penalties of intractability had been so deeply burned into the minds of all Frenchmen by the events of the "terrible year" that even a Clemenceau had lost much of his belligerence and learned the importance of collaboration. He still hated Thiers, but he recognized that the moneyed classes, whose loans were essential to pay off the indemnity and keep the government afloat, would trust no one else in equal measure. So Paris, and Clemenceau, bowed to the inevitable and accepted orders from the man who had crushed the liberties of the proudest of French communes. Fortunately there was little direct clash of personalities, for Thiers exercised his authority indirectly through the Prefect of the Seine, and to this key post he appointed the able and conscientious Léon Say.[3] The tact, moderation and prestige of this noted economist seduced the jealous council, and Say soon had the members busily at work on half a score of committees dedicated to various phases of civic reform.

The social services, particularly the care of the sick and indigent, attracted Clemenceau. Public hygiene, medical aid for the poor, vacations in the country for children of the slums, regulations against child marriage and the abandonment of newly born infants claimed his attention in turn. To vote appropriations or make gifts to a charitable institution, he insisted, was only a beginning. It was essential to come to close quarters with poverty and crime in order to understand and cope with them. Sanitation, education, health, and morality were all bound up together: an adequate water supply, free medical clinics, supervision and distribution of essential foods, milk in particular, adequate public schools and libraries, all these were admirable projects.[4] But too often a gap remained unclosed between the will and the deed, the project and its application, the charitable institution and the object of its solicitude. The most important thing was not a

[3] Léon Say had won attention by his criticism of Parisian civic economy under the Second Empire. He held the office of Préfect of the Seine from June 5, 1871, until December, 1872, when Thiers appointed him Minister of Finance.

[4] Jean Jules Henri Mordacq, *Clemenceau* (Paris: Les Éditions de France, 1939), p. 5.

hand-out to the needy: charity has its limits. The crux of the issue was to inspire the wretched to fend for themselves, and to do this it was necessary to win their confidence by comprehending and sharing their privations, and then to set them an example of courage, confidence, and self-help.

To prove that he could practice what he preached Clemenceau devoted two periods a week to medical service among the poor of Montmartre. His clinic at No. 3, rue de Trois-Frères, occupied two rooms, and the antechamber overflowed with patients and petitioners an hour before he strode in punctually at nine each Wednesday and Sunday morning. His professional skill and devotion to medical science, never very genuine or profound, declined after a few years; [5] even in his busiest days he regarded his dispensary as a clearing station in the battle of social hygiene, not as a hospital. Patients received more advice than medicine, or if a cursory examination revealed the possibility of a serious ailment, they left with a note referring them to a public hospital where they could receive more adequate treatment. Not only the sick but the maladjusted, the unemployed, and the indigent crowded into his office for aid and counsel and received it in generous if brusque terms. The trait which he had most admired in his father, the compulsion to serve the incapable, steeled him to hear their complaints and humor their foibles. Alert, smiling, friendly and indefatigable, he did his best to hide the contempt which he felt in his heart for many of the feckless specimens of humanity that drifted through his consulting room. Yet there can be no doubt that the time and energy which he dedicated to this urgent public service benefited him as much as it did the recipients of it. For it gave him an insight into the needs and mentality of the disinherited classes which he could have acquired in no other fashion, and it won him the respect, and the votes, of his constituents.

Another issue on which Clemenceau dared to proclaim his convictions, and won respect by his courage, concerned the fate of the communards. At a time when few ventured to defend the defunct Commune he invited criticism and obloquy by public pleas for the victims. The twenty thousand dead were past help. But the courts continued to try those accused of complicity in the insurrection and thirteen thousand received prison sentences or were exiled to New Caledonia. For these unfortunates an amnesty would mean restoration to civil life and a reunion with their families and friends. In November, 1871, before the Sixth Military Commission, Clemenceau argued that many Parisians had been misled into

[5] Mordacq, *Clemenceau*, pp. 172–173. Mordacq notes, however, that Clemenceau had some 600 works on medicine in his library at the time of his death.

The Bettmann Archive

This painting by J.-F. Raffaelli suggests the tense, dour inflexibility that distinguished Clemenceau in public debate. As a leader of the Radical Republicans he was a familiar figure at political rallies in the 1870's and 1880's.

supporting the Commune through patriotic motives, believing that it would be able to resist the German peace terms. He further insisted that the national authorities had provoked the events of March 18 and the subsequent civil war by their bungling deceptions and their self-righteous complacency. Given the lie direct by an irate officer, Major de Poussagues, he adjourned the issue to the dueling ground, where he had the good fortune to escape injury himself but wounded de Poussagues in the leg with his bullet.[6] Many Parisians, still unreconstructed rebels at heart, were secretly delighted to hear that a civilian had bested a military man in this fire-eating fashion. The incident furnished Clemenceau with a useful if somewhat exaggerated reputation as a duelist, and proved, if it needed proof, that he was a dangerous man to defy.

Hopes for a general amnesty were clearly premature in the autumn of 1871, and Clemenceau had doubtless known that his pleas would fall on deaf ears. The breach between Paris and the provinces, and between the bourgeoisie and the working classes, had left wounds too deeply envenomed to heal rapidly. Moreover, the Parisian electors, though chastened, were far from broken in spirit. In April, 1873, they chose the Leftist candidate, Barodet, and rejected Thiers' nominee, Rémusat, in a local election, an assumption of independence which needlessly alarmed conservative and royalist circles. Thiers resigned in May, to be succeeded by Marshal MacMahon, and the Republicans, despite energetic protests in which Clemenceau joined, were unable to check this swing to the right. The Royalists, both Legitimists and Orléanists, regarded the change as a victory, for they believed that MacMahon would yield the executive power to the legitimist candidate, the Count of Chambord, at the first appropriate moment.

But the refusal of "Henry V" to abandon the white flag of Henry IV and accept the tricolor alienated so many Frenchmen that the Republic survived *faute de mieux*. The ebb and flow of public opinion, the political juggling and ministerial crises, which filled the eighteen-seventies and finally left France a constitutional republic without a constitution, are too complex to analyze here. Readers curious to reconstruct the game, inning by inning, can do so in the histories of the period. It was an amusing game in its day and still makes good reading, though it has lost substance amid the harsher realities of the twentieth century.[7] By 1875 France was so evidently a republic *de facto* there seemed no longer any adequate reason

[6] Georges Suarez, *Clemenceau*, I, 122–123.

[7] For the English reader the best recent account of the founding of the Republic is D. W. Brogan, *France under the Republic* (New York: Harper and Brothers, 1940), Books I–III.

to refuse it the title *de jure*, and the National Assembly terminated the provisory era, and its own existence, by the adoption of three organic statutes. These constitutional laws provided for a Chamber of Deputies elected by universal manhood suffrage, a Senate the members of which were to be chosen by electoral colleges, and a President to be elected by a majority vote of the senators and deputies sitting together as a National Assembly.

This triumph of the parliamentary system necessitated an election which reopened the arena of national politics to Clemenceau. His labors on the Municipal Council had already won him the maximum recognition which he could look for in that restricted sphere: he had been chosen president of the council in November, 1875. Three months later, in February, 1876, the faithful electors of the Clignancourt ward sent him to the Chamber of Deputies, where he took his seat with the "radical" republicans of the Left. His forensic talents, which had been curbed in committees where debates were closed to the public, were to entertain and often to exasperate a larger audience.

From the outset party discipline remained light and loose among the republican majority of the new Chamber, but Gambetta could count upon their distrust of MacMahon and their suspicion of the royalist majority in the Senate to hold them in a general agreement. They had founded a republic but they had yet to secure control of it and the task required some unity of effort in their conniving and campaigning if it was to be carried through. Simple strategy dictated their first objectives: they must secure a majority in the Senate and control the presidency. With the elections of January, 1879, these goals were achieved, for MacMahon resigned the same month and the triumphant republicans replaced him by the more docile Jules Grévy. The colorless Waddington was chosen to head the reconstructed ministry, Gambetta became president of the Chamber and chairman of the important Committee of Finance, and Jules Ferry Minister of Public Instruction. The republic was to be run by republicans.

The wave which swept them into power also dissolved the superficial unity of the republican *mélange*, and Clemenceau was one of the first to desert. He had grown increasingly restless as the months passed, increasingly critical of his colleagues, increasingly impatient at the compromises and concessions which were, it appeared, the inevitable purchase price of public office. Gambetta had begun to flirt with the conservatives and truckle to the financiers. Waddington rejected an amnesty for the communards. The republic of which they had dreamed in the old imperial days, which they had founded in the midst of national defeat, and nursed through a critical minority, had come of age, but the more closely Clemenceau studied it the more easily he persuaded himself that it was a changeling. There was no definitive constitution, no Bill of Rights, no universal suffrage. The Senate was an excrescence which ought to be abolished. The educational system needed to be laicized, the army republicanized, the Church separated from the State. Astute opportunists like Gambetta knew that the time was not yet ripe for all these innovations; for some of them the time was never to be ripe. But Clemenceau, free from the responsibilities and restrictions of office, reminded the Chamber and the public that such projects were the timbers from which the republican platform had been constructed. As a radical he insisted upon hewing to the line and he let the chips fall among the moderates and compromisers who had sold their ideals, he hinted broadly, for a mess of ministerial pottage.

Possibly he was disappointed that there was no place for him in the new ministry, though he was subsequently to refuse offers of a post not once but many times. Perhaps he was sincerely heartsick at the tawdry edifice which he saw arising on the grave of the republican dream. Perhaps his years of conscientious service on the Municipal Council, and his fretful efforts to slow his pace to the tardy and straggling march of the republicans until they captured the Senate and ousted MacMahon, had exhausted his capacity for collaboration. Whatever his motives, or it might be fairer to say his rationalized impulses, may have been, they inspired him to a series of slashing attacks on the new republican ministers. He speedily made himself a marked man as the outstanding recalcitrant of the Chamber, attacking without pity, operating without anaesthetics, sparing no one, friend or foe. His associates of the old days were in exile, like Ranc, or in office, like Gambetta, and he noted with scorn how quickly the office-holders turned cautious and respectable, donning high hats, giving formal dinners, edging into society. It was easy to gibe at them, easy to recall the simpler days of plain living and high thinking when they made a meal of bread around a café table and drew plans for the new society. The Republic had arrived but social ills and economic inequality remained. Clemenceau was not alone in arraigning the popular leaders for pledges broken and ideals betrayed.

He might, of course, have harnessed himself once more to the obscure but honorable drudgery of committee work. He might have withdrawn to his study and limited his criticism to thoughtful editorials, or devoted himself to some genuinely creative writing. He might have retired to the country and become a Vendéean squire. But he preferred to remain in Parliament and make himself the conscience of the new régime, a terror to his colleagues. Yet this reputation, early acquired, of the tiger prowling up and down seeking whom he might devour, emphasizes the façade of his character and neglects the foundation. All his life, it is true, Clemenceau remained what Napoleon called "a phrase-maker," a master of mordant epigrams, and this skill with tongue and pen eclipsed and still eclipses his saner and sounder qualities of heart and brain. For Clemenceau was not only a talker, he was a worker, when necessary a painstaking, conscientious, and methodical worker. His epigrams, his flamboyant gestures, in a word his theatricalities, had their uses: they won attention for his ideas, they drove home his arguments, and they intimidated his opponents. But they also created and popularized a false impression, a two-dimensional caricature, of the man and the politician. He became for his generation the bad boy of French politics, giddy, impudent, and vindictive, a frivolous and irresponsible *gamin*, with the mind of Ariel and the heart of Caliban, who was capable of overturning a cabinet to gratify a grudge.

Such a judgment ignores the truth that cynicism is the armor of the disillusioned sentimentalist, and Clemenceau remained to the end of his life a sentimentalist at heart. The sardonic orator who appeared to thrive on hoots and catcalls as a matinee idol thrives on applause could break down and weep like a child when a battle ended and his taut nerves gave way. His dynamism, his frankness, his *bonhomie* were public poses maintained for the good of his morale. Alone (and he passed half his time alone) he could lay pretence aside, shrink into himself, and be what he was, a sensitive, vulnerable, and lonely man, often baffled and infinitely tired. At such moments he occasionally yielded to the temptation to self-pity which assails all solitary natures; and the Paris which applauded his insouciance would scarcely have recognized the neurasthenic who doctored himself for insomnia, adopted odd diets to humor his nervous stomach, visited spas to regulate his disordered liver, and resorted to massage and routine calisthenics to stimulate what he conceived to be a faulty circulation.

Clemenceau's perpetual youth and resiliency, therefore, his unquenchable *élan*, his iron constitution, are an inseparable element in his legend, but they rest as much upon fiction as upon fact. When he commenced his long parliamentary career in 1876 (his brief hours in the National Assembly in 1871 had been no more than a rehearsal) he was thirty-five. Fifty years later his admirers were still paying tribute to his courage, his youthful spirit, his iron constitution. But it would be equally just to say that Clemenceau at thirty-five was already old, that, in fact, he had never been young. The precocious child of the Vendée, the sophomoric medical student, the young fop who had impressed New York society with his fine clothes and his fine talk, the romantic teacher of French in a girls' school, the harassed mayor of a riotous Paris suburb, the father of a family, the city councillor — by 1876 he had already outlived all these roles, had exhausted the seven ages of man in half a lifetime and seemed as ready to discard them as if they had been a repertoire of plays. How little remained of all those successive impersonations! Childhood was a sentimental dream, America a not very amusing interlude, his medical career a disappointment, his marriage a failure. Half a century of political struggle full of sound and fury lay ahead of him, but in his heart he had already prefigured the grandeur and misery of victory. He might have confessed then as he did fifty years later that his hermit soul had never learned the secret of companionship, had never known an emotion so strong and single-hearted as the quest for solitude. "I don't know anyone any more. At times it's frightening. Frightening like the desert — and marvellously delightful like the solitude of high peaks."[8] Delightful, no doubt, this companionless intoxication, but also at times a little too desolate, a little too frightening. He was to see himself in the end as one with Demosthenes and Hammurabi, a being as dissociated from his time, as disenchanted and disillusioned as Henry Adams, and twice as lonely.

[8] Jean Martet, *Clemenceau*, p. 33.

CHAPTER IV

WRECKER OF MINISTRIES
1876–1893

Pour la chute de plusieurs cabinets je puis faire mon meâ culpâ, mais, au fond, c'était toujours le même ministère que je trouvais devant moi.[1]

CLEMENCEAU

CLEMENCEAU entered the Chamber of Deputies in 1876 as a Radical Republican. This meant, in terms of the party distinctions of the day, that he stood with the minority group of Left Wing Republicans who demanded the complete, the fundamental or radical, democratic program, the platform which Gambetta had promised the electors of Belleville in 1869. Separation of Church and State; universal lay education; freedom of the press, of assembly and of association; the substitution of a citizen militia for the professional army; modification of the fiscal system with the addition of an income tax; election of all public officials; amnesty for the communards; abolition of the death penalty; revision of the constitutional laws; abolition of the senate; and national ownership of banks, mines, and railroads.[2]

For his first important speech in the assembly Clemenceau chose a subject near his heart, a subject he had waited five years to plead before all France. He demanded an amnesty for the communards. Thousands of victims proscribed after the bloody suppression of the Commune were still in hiding, in jail, or exiles in the penal colonies of New Caledonia. The brief which Clemenceau submitted on their behalf was a humane, eloquent, and historic document. Moderate in tone, clear in organization, fortified with facts and figures, it remains even today a masterpiece of pleading. No one could disregard the character and ability of an orator who thus reproved his fellow Republicans for their lack of clemency, reminding them what agonies the Parisian people had endured in 1870–71,

[1] Georges Clemenceau, *Sur la démocratie: neuf conférences de Clemenceau*, rapportées par Maurice Ségard (Paris: Larousse, 1930), p. 83.

[2] Léon Jacques, *Les Partis politiques sous la IIIe République* (Paris: Recueil Sirey, 1913), p. 163.

what confusion reigned in their heads and hearts, how difficult it was for loyal Frenchmen in that time of trouble to distinguish their true allegiances. The amnesty failed to pass, but Clemenceau's great speech of May, 1876, brought the day of forgiveness nearer, and helped, in so far as the efforts of any one man could help, to close the gulf which the civil war of 1871 had dug between the French proletariat and bourgeoisie.[3]

It was easy baiting for the Radicals, while they remained in opposition, to attack Gambetta and his "Opportunist" bloc of Moderate Republicans for their failure to vote the amnesty and other radical demands. But Gambetta was a realist and a man of government; he saw clearly that he could not afford the luxury of pure doctrinaire policies.[4] In foreign affairs France had to humble her pretensions and act circumspectly and deferentially like a second-class power. In domestic matters the republican régime could not survive if it lost the support of the bourgeoisie. To perpetuate the valetudinarian republic it was essential to steer clear of crises, to calm apprehensions, to avoid making additional enemies. Had the Radicals gained control and filled the cabinet with men of Clemenceau's dogmatic and arrogant temper, they would, by demanding everything at once, have ended by getting nothing. It was necessary, Gambetta insisted, to be supple, to be pragmatic and opportunist, to lay aside for the moment the blueprints of that ideal republic which the Radicals sought to proclaim at once in its entirety.

Yet some positive item had to be selected from the republican program, and carried through with vigor, if only to divert the electors in the lower brackets from fundamental social and economic reforms. To promote labor associations, introduce an income tax, or nationalize the railroads, banks, and mines would alienate the wealthier classes. To abolish the senate, amend the constitutional laws, democratize the army, might alarm the Right and persuade the Monarchists to risk a *coup d'état*. These realities may well have guided Gambetta's thought when he chose in 1877 to stigmatize Clericalism as the enemy. With the Republican triumph of 1879 the way was opened for Jules Ferry, as Minister of Public Instruction in the Freycinet Cabinet, to inaugurate a campaign for the laicization of the schools.

To most Republicans the persistent popularity of the ecclesiastical

[3] *Journal Officiel. Chambre des Députés. Débats*, Session of May 16, 1876, pp. 3332–3341.

[4] J. W. Pratt, "Clemenceau and Gambetta: A Study in Political Philosophy," *South Atlantic Quarterly*, XX (April 1921), 95–104.

schools, particularly in the secondary grade, seemed an alarming development. That these clerical establishments won patronage by their greater efficiency and their attention to non-intellectual aspects of education made them no less a challenge to the state schools. Lay-minded Frenchmen felt that the young, boys in particular, ought to be reared in an atmosphere which would inculcate a patriotic love for the Republic. In clerical schools or under clerical teachers, such critics averred, the youth of the land might imbibe monarchist and ultramontane doctrines. Ferry denied that he sought to attack religion or separate the Church from the state. His aim was to modernize French education, render the curriculum, like that pursued in England and Germany, more practical, more progressive, and more scientific. Religious instruction was to be prohibited in state schools and national solidarity and patriotism stressed. Applicants for a teaching position henceforth must possess a state certificate. A "letter of obedience" from the local bishop, which had sufficed hitherto for members of religious orders, was no longer to be considered an adequate substitute. In its effect, such legislation meant the exclusion of teaching brothers and nuns from the state school system.

A cynic might be disposed to view the laicization program as a Republican campaign to secure the spoils of office. In the state primary schools alone one fifth of the men and two thirds of the women teachers were members of religious orders.[5] To supplant these by holders of state certificates would involve the removal (or retention under state approval) of some fifty thousand primary-school teachers. Furthermore, the introduction of compulsory education would necessitate the erection of many new schools and *lycées*, and the creation of more normal schools to train teachers for them, a program which, in its totality, would offer liberal opportunities for the exercise of political patronage. As a policy, therefore, laicization of the schools not only served to divert attention from other promised reforms, it aimed to bring a great public institution, the "University," the centralized educational machinery of the state, under the control of the political party in power. That this change would be accompanied by an improvement in educational methods, a rise in standards, a more practical curriculum, and an extension of literacy, was the hope of Republican idealists, but the more mundane and material benefits could hardly escape the attention of Republican tacticians.

As a policy lay education possessed the further advantage that it could

[5] D. W. Brogan, *France under the Republic* (New York: Harper and Brothers, 1940), pp. 152–153.

be adopted without antagonizing any of the Great Powers. Though it was impolitic to proclaim the fact, all French policies, foreign or domestic, had to be pursued with caution in the early years of the Republic because France remained diplomatically isolated. Patriots might dream dreams about a war of revenge and the reconquest of Alsace and Lorraine, but sober second thought assured them that for the present such a war would invite another defeat. The Republican bloc was constricted in its choice to a policy which would not create any new and powerful opposition, within France or without, and this consideration may well have provided a deciding argument in favor of the anti-clerical legislation. Measures which reduced the power of the Catholic clergy in France might be expected to placate Bismarck, for in the 1870's he was waging the *Kulturkampf* to curb Catholic influence in the Reich. Equally important, the adoption of anti-clerical legislation by the Third Republic would reassure the Italian government, for the Italians feared that the royalists and Catholics in France, if they came into power, might launch a crusade to restore Rome and the papal patrimony to Pius IX. Finally, Russia and Great Britain, as non-Catholic powers, would not oppose a program designed to limit clerical influence in France. All these considerations persuaded Jules Ferry, who excelled even Gambetta in his ability to read the political weather signs, that the laicization program would prove expedient and advantageous. It would, of course, further offend devout circles and royalist groups in France, but these were elements which the Republicans had no hope of conciliating and sought only to weaken, frustrate, and nullify.

Thus lay education became, after 1879, a major issue in French domestic politics. True to their policy of asking all or nothing, the Radical Republicans attacked it as a half-way measure and demanded complete separation of Church and state. But it served its purpose as a "red herring" and helped to hide the failure of the Opportunists to attack more fundamental social and economic issues.[6]

Nevertheless, French hearts still yearned to see the nation play some active role, however modest, in foreign affairs. As Bismarck's system of alliances made Europe practically a closed field, there remained only the colonial world. France already possessed bases in Africa (Algeria, the

[6] Evidence that the laicization program was adopted in part from motives of expediency, and designed to divert attention from more fundamental social and economic reforms, may be found well presented in Evelyn Martha Acomb, *The French Laic Laws, 1879–1889* (New York: Columbia University Press, 1941), pp. 73–82.

Senegal) and Asia (Cochin-China) which invited further expansion, and Bismarck encouraged colonial enterprise for Frenchmen, viewing it as a form of compensation which might seduce them from their vows to recover Alsace and Lorraine. To Clemenceau the fact that the Iron Chancellor approved it was the strongest argument that could be urged against French imperialism, but Ferry believed in meeting the Prussians half way, even though they came bearing gifts. Colonial expansion would open a field for ambitious French naval and military officers eager for active service; if successful it would thrill French hearts and shed lustre on French arms. The bourgeois investor would find new sources of profit, and even the clericals, alienated by the laicization program at home, might find some consolation in the support which French military and colonial expansion would afford Catholic missionary enterprise abroad. The peril attending the policy, the latent implication which Bismarck and Clemenceau foresaw with equal clarity, was that it must almost certainly bring France into conflict with Italy and Great Britain.

Ferry was prepared to take the risk, and Clemenceau, as spokesman for the Radicals, was prepared to fight him. In the outcome their fierce duel decided nothing, although Ferry was forced from office in disgrace in 1885. Yet the cold logic of facts, and perhaps the verdict of history, seems to lie with Clemenceau. He saw the danger of scattering French troops and resources on distant continents when France herself was open to invasion. He denounced the cost of imperialism, which burdened all taxpayers for the benefit of a small group of investors and administrators. And he penetrated the unacknowledged motives, the lust for power, the dissimulation and irresponsible manipulation of men and money, whereby an ambitious minister played the imperial game. Fundamentally, his fight with Ferry and other imperialists was a fight to determine the parliamentary responsibility of the President and the ministers.

Foreign affairs, the army, the navy, and the colonies were the departments least subject to cabinet control, least responsible to the Chamber of Deputies.[7] Though treaties had ultimately to be submitted to both chambers for approval, the negotiations leading up to them, military, naval, and diplomatic, might be withheld for a considerable interval if the interest and security of the State seemed to the cabinet to warrant such secrecy. It was always possible, therefore, that an ambitious Minister of Foreign Affairs might involve the Republic in risky commitments from which it

[7] Frederick L. Schuman, *War and Diplomacy in the French Republic* (New York: McGraw Hill, 1931), chs. i and ii.

was impossible to withdraw without loss of national prestige. The Chambers might repudiate his negotiations, but such a step, since it must be exercised belatedly and as it were posthumously, served to advertise the divisions within the government and weaken respect for it abroad.

Beyond this power to repudiate a treaty the only effective control the legislature could invoke against the Quai d'Orsay was the power of the purse: it might refuse appropriations for colonial or other enterprises which it considered unwarranted. But here again Clemenceau perceived how inevitably a screen interposed itself between the will of the electorate as represented by the deputies and the insulated officials who shaped the national destinies. The budget was prepared in detail and the taxpayers' money expended, not by the Chambers at large, but by two finance committees, one elected by the deputies and one by the senators. Such committees enjoyed a high degree of initiative and independence which tended to increase steadily under the Third Republic. They were the real working organs of Parliament, and their recommendations and decisions, based upon the labor and resources of a permanent personnel, largely predetermined many important questions, such as the allotment, for instance, of the national revenues. By adroit manipulation of the committee rules, or *règlements*, most of which were established by 1876, a few individual deputies might exercise great influence, for no quorum was required at committee sessions.[8] It became increasingly clear to Clemenceau that the functions of initiative and decision in matters administrative were passing insensibly into the hands of the ministers, the anonymous personnel of the permanent bureaucracies, and the standing committees of the Chambers. He believed it essential for the preservation of true democracy that the minority parties in particular guard against such canalizing of the legislative authority, and he constituted himself a watchdog, ready to rise bristling whenever he detected an encroachment upon the (theoretically) inalienable powers of the Parliament.

The Treaty of Bardo (May 12, 1881) provided a typical example of the imperialist activities of the ministry which excited Clemenceau's wrath. While dissimulating their intentions before a critical Chamber, Jules Ferry as premier and General Farre, Minister of War, dispatched a French force into Tunis and forced the Bey to accept an ultimatum which made the province a protectorate of France in everything but name. This treaty

[8] R. K. Gooch, *The French Parliamentary Committee System*, University of Virginia Institute for Research in the Social Sciences, Institute Monograph No. 21 (New York, 1934), p. 129.

the Chamber of Deputies and the Senate ratified, though Clemenceau pointed out that the cabinet had acted without authority, had kept the deputies in ignorance of the proceedings, and had committed the Republic to a policy of armed intervention in Tunis which antagonized Italy and Turkey. When it became apparent that the Tunisians were prepared to resist the attempted *coup de force* and that further expenditures in men and money would be required to pacify the territory, Ferry's gamble lost much of its appeal. On July 26 Clemenceau assailed the cabinet vigorously, but it survived, and the country went to the polls for the scheduled general election. The voters, concerned chiefly with domestic problems, returned a Republican majority. But attacks on the Treaty of Bardo continued. On November 8, as spokesman for the Left, Clemenceau condemned the whole Tunis expedition as a national misfortune dictated by private banking and commercial interests, and arraigned the government for the abuse of authority, the duplicity, and the costs which its policy had entailed. Ferry resigned a week later, but his determination and enterprise had given an historic turn to French colonial policy. France kept Tunis and continued to seek compensation overseas until by 1914 the French Republic administered the second largest colonial empire in the world.[9]

For the moment, however, French appetite for costly colonial ventures had been sated. It was a sobering sequel to the Tunis *coup* to see Italy, furious but impotent before the French achievement, throw herself into the arms of Germany to form the Triple Alliance. Economic depression, a mounting national debt, and the spread of phylloxera which almost ruined the wine industry, emphasized the truth that France had problems on the home front to conquer before shouldering the white man's burden abroad. When, in the spring of 1882, France was offered the chance to intervene jointly with Britain to pacify Egypt and guard the Suez Canal, the timid Freycinet cabinet hesitated and let slip the opportunity. The moment was not auspicious for another military parade undertaken to protect French holders of Egyptian bonds. So Great Britain intervened in Egypt unassisted, and proceeded to gather the land of the Khedive into her sphere of influence as a reward for the cost and risk involved, while France was left to realize that Freycinet was not Ferry.

The conflict between sentiment and common sense, the seesaw be-

[9] W. L. Langer, "The European Powers and the French Occupation of Tunis," *American Historical Review*, XXXI (October 1925), pp. 55–79; XXXI (January 1936), pp. 251–266. The debates in the Chamber of Deputies, excellent examples of Clemenceau's slashing mode of attack, are reported in the *Journal Officiel, Chambre des Députés, Débats*, sessions of June 26, 1881, pp. 1788–1791; and November 9, 1881, pp. 1967–1980.

tween the craving for a glorious foreign policy on the one hand and the quiet determination to cultivate their gardens in peace on the other, continued to plague and confuse the French heart and mind. The nation had been at once fascinated and repelled by the march into Tunis, and this divided mood gave Ferry another chance. The death of Gambetta in 1882 left him the most powerful figure in French politics, and President Grévy recalled him to office in February, 1883. To pacify the Left, the new ministry reëstablished divorce, legalized trade unions, permitted communes freely to elect their own mayors, and modified the system of choosing senators. These half-measures did not appease Clemenceau, for he suspected that Ferry threw them up as a smoke screen to conceal further audacious ventures in colonial conquest. The suspicion was justified. From his defeat over the Tunis expedition and the fall of Freycinet after fumbling the Egyptian issue, Ferry had learned, not to keep the Chambers better informed on matters of colonial policy, but to conceal even more carefully the secret diplomacy and hinterland strife whereby empires in Africa and Asia might be won. On the Niger and in Dahomey, French forces pressed forward with new assurance, while in Madagascar a stiff ultimatum precipitated a war which dragged on for two years. More serious yet, an insurrection in Tonkin and the attempts of the French to establish a protectorate over Annam resulted in an undeclared but costly and inconclusive war with China. To be approved Ferry's methods and policies had to be successful: he understood as clearly as his opponents the penalty of failure. In March, 1885, a French defeat at Lang-son threw Paris into a panic, and Clemenceau seized the moment to attack the cabinet with savage and exaggerated criticism. Once again, as four years earlier, the deputies were nervous with an election pending and repudiated Ferry once more, eager to disassociate themselves from an unpopular venture.[10]

The elections of 1885 opened a new and perilous phase in the history of the Third Republic. Defeat in Indo-China, economic depression at home, discontent on the Left at the meagre reforms, resentment on the Right over the anti-clerical measures, all these factors sent the voters to the polls in a rebellious mood. The result proved a blow to the "Opportunists," who emerged with some 220 seats against about 180 each for the Royalists and Radicals. The popular vote proved even more revealing; not in ten years had the Republic stood so low in the public estimation. To hold the fort and control the new Chamber the Opportunist bloc needed Radical

[10] *Journal Officiel, Chambre des Députés, Débats,* session of May 29, 1885, pp. 688–697.

support and this meant the acceptance of Radical nominees for the cabinet. At Clemenceau's suggestion, Freycinet, when he formed a cabinet in January, 1886, chose a Republican general, Georges Boulanger, as Minister of War.

This move marked a determined attempt on the part of the Radicals to edge their way into power. Through Boulanger they hoped to purge the high command of Royalists and to "republicanize" the army. The introduction of a new arm, the Lebel musket, created a need for new manufacturing machinery. Boulanger dispatched an agent, Léon Chabert, to New York, to negotiate for the patents; Chabert was an associate of Cornélius Herz, who in turn was part owner of Clemenceau's journal, *La Justice*. Herz, who liked to talk in millions and nurtured vast business projects, was also seeking a monopoly to create a telephone system, counting apparently upon another Radical nominee, the Minister of *Postes et Télégraphes*, Granet, for the concession. Boulanger sponsored Herz before his colleagues in the Cabinet, and Boulanger's under-secretary at the War Department was, like Herz, a part owner of *La Justice*.[11] These inter-relationships suggest that the Radicals were learning to combine business and politics, and it is impossible that Clemenceau could have remained ignorant of the combinations.

In the three years which followed (1886–1889) Boulanger's popularity was to soar like a rocket, only to die out in a trail of vanishing sparks. At its height *Boulangisme* constituted the gravest threat the democratic republic had yet faced: Boulanger incarnated the sort of mood which, fifty years later, was to install Hitler as dictator of the German Reich, a mood compounded of wounded nationalism, zeal for greater order, honesty and efficiency in government, a demand from the disinherited classes for social justice, from the industrialists for a more aggressive economic policy and wider markets, from the Right for a responsible executive after the evasions and pusillanimity of parliamentary strife, from the Left for the idealized social and political régime which they associated with the word Republic. The French heart and mind were still divided in 1886. Fear of war with its risks and losses, even a distant colonial war, had brought down the Ferry cabinet. There the head spoke. But General Boulanger, mounted on a black horse, was a symbol to stir the heart. His return from the review on July 14, 1886, brilliant in his uniform, surrounded by his staff, excited the crowds to a frenzy of enthusiasm which proved him a

[11] Adrien Dansette, *Le Boulangisme, 1886–1890* (Paris: Librairie Academique Perrin, 1938), p. 24n.

portent and a power. Leftists and Rightists both realized that in him they might find a lever which could shift a shaky government off its pedestal, provided the lever did not break or twist in the hands of those who grasped it.

To the initiated Boulanger was known as Clemenceau's man. He showed his response to Radical control by introducing military reforms popular with the conscripts, and banished from their commands all princes of former reigning families, a Jacobin gesture which seemed to demonstrate his Republican sincerity. But behind the scenes he was already flirting with the Right. Paul Déroulède, leader of the League of Patriots, saw in Boulanger the man to reform the constitution, establish a strong executive, and forge France into a unit for a war of revenge. Monarchists hoped to cast him in the role of a French General Monk who would clear the way for a royalist restoration. What Boulanger himself planned is not clear. He was ambitious but shallow, and his nerve failed him in moments of crisis. This lack of soldierly decision in the leader, more perhaps than any other single factor, saved France from a Boulangist *coup d'état*.[12]

So long as Boulanger remained outwardly obedient, and his reforms raised the morale of the conscripts and army staff, Clemenceau tolerated his equivocations. But popularity went to the general's head. Elevated suddenly to the role of "*Général Revanche*," he talked and acted with a flamboyance and light-headedness which endangered Franco-German relations, and Bismarck, who needed an argument to force through the German war appropriations, played up the peril. In diplomatic circles there was a widespread conviction by the spring of 1887 that a further increase in Boulanger's influence would mean a Franco-German war, and the danger exerted a sobering effect upon the Republican leaders. Boulanger had become a threat to the Republic: the problem was no longer how to use him but how to get rid of him. In May, 1887, Rouvier formed an "Opportunist" cabinet and Boulanger was not reappointed to the Ministry of War. Clemenceau had lost his lever; he could no longer come and go like a familiar spirit at the War Office in the Rue Saint-Dominique. But he did not let his personal disappointment blind him to the larger implications of the political situation. Bismarck's foresight had secured a renewal of the Triple Alliance with Italy and Austria the previous February, whereas French approaches to Russia still remained mere overtures. In the face of these realities, Boulanger's chauvinism

[12] Alexandre Zévaès, *Au temps du boulangisme* (Paris: Gallimard, 1930), p. 80.

with the popular excitement it aroused was a dangerous folly which alarmed moderate and conservative circles in Paris. Despite popular indignation, fanned by the suspicion that Boulanger's exclusion from the cabinet had been ordered from Berlin, Clemenceau accepted it and swallowed his chagrin.

By July the breach between the Radicals and the man on horseback whom they had helped to popularity became public knowledge, forcing Boulanger to rely more and more definitely on the Rightists and the League of Patriots for his support. Boulangism as a mood and a movement continued to spread: it infected the army staff, the royalist camp; it penetrated intellectual circles and inflamed popular passions. Deprived of his military command in March, 1888, Boulanger became a political candidate and rolled up impressive majorities in multiple elections. But the deepening threat of a dictatorship kept the Republicans from opening a rift in their ranks wide enough for Boulanger to wade through it to a throne. And Clemenceau, Boulanger's protector in 1886, had become his nemesis by 1888. On May 25 he joined with the Opportunist Ranc and the Socialist Joffrin to found the *Ligue des Droits de l'Homme*, pledged to combat Caesarism and promote the Radical reform program by more democratic means.[13]

Because the Third French Republic weathered the tempests of the 1880's it is difficult in the aftermath to conceive how real the perils were. The fate of the Weimar Republic in its fifteenth year, when disgust at an ignominious foreign policy and economic distress at home lifted Hitler to power, throws a retrospective light on the arena of French politics in 1885. More than ever the political farce threatened to become a tragedy in which heads were to roll, figuratively at least, in the dust. To be prominent meant to be vulnerable, to be vulnerable meant, sooner or later, to be attacked, exposed, pilloried without pity. Unlike the First Republic, the Third Republic spared the lives of its political victims but it spared little else. Charges of graft, favoritism, immorality, and even treachery, publicized by a free, vigilant, and scandal-loving press, long surrounded French parliamentarians with an aura of corruption which denied them the respect usually accorded legislators in other lands.

Had Boulanger's private life been more reputable, his word more dependable, his self-discipline more austere, he might have achieved a moral victory over the scandal-smeared chambers and unpopular ministers. The "Wilson Scandal" of 1887, which implicated President Grévy's son-in-law

[13] Adrien Dansette, *Le Boulangisme, 1886–1890*, pp. 222–223.

in the sale of medals and decorations, disgusted men of honor and discredited the presidential office itself. But a scandal of far greater proportions hung momentously over the political life of the Republic during these formative years. If the inside story of the Panama Company with its astounding record of bribery and blackmail had come before the public a little earlier, popular disgust might have swept the Republican régime out of existence in one hot breadth of indignation. Even Clemenceau, for all his intrepidity and skill, was to find himself badly scorched in that blast of shame. But time, procrastination, and hush-hush tactics protected the Republicans. Though the Panama Company failed in 1889, the public did not learn the unsavory details until November, 1892, and by that time Boulanger was dead and Boulangism discredited.

The *Compagnie du Canal Interocéanique* had been a risky and overoptimistic enterprise from the start. Ferdinand de Lesseps's superb confidence, and his popular reputation as the "Great Frenchman" who had cut the Isthmus of Suez, blinded investors and even engineers to the difficulties and dangers of the new venture. Lack of sufficient capital, tropical diseases, miscalculations and mismanagement, all contributed to the financial collapse of the company. But the most serious drain on its credit and vitality was the blackmail practiced in Paris. Journalists who caught wind of the financial plight of the directorate had to be bought off. Deputies, even ministers, whose support was required to authorize new expedients for raising capital profited profusely and shamelessly. A German Jew who had gained an *entrée* to the highest business and social circles in Paris, the Baron Jacques de Reinach, acted as intermediary in holding the Opportunist deputies in line. Criticism from the Radical benches and Radical press was bought off by another Jew, the wealthy speculator, audacious promoter, and enigmatic go-between, Dr. Cornélius Herz.

Like Boulanger, Herz benefited in his early rise to influence and affluence from a carefully cultivated and judiciously advertised association with Clemenceau. How close the relationship became Clemenceau later found it expedient to forget, but at one time he contemplated appointing Herz the guardian of his children in the event of his death.[14] Early in 1880, when *La Justice* was founded, Herz apparently agreed to underwrite the expenses of the journal. By 1883 the advances had increased to a point where Clemenceau signed over a half interest to this obliging sleeping partner whose interest was so easily aroused, whose purse-strings

[14] Georges Clemenceau, *Le Silence de M. Clemenceau*, pp. 212–213.

were so readily released. The exchange of favors continued in one form or another throughout the 1880's; how much Herz contributed in actual cash cannot be established with certainty; estimates have run from 400,000 to 2,000,000 francs.[15] It does not follow of necessity that Clemenceau as director and Herz as investor always saw eye to eye in matters of editorial policy. The association remains, like so many relationships among businessmen, journalists, and politicians, obscure and intangible.

When the Panama scandal broke openly at the close of 1892 it was inevitable that Clemenceau would be dragged into the proceedings. His long association with Herz was public knowledge. But the situation was further complicated by the fact that Herz had been blackmailing Reinach and threatened to expose the Baron's activities on behalf of the company. Deputies who had profited by Reinach's generosity begged the Baron to placate Herz lest the implacable doctor reveal more embarrassing details. On November 19, 1892, when the Minister of Justice was finally moved to order the arrest of directors and agents of the defunct company, Reinach paid a final visit to Herz, accompanied by the Minister of Finance, Rouvier, and Clemenceau. Herz remained adamant; and Reinach, faced with arrest, returned to his home in despair and was found dead in bed the next morning. Clemenceau was one of the last persons to see him alive.

The Chambers could no longer postpone an enquiry, and the Boulangists had their chance to avenge themselves against the ruling bloc, the *République des Camarades*, which had repudiated and broken their idol, Boulanger. Five deputies and five senators were indicted for accepting bribes. Clemenceau escaped a formal arraignment, but he was not destined to escape disgrace. The leader of the League of Patriots, Paul

[15] Bruno Weil, *Panama* (Berlin: W. Rothschild, 1933), pp. 235–245. Ernest Judet, *Le Véritable Clemenceau* (Berne: F. Wyss, 1920), p. 183. In his defense offered August 8, 1893, at Salernes, Clemenceau ironically named three to five million francs. V. Georges Suarez, *Clemenceau*, I, 256. The report on Herz compiled by the parliamentary Commission of Investigation can be read in the *Rapport général fait au nom de la commission d'enquête sur les affaires de Panama.* Par M. E. Vallé. Chambre de Députés, Paris, 1898. Item No. 2945. Charles de Lesseps testified: "Je ne pouvais pas me faire un ennemi de Herz, auquel on attribuait une grande influence, dont le rapide avancement dans la Légion d'Honneur, dont la situation comme gros actionnaire de *La Justice* faisaient craindre l'hostilité. Je payais donc le 600,000 francs en question." De Lesseps was defending himself and some of his inferences were unwarranted by the facts. Clemenceau's defense was based in part on a statement published in *La Justice*, November 3, 1886, that Herz had then ceased to be a stockholder in the journal. The public honors which Herz received are not easily accounted for by any known services to the Republic. He was named Chevalier of the Legion of Honor in 1879, Officer, 1881, Commander, 1883, and Grand Officer, 1886.

Déroulède, had marked his prey: in a philippic of unparalleled venom and virtuosity he assailed Clemenceau before a fascinated Chamber, accusing him not only of collaboration with Herz, but of acting as a paid agent and spy for the British government. In overturning cabinets and thwarting French colonial expansion, Déroulède insisted, Clemenceau had consciously and consistently played England's game. In the atmosphere of bitterness and resentment against foreigners then widespread in France, such insinuations took on added malignity, and the mere fact that Clemenceau spoke English and had visited London gave the charges an appearance of verisimilitude.

There was only one retort possible, and Clemenceau made it: he gave Déroulède the lie direct. On December 22 the two sought a solution on the dueling ground. But on this occasion, perhaps the most serious in his career, when life, reputation, and honor hung in the balance, Clemenceau's customary skill with the pistol deserted him. Six shots were exchanged without result, and nothing was settled, but Déroulède emerged the hero of the duel in the opinion of the public.

Pressing their advantage, Clemenceau's enemies attempted to implicate him explicitly in treasonable negotiations with the British. An ally of Déroulède, Lucien Millevoye, produced before the Chamber a sheaf of documents furnished by a negro employee of the British Embassy named Norton. The documents were palpable forgeries, and Clemenceau brought legal action against Norton and against a journalist, Ducret, for defamation of character. The court sustained the charges, and the defendants were sentenced to fine and imprisonment. But though legally cleared of the charge of treason, and awarded two francs damages for the injury to his reputation, Clemenceau could not escape the shadow cast by the charges. In the elections of August, 1893, when he offered himself as a candidate in the Department of the Var, he was decisively repudiated by the electors. Political circles in Paris exhaled a sigh of relief. The Tiger had been banished from the arena.

CHAPTER V

POLEMICIST
1893–1902

Mais il y a quelquechose de supérieur à l'esprit de corps, c'est la vérité, c'est la justice.[1] CLEMENCEAU

HISSED and mocked in the Chamber, repudiated at the polls, deserted by his friends and hounded by his creditors, Clemenceau withdrew into himself in the fall of 1893, his spirit crushed by the wave of enmity which had overwhelmed him. In that dark spring and summer the rancors he had stirred up so recklessly in twenty years of combat were turned against him. He suddenly became one of the most unpopular and calumniated figures in French public life, not only stigmatized as a grafting politician, but widely suspected of treasonable relations with the British.

Once before, when he escaped from Paris in 1871, cursed by the communards as a traitor and pursued by the Versailles police as a radical, he had known the isolation and bitterness of failure and obloquy. But then he had youth and resiliency on his side: he was thirty, and a few weeks in his beloved Vendée had revived his spirit. Now, at fifty-three, his political career seemed blasted beyond repair. Life no longer beckoned; his health declined; he lost color and animation and self-assurance. To a few intimate friends he admitted that he was at the end of his financial and physical resources, without the will or the spirit to resume the struggle.[2]

His haughty independence, his obstinate pride, fed on its own bitterness and frequently impelled him to rebuff the friends who sought ways to help him. More than once in his long career he was to know these spells of sudden exhaustion and disgust when all his fibres renounced the will to live and he came face to face with the truth that death might be a supreme contempt for oneself.[3] The world, which had been too much with him

[1] Georges Clemenceau, *L'Iniquité* (Paris: Stock, 1899), p. 11.
[2] Georges Suarez, *Clemenceau*, 2 vols. (Paris: Les Éditions de France, 1932), II, 7–11.
[3] Suarez, *Clemenceau*, II, 56.

during his years of ambitious strife, had cast him forth, and his numb spirit turned but slowly to neglected fields for sustenance — to nature, to sculpture and painting, to philosophy and science and history, and above all to books. The shelves which lined his study became his rampart against a hostile world and the books his ideal companions, patient, loyal, unreproachful, making no demands upon his exhausted nature but forever ready to serve his requirements. He lived with them for long months, drawing on them now as a narcotic for his exacerbated nerves, now as a stimulant for his questioning mind, and very slowly he won back some equanimity and some zest for life.

Exile from the forum not only brought the leisure for reading and contemplation, it provided an incentive for improving his prose style. In the years which followed 1893 Clemenceau demonstrated that his pen could compel as much respect as his tongue or pistol. In his new role as observer and commentator his perfectionist complex goaded him more imperiously than ever: he strove with all his ardor to think clearly and to write effectively, and the triumph which he achieved was no easy, unearned laurel. The man of action, the duelist, the orator whose electric phrases had singed reputations and shattered cabinets, became a studious recluse, delighting in meditative walks, in solitary train rides, in long ardent days among his books, the world almost forgetting, almost by the world forgot.

Almost, but not quite. For there was still a mood of anger and bitterness in his heart which projected itself upon society, seeking a local habitation and a name. In his misanthropy he found himself at once angry and tender, contemptuous of individuals but sensitive to the still, sad music of humanity. Even in his retirement the day's journals washed up at his feet the flotsam of a great city's obscure agonies. From casual items his clairvoyant mind framed indictments of the social order, concise in phrasing, caustic in mood, cruel as caricatures in their stark enunciation of unpleasant truths. Writing not only for *La Justice*, but for *L'Echo de Paris*, *Le Matin*, *L'Illustration*, *Le Dépêche de Toulouse*, and *La Nouvelle Presse Libre*, he soon became famous as one of the most influential columnists of the day. No longer the voice of conscience in parliament, he had become the voice of conscience in the press. Hunger, poor relief, work houses, juvenile prisons, orphanages, bastards, beggers, prostitution, public sanitation — week after week he forged his compact paragraphs, forcing these unattractive aspects of city life upon the attention of the complacent classes. The unemployed, the eight-hour day, conditions in mines and factories, labor unions, strikes, anarchists, each topic in turn was culled from the day's news to bear witness to the truth that life was a relentless struggle for survival too seldom tempered by pity or charity. "Let us preach peace," he urged, "because there is little but conflict; justice, because iniquity surrounds us; happiness, because hate abounds." He could not forget, or allow others to forget, that life ought to be a fervent fight to remold ourselves and our surroundings into something nearer to the heart's desire. "To comprehend things as they are, that is a worthy aim no doubt. But how much more stupendous the faculty of conceiving things as they ought to be."[4]

As the months passed these new activities brought him some softening of mood, some rejuvenation of spirit. In the world of literature and art he came to know rare spirits more worthy of his measure than the political associates with whom he no longer consorted. He was not a man with whom it was easy to become familiar; he had none of that magnetism which gave Jaurès power over individuals and multitudes; he treated his acquaintances as colleagues or allies rather than as friends. But what superior acquaintances he found!—Edmond de Goncourt, Gustave Geffroy, Émile Zola, Alphonse Daudet, Jules Renard, Anatole France, Georg Brandes, Claude Monet, Auguste Rodin. From such men he learned timeless values and imbibed a new conviction of the dignity and tragedy of life, a conviction which diluted and objectified his personal rancor and chagrin.

From the income which journalism provided he strove to pay off the obligations of *La Justice* and provide for the support of his children, now reaching maturity. As his mastery of the writer's craft increased he looked on life with a fresh vision and found it more tolerable. Clemenceau's inkwell, Léon Daudet observed with a writer's love of hyperbole, was his fountain of youth. The first harsh and critical essays, collected as *La Mêlée sociale* (1895), were followed by a gentler series, broader in vista, more genial in tone, more philosophical in spirit, published under the title *Le Grand Pan* (1896). Quaint characters, landscapes, travel, Greek antiquities, books, plays, paintings, a miscellany of cultural topics, were mingled with sage and lively comments on contemporary events. Clemenceau was once more coming to terms with the world and himself, was perfecting a role which he could conceive himself filling with success and dignity. The most influential man, he proclaimed, in a passing analysis of

[4] Georges Clemenceau, *La Mêlée sociale* (Paris: Bibliothèque Charpentier, 1895), Introduction, xxxvii-xlii.

Ibsen's *An Enemy of the People*, is the man who stands most completely alone, and he saluted the solitary thinker, "who, from his silent study, guides the world with black lines on white paper." [5]

This reverence for the independent artist found even more eloquent expression in a generous tribute which he composed in honor of Edmond de Goncourt.[6] In the ideal world of great literature it seemed to him possible that a writer could formulate his concepts, in all their logic and passion, with unfettered ease, free from the compromises which vitiated all mundane activities. This faith, and perhaps a secret wish to emulate an Ibsen or a Zola, induced him to attempt a novel and two plays. The novel, *Les Plus forts*, and the more important play, *Le Voile de Bonheur*, were published in 1898; both appeared in later editions and are available in English translations. But Clemenceau, despite his keen observation of men and affairs, despite his determination and his literary zeal, was not greatly gifted for creative writing. He could analyze and dissect with a cool aseptic pen, he could ridicule with lively irony, he could expose dishonesty and insincerity with unsparing logic. But his plots creaked, his scenes lacked spontaneity, the characters had ink rather than blood in their veins, and a didactic or forensic note marred the naturalness of the dialogue. Despite his admiration for the lonely thinker, Clemenceau himself was better fitted for action than for speculation, for polemics than for philosophy, and he found that the castle of *belles-lettres* is not easily taken by assault.

His cluttered private study at his house on the Rue Franklin was, after all, no more than a sanctuary to which he could retire to lick his wounds; even in these years of defeat and depression he was still the Tiger. The glimpses which may be caught of him, coming and going at the offices of *La Justice* and *L'Aurore*, suggest the eagerness with which he still sniffed the smoke of battle. He liked to drop in late in the evening and pace back and forth, chatting and culling over the proof, while the staff put the paper to bed. Stray items of news which the reporters and compositors tossed back and forth, especially those which were off the record, often carried for him a kernel of hidden significance which occasionally he shared with others but more frequently kept to himself. Sometimes on a Saturday night he would arrange an outing with the younger men, and

[5] Georges Clemenceau, *Le Grand Pan* (Paris: Bibliothèque Charpentier, 1896), article "Ibsen." Clemenceau's admiration for Ibsen led him into a dispute with Jaurès on the role of the individual *vs.* society.

[6] George Adam, *The Tiger: Georges Clemenceau* (London: Jonathan Cape, 1930), p. 278.

take them for a ten-mile walk in the country on Sunday morning, the aim being to work up a worthy appetite for the huge pot of soup which had been ordered in advance at a convenient inn. At other times the restlessness in his veins, which middle age had not calmed, drove him to a gymnasium for fencing exercise, or excited him to seek amorous adventures. But on this last subject, as on his domestic problems, he preserved a silence so complete that his biographers have little save gossip to build on, and all but the most hostile have respected his reticence.

The political arena still drew him like a magnet, though he fought to free himself from its fascination and to avoid political issues in his columns. The ship of state, after weathering the stormy tumult of Boulangism and the miasmic fog of Panama, had emerged into calmer waters, but its course pleased Clemenceau no better than formerly. Internationally France enjoyed a somewhat stronger position. By 1894 the *rapprochement* with Russia became an alliance, but an alliance directed as much against Great Britain as against Germany, and likely, as Clemenceau feared with prophetic insight, to involve the Republic needlessly in the Balkan imbroglio. On the domestic front the revival of socialism in the nineties created a new political party to the left of the weakened Radical Republican group, thus preparing the way for that alliance of Socialists and Left Wing Republicans which was to control the government after 1899. But more significant to Clemenceau's observant mind was the *Ralliement* which brought a group of Royalists and Catholics to the support of the Republic after 1892. The *ralliés* as a group were to be transformed a decade later into the Party of Liberal Action, and included Catholics who, after the fiasco of Boulangism had discredited the Royalist cause, followed the adjuration of Leo XIII to accept and support the Republic. It was their hope that they might moderate the anti-clerical legislation, promote Christian socialism as an antidote to the Marxian doctrines which were spreading among the working classes, and alleviate the labor unrest by a sincere attempt to apply the principles advocated in the Encyclical *Rerum novarum* of 1891.

Unhappily, this essay in conciliation, which promised briefly to ease the conflict between Church and State and to unite all but the most refractory clericals and recalcitrant socialists in a mild and well-meant program of social reform, was promptly vitiated by "The Affair." To be understood, the Dreyfus Case must be considered as a state of emotion rather than a set of events. France a generation after 1870 was still a nation with an inferiority complex. Like the National Socialists in Germany forty years later, Frenchmen were seeking a formula which would explain the relative weakness, division, and impotence of *La Patrie*. Patriotic orators always urged, it is true, the need for a more selfless devotion to the Republic, a deeper unity of spirit, a more elevated morale. But self-criticism and self-castigation have a limited appeal at political rallies. What Frenchmen wished to find was a scapegoat, a Jonah who could be blamed for the misfortunes which had overtaken the ship of state. The will to believe that secret and inimical forces were at work within French society had vented itself during the seventies and eighties in the duel between the Royalist-Clerical forces and the Republicans. By 1879 the Republicans had gained the ascendency; by 1889 Royalists and Clericals had been weakened in numbers and influence and thrown on the defensive. But the Republicans, after a decade of power, had failed to carry through the social and political reforms which radical leaders like Clemenceau continued to demand, and the Panama scandal revealed the cynicism and the corruption which prevailed in official circles. Boulangism had demonstrated that a number of French chauvinists were fools. Panama proved that a number of French politicians were knaves. France as a nation of patriots was suffering from wounded vanity.

The suspicion that German intrigues and English gold kept the nation divided and thwarted its foreign and domestic policies was deepseated though seldom openly avowed. It was widely believed that Boulanger had been dropped from his post as Minister of War at Bismarck's demand. Clemenceau had been driven from political life after the Panama scandal because of his supposed activities on behalf of the British government. And Clemenceau had been intimate with Cornélius Herz and Jacques de Reinach. Ruined investors have long memories. The failure in 1882 of *L'Union Générale*, a banking corporation in which many Catholic investors had deposited their life savings, had been attributed to the enmity of Jewish and Protestant financiers. Now thousands more small French investors saw their savings swept away in the collapse of the Panama Company, and listened credulously to the suggestions that British jealousy and the machinations of international Jewry had hastened the ruin of this great and humane French enterprise.

In such a climate of opinion the growth of anti-Semitism was perhaps inevitable. As early as 1886 a journalist, Edouard Drumont, had published a long work, *La France Juive*, which pictured France as a defenseless society bled white through the intrigues and extortions of Jewish financiers. Drumont liked to represent the Jews as avaricious aliens who felt no loyalty towards the nation which they corrupted, pillaged, and betrayed. It was easy for him to edit the unsavory details of the Panama blackmail so that they seemed a confirmation of his thesis, and in 1892 he founded a new journal, *La Libre Parole*, to publicize his views. Millions of Frenchmen were thus indoctrinated with the argument that, if something was rotten in the state, Jewish intrigue and Jewish agents, working in the interest of foreign powers and international finance, were to blame for it.

In the autumn of 1894 Drumont shocked his readers with fresh allegations of Jewish perfidy. A captain on the French general staff, Alfred Dreyfus, had been arrested, allegedly for selling military secrets to the Germans. To readers of *La Libre Parole*, and, indeed, to most Frenchmen who heard of it, the speedy conviction of Dreyfus before a military court, and the sentence confining him for life to close imprisonment on Devil's Island, appeared lenient. Death before a firing squad would not have seemed too severe for a French officer guilty of such a crime. "Alfred Dreyfus has been condemned to the maximum penalty, by the unanimous decision of the judges," Clemenceau announced in *La Justice* on December 25, 1894. "Without article 5 of the Constitution of 1848, which abolished the death penalty in political cases, he would have been shot tomorrow." No hint of pity colored the ruthless phrases in which Clemenceau denounced "this appalling crime"; no mood of Christmas charity awakened a sigh for the bereft wife and children of the defendant. "As for me," he concluded, "I rate perpetual imprisonment a punishment worse than death. Who will object if the traitor is to wear the chains of a convict?" [7]

Three years were to pass before the Dreyfus incident expanded into the Dreyfus Affair, three years during which Clemenceau perfected his sinewy, incisive, columnist's prose as if preparing himself for the conflict which was to divide France into two camps. Then, in October, 1897, he joined a newly founded daily, *L'Aurore*, and commenced a series of articles which probed the Dreyfus case as a surgeon might probe a tumor. Layer by layer he parted the tissue of lies, deceptions, illegalities, forgeries, and *a priori* judgments whereby an innocent man had been convicted, condemned, and denied the chance to appeal. With a guile worthy of Socrates he allowed himself to be led, seemingly against his preconceptions and against his will, from one logical conclusion to another, from one fact to its ineluctable sequel, until his readers like himself came face

[7] Clemenceau, *L'Iniquité*, pp. 1–3.

to face with the appalling truth that the man condemned to a living death on Devil's Island might be, indeed almost certainly was, innocent.

Reconstructed as a cold series of facts, the Dreyfus Affair sounds impossibly one-sided. The famous *bordereau* on which Dreyfus was convicted was not in his handwriting but in that of another officer, Major Esterhazy. Some of Esterhazy's superiors suspected him; it is possible that Colonel Henry actually knew he was the guilty man; yet these superiors protected him and opposed a revision of the case. When the conscientious Colonel Picquart discovered that the *bordereau* was in Esterhazy's hand and notified his superior, General Gonse, Gonse told him to keep the information to himself. Shortly thereafter Picquart was transferred to a frontier post in Tunis. Mathieu Dreyfus, learning independently that the *bordereau* was in Esterhazy's script, demanded justice for his brother. Esterhazy was tried and acquitted by a military court, while Picquart, who had returned to testify against him, was kept under arrest. At each turn it seemed that power and prestige stifled anew the voice of truth and justice.

All the monstrous implications that darkened like a thunder cloud above this sequel of events had been exploited by Clemenceau in his daily articles with deft allusiveness, though he had carefully avoided actionable statements. But on January 13, 1898, *L'Aurore* published Émile Zola's letter to the President of the Republic, that vigorous indictment for which Clemenceau suggested the famous title *J'accuse*. From the illegality of the first court martial, which had condemned Dreyfus on evidence withheld from the defendant and his lawyer, to the acquittal of Esterhazy two days earlier on January 11, Zola laid bare with a novelist's skill the action and motivation of the plot. It was a courageous act at a time when defenders of Dreyfus were being attacked as hirelings of the Jewish syndicate. Summoned before a court on February 23, Zola was convicted of libel and sentenced to a year's imprisonment after the witnesses for the defense had been jeered at and shouted down. Even Clemenceau, who attempted to plead for the freedom of the press, was daunted by the fury of the popular anger. "I was there when he was condemned," he recalled years later, "and I swear I was not prepared for such an explosion of hatred. If Zola had been acquitted that day none of us would have come out alive." [8]

Fortified by the verdict, the military chiefs rode on their triumphant way. Zola was deprived of the Legion of Honor; Picquart was dismissed

[8] Louis Leblois, *L'Affaire Dreyfus* (Paris: Librairie Aristide Quillet, 1929), p. 49.

from the army; Louis Leblois, Picquart's attorney, was stripped of a minor political office. But as Zola had warned, Truth, too, was on the march. Though the Minister of War, Godefroy Cavaignac, reassured the Chamber of Deputies that Dreyfus was guilty, and even proposed to arrest leading Dreyfusards including Jean Jaurès, Scheurer-Kestner, Mathieu Dreyfus, and Clemenceau, the Olympians had overstrained their authority, and the tide of public opinion was beginning to turn. At the end of August, 1898, Colonel Henry, after confessing that he had forged some of the evidence against Dreyfus, committed suicide. Two of his superiors, General de Boisdeffre and General de Pellieux, resigned, and Cavaignac, the Minister of War, followed them. The revisionists, who demanded a new trial for Dreyfus, were gaining the day.

On June 3, 1899, the Cour de Cassation ordered a reopening of the case. Dreyfus was brought back from Devil's Island and faced a second court martial at Rennes, which once again found him guilty, this time "with extenuating circumstances." His punishment was changed to ten years' imprisonment, of which he had already served five. But the passions aroused by the case had so tragically divided French society that many earnest leaders conceived that the most important need was to silence the clamor on both sides. The new Ministry of Republican Defense, under Waldeck-Rousseau, promptly offered Dreyfus a pardon. Broken in health and spirit, Dreyfus agreed, though to accept a pardon for a crime which he had not committed seemed to justify his accusers and protected them from prosecution.

Clemenceau, more concerned for the principles at stake than for the fate of one man, was furious over what he perceived at once to be a tactical error on the part of the defendant. His political instinct was justified. It required another seven years of patient pressure before the Cour de Cassation finally set aside the earlier verdicts, and a repentant nation accorded Dreyfus and the leading Dreyfusards a frank and official atonement for the misjudgment and the opprobrium from which they had suffered.

Today the outstanding fact remembered about the Dreyfus tragedy is that Dreyfus was an innocent victim of judicial error and anti-Semitic prejudice. But for French society the tragedy was national in scope. Millions of Frenchmen believed in all sincerity that, innocent or guilty, Dreyfus had become the excuse for a Jewish syndicate, drawing funds from all over the world, to discredit the army, divide the nation, disrupt the republic. Men like Zola and Clemenceau, the Anti-Dreyfusards implied, were paid to keep the case before the public, to cast doubt upon the competence of the military courts and the capacity of the general staff. Whatever their motives, there can be little doubt that they succeeded in this: French military prestige suffered at home and abroad. The disorder and uncertainty, the rancor and resentment, engendered by the controversy exposed France to the humiliation of the Fashoda incident in 1898. The British Cabinet, strong in the conviction that the French were too distracted to risk a war, took an arrogant stand when they learned that Marchand's expedition had penetrated to the Upper Nile, and insisted upon his withdrawal. It was a signal humiliation for France, and exposed the Dreyfusards to the accusation that they had played into the hands of the British by weakening *La Patrie* at a critical time. Clemenceau discovered that his suspected relations with the British embassy, which had cost him his seat in the Chamber of Deputies five years earlier, had not been forgotten.

The Affair could not fail, likewise, to intensify the feud between France and Germany. That the German military attaché should seek to purchase secret information from a member of the French general staff was a nightmarish thought to haunt the public imagination. The resulting tension and suspicion nullified all efforts to establish the innocence of Dreyfus from German sources.[9] The fact that the trial had been held *in camerâ*, the hints that some of the evidence against Dreyfus was too pregnant with international complications to be produced, the appeal to "reasons of state" to excuse arbitrary acts of the court, all this helped to rasp nerves tautened periodically since 1870 with the fear of a fresh invasion. The outcome verified Clemenceau's reading of political realities. Enduring fear of Germany drove the French to forget Fashoda and seek after 1900 a closer understanding with Great Britain. The scar left by the amputation of Alsace-Lorraine counted more than all the rebuffs Britain had administered to French colonial aspirations.

On French domestic politics the influence of the Dreyfus Case was even more definitive. Convinced that the Republic, and with it the heritage of the great Revolution, was endangered, Frenchmen reëxamined the ideals of Liberty, Equality, Fraternity, and found them worth preserving. The

[9] The concern felt for Dreyfus in German diplomatic and military circles, among those officials in a position to know the truth but powerless to proclaim it, only came to light after World War I. The most important material on the Affair from German sources can be found in *Die grosse Politik der europäischen Kabinette, 1871–1914*, 40 vols. (Berlin, 1922–26), vols. IX, 387–399, and XII, 576–628; and in the notes of Maximilian von Schwartzkoppen, *Die Wahrheit über Dreyfus* (Berlin, 1930).

"League of the Rights of Man" organized in 1898, the alliance of Socialists, Moderates, and Radical Republicans to form a government of republican defense in 1899, and the perpetuation of this alliance through a permanent steering committee after 1902, were all developments fostered by the Dreyfus agitation. The groups of the Left and Center, organized as a "Bloc," took the offensive and carried through a program designed to secure control of all branches of the civil service, republicanize the army and subordinate it to the civil power, and weaken the influence of the Catholic Church by curtailing the educational activities of the clergy. The Associations Law of 1901, restricting the activity of the congregations, the attack on and suppression of teaching orders, the embitterment of Franco-Papal relations, and the Law on the Separation of Church and State (1905) were all a reflection of the intellectual and emotional resurgence of anti-clericalism.

To Clemenceau personally the Affair brought journalistic fame, the excitement of battle, and in 1903 the chance to reënter politics. He had earned the reward, although it is true that his role as a Dreyfusard had sometimes seemed more intractable than constructive. History often exaggerates the influence of great men in their minor moments. To many of his contemporaries, Clemenceau at sixty seemed no more than an aging politician, embittered because he had been defeated and left behind in the race. He may even have seen himself in that guise now and then: his vanity drove him to seek the limelight and yet pretend to shun it, like an actress attempting to renew past triumphs. His speech at Zola's trial was superfluous, for he was not involved in the action, and his duel with Drumont a few days later was injudicious considering the state of public opinion. Both antagonists missed three times, and as Clemenceau in practice could put nineteen balls out of twenty into a lead figure his inaccuracy can probably be ascribed to generosity. Or to prudence. It would have done the Dreyfusard cause no good to make the influential but near-sighted author of *La France Juive* a martyr.

There can be no question that Clemenceau's intractable temper was making him, as always, a difficult colleague and an implacable foe in comparison with such temperate, courageous, and disinterested Dreyfusards as Picquart, Scheurer-Kestner, and Louis Leblois.[10] To clarify and

[10] The Dreyfusards were far from unanimous in their aims and their motives. Some, like Clemenceau, were most concerned to attack the military court and the general staff for overriding legal forms and defying civil rights; for them Dreyfus' guilt or innocence, and his fate, were matters of secondary importance. Some, the Dreyfus family in particular, were most anxious to clear away the stigma of treachery from their name and to free the Jews as

intensify the conflict remained his aim; and in pursuit of it he often proved opinionated and heartless. He would even have sacrificed the central character to the dramatic possibilities of the plot, would have persuaded Dreyfus to refuse a pardon and prefer death on Devil's Island, that the denouement, the final establishment of his innocence, might appear the more tragic and damn his accusers the more drastically. For Clemenceau was a fighter, with that rare two-edged courage which enables a man to sacrifice others as readily as he would sacrifice himself if the cause demands it. He did not believe it possible to found the republic by halves, and he foresaw the perpetual danger of a military *coup d'état* so long as the army remained under the control of a clique of royalist officers. For him the Dreyfus Affair was in essence a renewal of the campaign initiated ten years earlier when he nominated Boulanger Minister of War, the campaign to republicanize the high command and subdue it to civilian control. A deep resentment against those arrogant and independent generals had burned in his heart since the days of the Commune, and he was not disposed to spare the pride of the military now that a chance had come to pay back part of the score.

Nor should it be forgotten in Clemenceau's defense that his health was poor in these fretful years at the turn of the century, and a load of debts weighed him down. In the circumstances his persistent contributions to the press were a triumph of concentration. His daily articles on the Affair, reissued by his publisher friend, Pierre Victor Stock, in seven volumes,[11] remain a monument of journalistic clarity, verve, and political

---

a group from the undeserved odium. Still others, like Colonel Picquart, Scheurer-Kestner (the vice-president of the Senate), and Louis Leblois, as well as intellectuals like Zola, endangered their professional careers and endured intense unpopularity because their consciences would not let them acquiesce in what they decided had been a miscarriage of justice. An admirably clear analysis of the Dreyfusard campaign, especially the fight for revision, is now available in English: *The Dreyfus Case. By the Man — Alfred Dreyfus and his son — Pierre Dreyfus.* Translated and edited by Donald C. McKay (New Haven: Yale University Press, 1937). For further literature on the Affair see the bibliographical notes.

[11] Clemenceau's articles on the Affair were collected and edited by Stock between 1899 and 1903 and form a vivid day to day comment on the successive developments. The dramatic irony implicit in the situation, the inexorable manner in which the leading characters obeyed the dictates of their loyalties and prejudices, the shattering denouement, all seem to have foreshadowed themselves in Clemenceau's mind as early as 1898. His dissection of scenes and motives has at times a fated quality like the utterances of a Greek chorus. "I must bear witness," he insisted more than once, "that there is an implacable logic chaining together the succession of events which are unfolding before us" (*L'Iniquité*, p. 163). Of his seven volumes on the Affair, *L'Iniquité* and *Vers la Réparation* appeared in 1899, *Contre la justice* in 1900, *Des juges* and *Justice militaire* in 1901, *Injustice militaire* in 1902, and *La Honte* in 1903.

acumen. He commenced them shortly after joining the contributing staff of *L'Aurore* in 1897 at the invitation of Ernest Vaughan (his own paper, *La Justice*, went into liquidation in October of that year); he continued them in a new weekly of his own, *Le Bloc*, after a break with Vaughan in 1899, but returned to *L'Aurore* when *Le Bloc* ceased publication in 1902.

Here once again the knotty problem of Clemenceau's finances beclouds the discussion. When Vaughan invited him to write a daily column for *L'Aurore* he agreed that part of his earnings should be assigned monthly to the creditors of *La Justice*. At the close of 1899 the staff of *L'Aurore* agreed to accept a reduction in salary, but Clemenceau, bound by his agreement, objected. He had quarreled with another contributor, Urbain Gohier, and refusing all overtures he broke with Vaughan in a note dated December 17. A year of poor health and increasing irritability followed during which he strove to support himself by free-lance writing, discouraged, it may well be, to see his Radical Republican group sharing power in the cabinet of Waldeck-Rousseau while he stood on the side lines. His father's death had left him more lonely than ever; and the small inheritance which it brought him went to appease his creditors.[12] Some 20,000 francs in royalties which accrued from his volumes published by Stock was largely distributed in the same cause.[13] Despite the prevalent belief that the champions of Dreyfus were being well paid for their services, Clemenceau seemed to have lost rather than gained by his labors. In 1902, however, his prospects brightened. Stock and other friends urged him to reënter the political race as senator for the Department of the Var, and although he had frequently advocated the abolition of the upper chamber he modified his scruples and accepted the nomination. He was elected April 6, 1903. Joseph Reinach, who saw him frequently during these months, found him greatly improved in spirits. Louis Leblois had come to his aid financially, contributing, apparently, 60,000 francs to *L'Aurore*, now under new direction, on condition that Clemenceau resume his contributions.[14]

[12] Georges Clemenceau, *Le Silence de M. Clemenceau*, ed. by Jean Martet, p. 240.

[13] Pierre-Victor Stock, *Mémorandum d'un éditeur. Deuxième Série* (Paris: Stock, Delamain et Boutelleau, 1936), p. 45.

[14] Paul Desachy, *Une grande figure de l'affaire Dreyfus: Louis Leblois* (Paris, Rieder, 1934), pp. 180–181. Clemenceau admitted this indebtedness to Leblois years later, recalling that Leblois brought him "I don't know how many thousand francs. . . ." But he did not remember the contribution with any expression of gratitude; indeed he insisted that Leblois was a man "against whom it was necessary to be on one's guard" (*Le Silence de M. Clemenceau*, pp. 212, 240).

With a senator's status and salary, money behind him, and an assured public for his pen, Clemenceau reëntered the arena, a *vieux débutant* as he liked to style himself, often in opposition but never in office. His long apprenticeship in medicine, journalism, and politics had not greatly modified his thinking; he remained the ferocious idealist, "a blend of anarchist and conservative," who contemplated his fellow men with a great admiration and a great contempt, admiration for what they might be and contempt for what they were. He still believed that the purpose of life was to strive for "things as they ought to be"; he still sought integration amid the hammer blows of strife; he still clung to his Jacobin faith in democracy and right reason, in education and enlightenment. "The true mission of the press," he insisted, "is to react against prejudicial influences."[15] And the true aim of democracy was to liberate the potentialities of the individual within the framework of a harmonious and integrated society. "Democracy alone is capable of making the citizen complete. To it alone belongs the magnificent role of reconciling all citizens in a common effort of solidarity."[16]

Solidarity. The word had taken on an almost mystical sanctity for French liberal thinkers in the early nineteen-hundreds. Though never formulated positively enough to be called a political philosophy, it none the less represented as nearly as any school of thought could do, perhaps, the faith to which Clemenceau subscribed. In 1903 he had completed half his thirty-five years of parliamentary activity, but he had not yet entered a ministry, had not yet emerged *dans les champs du pouvoir*, had not yet become one of the makers of modern Europe. But he had completed his long political apprenticeship. It is time to attempt an assessment of his philosophy, if it may be called a philosophy, and to analyze his program, if it may be called a program. This, however, is a task reserved for the following chapter.

[15] Georges Clemenceau, *Sur la démocratie: neuf conférences*, rapportées par Maurice Ségard (Paris: Larousse, 1930), p. 59.

[16] Clemenceau, *Sur la démocratie*, p. 98.

CHAPTER VI

SENATOR
1903–1906

All social activity is a resolution of forces, an association of interests, in which the individual and the group cannot serve one another to advantage, cannot prop one another up, except by a mutual thrust and counter-thrust.[1]

CLEMENCEAU

WHILE still a medical student Clemenceau had pondered the origin of life and the laws which determine the harmonious growth of living organisms. His early positivism was later modified by the Darwinian theories on the struggle for existence and survival of the fittest; and his faith in democracy resolved itself into the concept of a fair field and no favors, with the state as umpire assuring the maximum equity and opportunity for legitimate self-development to each citizen. Progress he conceived as a product of the contest of individual and group efforts in the political, economic, cultural, and intellectual spheres. He liked to proclaim his profound confidence in the ultimate filtering out of truth through the free play of the human spirit. But this optimistic faith, inspired by the eighteenth-century *philosophes*, was tempered by a realistic conviction that there was no progress without effort. Democracy, for Clemenceau, was a fighting faith, a perpetual crusade on the part of society to improve itself.

How much of his thinking was borrowed from Comte, Darwin, Spencer, or Durkheim it is not easy to determine, for Clemenceau seldom cited authorities save to dispute their conclusions. He accepted the fact of the increasing complexity of modern society, involving that specialization of labor which Durkheim emphasized, and he shared the latter's hope that law, as civilization advanced, would be less *retributive* and more *restitutive*, that legislation would, in other words, more nearly approximate the dictates of the intelligence and the moral sense. But his mind distrusted the abstract and metaphysical, and he had scant sympathy with

[1] Georges Clemenceau, *Au soir de la pensée*, 2 vols. (Paris: Plon, 1930), II, 375.

the tendency to distinguish phases or stages in evolution or history. In his voyages on the seas of thought he preferred to cruise within sight of the concrete and hug the shores of the empirical. Perhaps for this reason he does not seem to have found Schopenhauer or Bergson particularly stimulating, although one would have expected him to enjoy Schopenhauer's sardonic insight into character and to approve Bergson's emphasis on the role of creative evolution.

That wars and revolutions were the growing pains of a better world order Clemenceau could not demonstrate even to his own satisfaction, but he accepted this thesis as an article of belief and verified it, in his own experience, by driving himself to action whenever he felt doubtful or discouraged. Reversing the old admonition to be sure you are right and then go ahead, he found that if he pushed ahead stubbornly he usually felt increasingly certain that he was right. Other French thinkers of the time, pondering the same problems more profoundly, and equally eager to formulate a philosophy which would provide an acceptable answer, developed the concept of Solidarity. The honor of enunciating this doctrine in popular terms is usually awarded to Charles Gide and Léon Bourgeois. In reality it was no man's brain child; rather it was a spontaneous whorl or vortex formed in the currents of French thought as they turned from the nineteenth to the twentieth century. The French Revolution of a hundred years earlier had been, in one aspect at least, an attempt to disengage society from its dependence upon organized religion and to found theories of statecraft upon scientific deductions. Solidarity drew its strength from a similar merging of two contemporary intellectual trends. "This idea of social solidarity," Léon Bourgeois proclaimed, "is the resultant of two forces long alien to each other, today reconciled and combined among all the nations which have reached a superior stage of evolution: namely: *the scientific method and the moral idea.*"[2]

French intellectuals of 1900, especially those whose anti-clericalism had been intensified by the Dreyfus controversy, embraced the formula with enthusiasm and gave it wide currency. The political theories of the Radical Republicans and Socialists lacked an authoritative moral philosophy and Solidarity promised to supply the lack. The word acquired a sudden popularity, became a slogan, inflated and magniloquent. "Every nation is a great solidarity," Renan had affirmed. "History is nothing

[2] Léon Bourgeois, *Solidarité*, 7th ed. (Paris: Librairie Armand Colin, 1912), p. 6. Bourgeois had formulated his ideas on the subject before 1900; the first version of *Solidarité* was published in 1896, and an *Essai d'une philosophie de solidarité* in 1902.

other than the study of solidarity," Seignobos added.[3] But to its formulators Solidarity remained a more precise, a more strictly contemporaneous concept. "It is the product," Bourgeois insisted, "of the joint advance of minds and consciences, and it constitutes the basic warp and woof underlying the developments of our age."[4] Modern science, which was endowing society with a new muscular system in machine production and steam and electric power, a new nerve system in the telegraph, telephone, and rotary press, a new alimentation through the increase and distribution of the food supply, this same science, its devotees affirmed, would provide a solution to the problems of social hygiene, education, distribution of wealth, regulation of population, and class conflict, problems which the closer coherence and integration of society had aggravated and multiplied.

Could such a rectifying principle be discerned in the working of secular society? The philosophy of Solidarity seemed to furnish rational arguments for the belief that such a principle did exist and that science, guided by ethical ideals, could discover and invoke it. "Thus the definitive truth emerges," Bourgeois wrote. "Individual activities, isolated, produce little and that but slowly. In conflict, they destroy one another. Side by side they add only to themselves. None but associated activities interact rapidly, persist and grow. Association is creative. . . ."[5]

Clemenceau was more skeptical and more realistic. He recalled that Darwin had often found the struggle for existence fiercest among closely related species, and he insisted that social collaboration, even when most productive and progressive, remained critical and competitive. He did not believe that modern science would give man something for nothing, or add a cubit to his stature while he took no thought of the morrow. The Socialists seemed to him too frequently to reduce themselves into a mutual admiration society and to expect the proletariat to do the same. Clemenceau had more respect for the Syndicalists, with their pragmatic program of bargaining backed by the threat to strike and the threat of violence. And it is worth noting that Georges Sorel, in his *Réflexions sur la violence*, quoted Clemenceau more frequently and approvingly than any other commentator. The two men shared a common dislike for that eloquent gift of euphemism which Jaurès invoked so gracefully, for they recognized that in politics the art of bargaining was often one half seduction and one half blackmail.

[3] Charles Gide, *La Solidarité* (Paris: Presses Universitaires de France, 1932), p. 3.

[4] Bourgeois, *Solidarité*, p. 6.

[5] Bourgeois, *Solidarité*, p. 25.

Clemenceau's youthful acquaintance with the harsh and narrow life of the Vendéean peasant, his critical initiation into politics as mayor of Montmartre, his medical activities among the destitute families in Paris, all had reinforced his preference for a pragmatic approach to social problems. In judging a character or a situation he applied a realistic norm, illustrated his comment with a concrete example. He remained a perpetual foe of platitudes, complacency, selfishness, and humbug; to call his splenetic fault-finding, his brutal flair for deflating a pompous ego, constructive criticism is too generous; his life, as he confessed himself, was a complex of friendship and vituperation, an unstable mixture which constantly threatened to dissolve into mere acid scolding. But he could not withhold his reprimands. He was haunted by the pressure of time, by the chariots of retribution which he heard drawing near, by the miseries of the under-nourished, disease-ridden dwellers in the slums, by the unregarded and unrewarded labors of millions of conscientious and anonymous servants of society, clerks and cooks and carpenters, parents, teachers, doctors. "There are other types of bravery besides military courage," he once observed, his father's example, perhaps, coming to his mind. "The physician, the simple hospital attendant, who for fifty years walks hand in hand with death, caring for contagious cases, reveals a courage of a higher order." [6]

The essential problem in any régime, Clemenceau came to believe, was to keep all functionaries up to the mark; in a democracy, where responsibility was most widely divided, this problem outweighed all others. To expose and demote the lazy and incompetent, to distinguish and advance the capable and conscientious, here, if anywhere, he was persuaded, one touched upon the self-rectifying principle of politics. The secret of the good society was a steady, unsparing, winnowing wind of criticism, sifting the chaff from the grain. Every régime, institution, business, club, committee, or family was leavened by the unselfish devotion of a conscientious minority. The members of this minority were the elect, and Clemenceau liked to believe that authority gravitated naturally into their hands, or that, even when they took no active part in affairs, their strength of character shed a profound influence around them. "Democracy," he wrote, "is essentially the régime in which the people is governed by *élites*. To find the best method of forming these *élites* is the primary problem which confronts a democracy." For the members of an *élite* could not be per-

[6] Georges Clemenceau, *Sur la démocratie: neuf conférences,* rapportées par Maurice Ségard (Paris: Larousse, 1930), p. 119.

mitted to entrench themselves in power, to transform a little brief authority into an office, to become an aristocracy, a caste. "The *élite* is essentially fluid, changing. It is in perpetual flux, emerging each moment from the depths of the populace, appearing on the surface, playing its role and vanishing, to provide a place for the new *élite*."[7]

As an illustration of the emergence of such an *élite* Clemenceau cited the activity of the Dreyfusards. Their indignation at a miscarriage of justice forged a bond among them and crystallized their mood. The group became a powerful catalytic agent within the body politic, produced a ferment which established a new bloc in power; then, its function accomplished, the group dissolved. Out of the minor political revolution thus stirred up flowed a number of reforms, traceable, in their inception, to the initiative of the Dreyfusard *élite*.

It was true that a few courageous individuals, endowed with sensitive consciences, had awakened France to a miscarriage of justice, reversing the tide of popular opinion. It fell to the politicians of the Left, however, to seize the pliant hour and inaugurate long-nurtured reforms like the separation of Church and State and the republicanization of the army. Their task, inevitably, involved a descent from the high level of abstract justice and the rights of man and the citizen to the mundane sphere of practical politics. The consequences, it must be confessed, were disillusioning. Waldeck-Rousseau, who formed a ministry of pacification in June, 1899, sought to steer a moderate course and let rancors die. But the republican bloc of the Left, supported by Socialists, Radical Socialists, Radical Republicans, and some Moderate Republicans, had a score to settle with the Clericals, the Patriotic Leagues, and the Army command.[8] Unfor-

[7] Here, as elsewhere, it is not easy to trace the origin of Clemenceau's ideas. He agreed with Herbert Spencer that all government rests to a large degree on the consent, tacit or manifest, of the governed. His thinking with respect to an *élite* may have taken form in his student days when he meditated Blanqui's projects for organizing a secret revolutionary group; but the ideal as Clemenceau later formulated it has been adapted to an evolutionary instead of a revolutionary society. Historically this concept of government of an *élite* by an *élite* for the people was to achieve its most striking expression in the Russian Communist Party. Between 1909 and 1912 Clemenceau meditated a seven-volume work on government, law, morality and culture, to trace the growth of the democratic ideal from prehistoric times, but politics reclaimed his attention too powerfully and the project was laid aside. Part of the material and some of the conclusions were later incorporated in *Au soir de la pensée*. See Léon Abensour, "Un grand projet de G. Clemenceau," *Grande revue*, CXXXI (1930), 529–550. The quotations cited are taken from notes and comments which Clemenceau prepared in collaboration with Abensour.

[8] R. A. Winnacker, "The Délégation des Gauches," *Journal of Modern History*, IX (December 1937), 449–470.

tunately, some of the religious orders, notably the Assumptionists, had been active in the campaign against Dreyfus, and this served as an excuse for a renewed attack upon them. The period of the *Ralliement*, with its aspiration towards a working agreement between servants of the Church and servants of the State, had passed. The years between 1901 and 1906 saw the passage of an Associations Law which placed the religious orders at the mercy of the government, the abrogation of the *Concordat*, and finally the separation of Church and State. The leaders of the *Bloc des Gauches* had reverted to the projects of Jules Ferry, eager to place all Church property at the national disposal, and to draw or drive students still attending clerical schools into secular institutions with secular instructors. If carried through rigorously, such legislation would lead to a state monopoly of education. Clemenceau foresaw the trend and refused to condone such a consummation. Monopolies breed dogmas, he warned his senatorial colleagues in November, 1903.[9] In its hour of mastery the *Bloc des Gauches* was developing the vices of intolerance and bigotry which its leaders never tired of denouncing in their clerical and conservative opponents.

The patriotic organizations, especially Déroulède's *Ligue des Patriotes*, which had defended the army chiefs in their fight with the Dreyfusards, were likewise marked out for dissolution once the *Bloc des Gauches* assumed power. Déroulède had rendered himself ridiculous—and vulnerable—through a farcical attempt at a *coup d'état* in February, 1899. Acquitted by a jury, he was retried by the Senate, imprisoned, and then exiled. Guérin, a lieutenant of Edouard Drumont, even more prejudiced against the Jews than his chief, was likewise convicted of conspiring against the Republic. In their zeal to secure a conviction the prosecutors did not hesitate to use shady police methods, and they pressed towards their goal with a cold ruthlessness reminiscent of the Dreyfus proceedings. Their goal was the "purification" of the government services, and functionaries were left in no doubt from which direction the wind of official favor was now blowing.

It is not easy for men long seated in the ranks of the Opposition to lay aside old loyalties and prejudices on stepping into a cabinet office, to widen the focus of their mind from a party concept to a national comprehension. Camille Pelletan, an old associate of Clemenceau, one of the original group which founded *La Justice* in 1880, demonstrated this when he became Minister of Marine under Combes in 1902. Anxious, as a

[9] Georges Suarez, *Clemenceau*, 2 vols. (Paris: Les Éditions de France, 1932), II, 68.

good Socialist, to befriend the dockyard workers, and, as a good Republican, to promote deserving Republicans, Pelletan pursued a partisan policy (Combes permitted his cabinet associates unusual freedom of action) and the efficiency of the French navy suffered in consequence. A Committee of Enquiry, appointed in 1904 to investigate charges of favoritism and incompetence in this branch of the national defense, took no resolute action, and the decline of the navy continued. As chairman of this committee, Clemenceau may be accused of partiality and blindness for his failure to report the evidences of neglect, false economy and faulty design in naval construction which the enquiry revealed. But the navy was associated in his mind with the colonies (indeed the two departments had been united until 1890) and he looked upon both with a jaundiced eye as enterprises which diverted French attention, income, and energy from the Rhine frontier where the future of the Republic would one day be decided.[10]

The efforts to republicanize the army command produced a more dramatic scandal, a political crisis which split the *Bloc des Gauches* and resulted in the resignation of the Combes cabinet in January, 1905. The victory of the Dreyfusards had brought a new minister of war into office in 1900. General André was a good Republican who conceived it to be his responsibility, in the spirit of the new régime, to promote Republican officers of sound opinions. But how to discover their true opinions was the problem. André decided to utilize the resources of the anti-Catholic section of the Freemasons, and a member of his staff, Captain Mollin, was soon receiving daily reports, or *fiches*, from the secretary of the Grand Orient lodge. The men employed in this secret system of espionage conceived themselves to be dutiful sons of the Republic, working for the improvement of the army staff and army morale, but the effect of the system was to violate the revolutionary ideal of "careers open to talent" and to handicap clericals and conservatives to the advantage of anti-clericals, Protestants, Freemasons, and Jews. This was the more serious for the sons of good Catholic families because by 1900 the army was the only important branch of public service in which Catholics were not likely to find their religion a bar to advancement.[11]

Rumors soon spread that new influences were governing the system of military promotion. When a subordinate at the Grand Orient betrayed

[10] This neglect and maladministration of the navy, though ignored for some years, was a buried bomb. When it burst in 1909 it wrecked the Clemenceau ministry.

[11] D. W. Brogan, *France under the Republic* (New York: Harper and Brothers, 1940), pp. 380–382.

the machinery of recommendation to the secretary of the *Ligue de la Patrie Française*, the Nationalists of the Right had proof of what had become an unverified surmise. The Minister of War faced a sudden critical interpolation in the Chamber to which he dared not answer yes or no. Then the details came out, too substantial to be denied, and the officers concerned passed the responsibility back and forth in undignified confusion.[12] After several marginal votes, the Combes ministry resigned in January, 1905. The Freemasons involved in the exposure protested, with mortification, that the politicians of the Left might have passed them a vote of thanks for "deserving well of the Fatherland." Perhaps they regarded themselves, in Clemenceau's definition of the term, as an *élite*; if so, they were consistent in following his prescription, for they dropped from the public view when the scandal was over.

The *Bloc des Gauches* had risen to power on the tide of national indignation which followed the denouement of the Dreyfus Affair. For five years, from 1900 to 1905, it controlled the Chamber of Deputies. The slogan of the *Bloc* was social justice, its intellectual creed was Solidarity. But inevitably practical considerations and stubborn obstacles tarnished and mutilated the ideal program. The quest for Solidarity ended in disunity and schism. Between Church and State the rift widened into an open break. Class antagonism deepened, Syndicalism waxed stronger, and the *Confédération Général du Travail* threatened to become a state within a state, dictating its will to the government under the menace of a general strike. The army was weakened by a cut in appropriations, by the new modes of promotion, and by the reduction of the period of service from three years to two. The efficiency of the navy declined. Even within the cabinet there was, if not disunion, a dispersal of authority, for Combes allowed the various ministers a free hand in running their departments and the independence of the bureaucrats increased.

One consequence of this division of cabinet responsibility was a disjunction of French foreign and domestic policies. While French Socialists, under the inspiration of Jaurès, were fraternizing with their fellow Socialists in Germany, and laying plans for an international strike which would make an imperialist war impossible, Delcassé, as French Minister for Foreign Affairs, strengthened the Franco-Russian military alliance, har-

[12] Captain Mollin, "Who Started the Spy System in France?" *Catholic Mind* (New York, April 22, 1905), pp. 179–201. Mollin's superiors asked for his resignation in an effort to shield themselves, but he fought back, proving that he had acted throughout on their instructions and with their approval. In preparing his defense Mollin sought the advice of Clemenceau's brother Albert, who, as a lawyer, had volunteered his services in the Dreyfus case.

monized disputes with Italy, and fostered an *entente* with England which by 1904 became an alliance in all but name. Delcassé's patient and successful diplomacy reëstablished a balance of power in Europe, creating a *Triple Entente* to offset the Triple Alliance. But his commitments presupposed that France would maintain her armaments and support her allies. Meanwhile, on the home front, the Socialists were preaching internationalism, paring military budgets, and protecting the labor unions. By 1905 the contradictions implicit in these divergent policies produced a crisis. Russia, having turned from the west to the east, had suffered defeat in the Russo-Japanese War and was temporarily useless as an ally. Germany seized the opportune moment to demand compensation for the spread of French influence in Morocco, and France had to yield. Delcassé's ambitious policies and independent course had invited the reverse and he paid the penalty: he resigned. A shock of resentment swept through the French nation and the nationalist leagues began to agitate with new energy. The reign of the *Bloc* was over, the sterner realities of the class conflict were threatening the internal peace of France, and grim shades of an international war had begun to cast their warning athwart the domestic scene. The French people paused to take stock of realities.

It seemed clear that the dangers, internal and external, called for a stronger cabinet with a more concerted and resolute policy. Yet when Combes resigned in January, 1905, his successor, Rouvier, was able to form only a stop-gap ministry. He hung on for a year, weathered the humiliation over Morocco and Delcassé's resignation in June, reshuffled his cabinet in February, 1906, then gave up in March and yielded his office to Sarrien. Sarrien's cabinet lasted seven months, while on the left the *Confédération Générale du Travail* grew more radical and on the right the *Action Française* grew more royalist. In October, 1906, Sarrien was superseded by Clemenceau, who established a cabinet which lasted longer than the Combes ministry had endured—lasted, in fact, almost three years, until July, 1909. The fall of three cabinets between January, 1905, and October, 1906, signalized the fact that the *Bloc des Gauches* had collapsed. The persistence of the Clemenceau cabinet from October, 1906, to July, 1909, demonstrated that the Radical Republicans had rallied the center against the Right and the Left. France had passed through a period of instability and returned to the middle of the road. Clemenceau, the empiricist, the critic, the man of action, had been chosen to steer the government on a firm but moderate course. It was a mandate to govern and to govern prudently. It was not a mandate to improvise or to experiment.

CHAPTER VII

PRESIDENT OF THE COUNCIL: DOMESTIC PROBLEMS 1906–1909

Lorsque M. Jaurès, du haut de la tribune, me demandait mon programme, j'avais quelque peine à me tenir de lui répondre: "Mon programme? Il est dans vôtre poche; vous me l'avez pris." [1]

CLEMENCEAU

IN 1906, when Clemenceau became a cabinet minister, the mood of France mirrored the hopes and fears which ruled all the leading European peoples: hope that means could be found to assure peace and disarmament, so that taxes might be reduced or diverted to the social services; fear that national rivalries would grow sharper and more costly until they ended in a ruinous war. While Socialist delegates hurried from one congress to another, planning an international strike to paralyze mobilization if hostilities threatened, the diplomats at Algeciras sought a formula to ease Franco-German tension over Morocco. In February, Great Britain opened a new and more costly phase of naval construction by launching the first *Dreadnought*; Germany responded with an augmented naval program in May. During the year which followed the strains and contradictions implicit in European society grew more pronounced. Germany, Austria-Hungary, and Italy renewed the Triple Alliance; France, Russia, and Great Britain drew together in a Triple *Entente*; while at the Hague a Peace Conference representing all the powers labored to limit armaments, protect neutrals, and promote international arbitration and good will.

It is not easy to establish a connection during this period between the crises in French domestic and foreign affairs. Théophile Delcassé was repudiated by the press and by the parliament in 1905 because, after seven years at the Foreign Office, his brilliant alliance-building had alarmed the German government and invited war. Rouvier's cabinet, on the other hand, was overthrown in March, 1906, because it stirred up internal disorder by the rigor with which it attempted to enforce an inventory of Church property. It may be noted, however, that in the weeks before

[1] Georges Suarez, *Clemenceau*, II, 88–89.

Rouvier's fall the Chamber of Deputies had been wrangling over the budget, especially the military and naval estimates. Both deputies and senators voted the budget for the succeeding Sarrien ministry with a confidence they had not felt, apparently, in Rouvier's assemblage of mediocrities. This sequel suggests that their basic desires at the moment were stronger government, cheaper government, and adequate national defense, not an easy program to execute, but one which was typical of the nation's divided sentiments.

Compared to the ministry which it replaced, the Sarrien Cabinet of 1906 reads like a roll of fame. With Léon Bourgeois at the Quai d'Orsay, Clemenceau at the Ministry of Interior Affairs, Poincaré handling the finances, and Aristide Briand Public Instruction and Cults, it included men of established reputation for whom fate reserved still greater tasks. But the list comprised other notables in addition to these four, for Sarrien persuaded Louis Barthou to head the Ministry of Public Works, Posts and Telegraphs, and Gaston Doumergue that of Commerce and Industry. The War Department was left to Étienne and the Navy to Thomson, while Leygues was responsible for the Colonies and Ruau for Agriculture.

The French people were weary, in 1906, of their government's timidity in foreign affairs, disturbed by the long controversy between Church and State, and alarmed by the spread of syndicalism. By luck or judgment Clemenceau read the mood of the nation aright and from his first days in office his resolute course of action marked him out as the man of the hour. The rise of Socialism and the spreading strikes had thoroughly frightened the middle classes. In March, 1906, a tragic mining disaster in the Pas-de-Calais buried a thousand miners alive; the mining companies had neglected adequate safety measures, and the workers' response was a particularly bitter strike. Full of fine sentiments and bonhomie, Clemenceau plunged into the mêlée in person, but contact with the inflamed workers and obstinate mine owners quickly dissipated his conciliatory mood. He returned to Paris persuaded that, to arbitrate, the government must be strong, and he sent troops to patrol the disaffected regions. The soldiers had orders to show consideration and above all to avoid bloodshed unless the provocation became very great, but several clashes occurred with loss of life on both sides. It was a critical test. The sympathy of the soldiers lay with the working classes, several battalions were in a mutinous mood, and timid bourgeois citizens half-expected another 1789 and a collapse of army discipline. As May 1 approached proletarian agitators planned mass demonstrations in Paris, and the Confédération Générale du Travail hoped for a show of working class solidarity which would overawe the government. But Clemenceau put his trust in firmness and the soldiers' habit of obedience. He advised the Prefect of Police to call out special reserves, and he arrested the leaders of the Confédération on the charge that they were conspiring against the public order. For the sake of impartiality he also took into custody the most militant spokesmen of the patriotic and reactionary leagues, which planned to hold counter demonstrations.

Such ruthlessness angered the Socialists, but it reassured millions of sober citizens throughout the country. Jean Jaurès vigorously assailed Clemenceau in the Chamber, hurling back at him the accusations of blindness, brutality and arbitrary rule which he had himself so often urged against previous ministers. In reply Clemenceau admitted frankly that he was now "on the other side of the barricade." He had become a member of the government, and the first duty of a government was to maintain order and to protect property. After that, as opportunity permitted, the long awaited reforms: an eight-hour day, unionization of all workers including state employees, sickness, old age and accident insurance, nationalization of monopolies, progressive income tax, proportional representation. But first, as an essential prerequisite to any progress, the maintenance of law and order.

The exercise of authority sobers most men, and Clemenceau in office had to lay aside the distant vision for the present duty. The evangelist had become a policeman. To get the world up in the morning, start it on its way to work, supervise its labors, assure its sustenance, see it safely home again at evenfall — such duties soon seemed responsibility enough for any government. From time to time the new minister exploded in a burst of nervous frustration as he saw from the inside the sterile and unimaginative methods of a government bureaucracy at work. He deplored the consecrated apathy, the invincible indolence of the public functionaries. He rebelled as other reformers before him had rebelled at the pious interment of generous ideals in a bottomless sea of paper projects. Then he took a firm hold on his irascible temper and geared himself down to the daily stint of conciliation and intimidation, of promise and compromise, which was the art of politics.

Despite the attacks of Jaurès, he gained respect if not popularity by his firmness. His resolution in calling out the soldiers and in arresting the syndicalist leaders won the approval of the Chamber and a great part of the nation. When the Socialists had exhausted all their eloquence in criticism, the Sarrien ministry asked a vote of confidence and received it,

410 to 87.[2] Having successfully demonstrated that "the velvet scabbard held a sword of steel," Clemenceau and his colleagues then reverted to gentler tactics. As July 14, 1906, approached, the Cabinet announced a general amnesty for all infractions of the law arising from strikes, election riots, journalistic imprudence, and violation of the legislation on religious affairs. This gesture at conciliation was misunderstood in some quarters, mocked in others: the intention, at least, was generous.

After six months as nominal head of a ministry in which he felt himself a pigmy among giants Sarrien pleaded ill health and resigned. Clemenceau took over the leadership promptly, reconstructing the cabinet (October 18–22, 1906) with an assurance that indicated prearrangement.[3] Elections the previous spring had strengthened the parties of the Left in the Chamber, particularly the Radical Republicans, and the financial policies of the government had been under attack. In the Clemenceau ministry the more adroit and radical Caillaux (he favored a progressive income tax) replaced the precise and conscientious Poincaré. For two weeks before Sarrien retired the powerful Committee on Finance had been tearing to pieces Poincaré's trial budget for 1907. Caillaux slashed expenditures, reallocated obligations, and reduced the anticipated deficit, on paper at least, from 353 to 62 million francs. Clemenceau persuaded both chambers to pass the amended budget by comfortable majorities.

In return he offered a program of reform full of eloquent promises but vague regarding the time and manner of their implementation. An adequate program of national defense would be mandatory. The religious question was to be settled in conformity with the laws of 1901 and 1905 suppressing the teaching orders and separating Church and State. Legislation would be drafted to provide for a progressive income tax, an eight-hour working day, old age pensions, extended power and protection for the *syndicats*, proportional representation, a law guaranteeing individual liberty, and sharp restrictions on the scope and authority of the military courts. As a final sop to the workers a new Ministry of Labor was created and this twelfth portfolio in the cabinet was entrusted to the independent Socialist, Réné Viviani. It was a fine program, but nothing, as the German proverb has it, is eaten as hot as it is cooked. When Clemenceau left office three years later nine-tenths of it was still in the future tense.

[2] *Revue politique et parlementaire*, XLIX (June 1906), 218.

[3] As early as March 14, 1906, the German ambassador at Paris, Fürst Radolin, informed his government that it was considered likely that Clemenceau would supplant Sarrien, or at least dominate the cabinet (*Die grosse Politik der Europäischen Kabinette, 1871–1914*, ed. by Johannes Lepsius, Albrecht Mendelssohn Bartholdy and Friedrich Thimme, 40 vols., Berlin, 1922–26, XXI, 291).

The reorganized cabinet of October, 1906, Clemenceau insisted before the Chamber, was a continuation of the Sarrien Ministry. The charge that Clemenceau had forced Sarrien out and usurped almost dictatorial powers in his place is part of the "Tiger's" legend, and is not borne out by the facts. In addition to Sarrien's post (he was supplanted at the Ministry of Justice by Guyot-Dessaigne) four other portfolios changed hands. Léon Bourgeois yielded the Foreign Office to Stephen Pichon. Joseph Caillaux, as already noted, replaced Raymond Poincaré as Minister of Finance. Georges Picquart followed Eugène Étienne in the War Department, and Milliès-Lacroix succeeded Georges Leygues in the Colonial Office. Evidently Clemenceau planned from the first to keep the Ministry of War and the Ministry of Foreign Affairs under close control, for he chose the Dreyfusard Picquart and the tractable Pichon for these respective posts. Such an aim, however, scarcely justifies the accusation that he sought to create a one-man government; it merely reflects his determination to keep these two powerful and independent ministries subservient to the head of the council. The fact that he induced men of the ability of Aristide Briand, Louis Barthou, Gaston Doumergue, Réné Viviani and Joseph Caillaux to collaborate for three years in a cabinet of "republican concentration" demonstrates his capacity for promoting effective team work. A leader who selects five future prime ministers for his colleagues is no mean judge of political ability. And a President of the Council of Ministers who keeps such colleagues with him and keeps his cabinet in office for nearly three years is no mere irascible autocrat who has surrounded himself with puppets.

Despite the undoubted capacity of its members the achievements of the Clemenceau Ministry in domestic affairs proved a record of frustrations and disappointments. Social reform languished. The deputies, prompt to raise their own salaries from 9000 to 15,000 francs a year, proved less ardent in their concern for the destitute. "The interests of the *beati possidentes* and the ignorance of the masses whom they exploit: these are the two great determining forces in conservatism-at-any-price."[4] So Clemenceau had written in 1902; and more to the same effect before 1902 and after 1902. But in accepting office in 1906 he deserted the ranks of freelance critics to become a defender of the *status quo*. His cabinet owed its lease of power to the dominent group in the assembly, the Radical Republicans. This group had decided the choice of Armand Fallières as President of the Republic at the beginning of 1906. It had increased its

[4] Georges Clemenceau, *La Honte* (Paris: Stock, 1903), p. 352.

representation in the election of new senators in January and the general election of deputies in May. A politician of Clemenceau's acumen could not misread these returns. The Socialists, who were likewise increasing their forces, would have to be lulled with promises in order that the property owners, particularly the *petit bourgeoisie*, the *rentiers*, the millions of peasant proprietors, might be safeguarded in their possessions, their privileges and their investments. His heart remained with the disinherited classes in their struggle for social justice. But as a realist he recognized that his Ministry must follow a Radical Republican policy, which meant, primarily, that it must maintain peace and order, protect private property, and keep taxes as low as possible. To profess zeal for social reform was in the spirit of the time but such zeal must not lead to crushing taxation or collectivist experiments, it must stop short with token reforms. To govern was to dissemble and politics remained "the art of the possible."

The Socialists, and the leaders of the more militant *syndicats*, were not readily placated with a program of promises and an expression of benevolent intentions. Strikes continued, with growing violence, and in 1907 a workers' conference at Marseilles condemned militarism, adopted a plan for spreading socialist propaganda among army recruits, and formally denounced the government for arbitrary and illegal use of power. Clemenceau responded by despatching troops wherever violence threatened; there were more fatalities in 1907 and 1908 from strike battles; and the *syndicat* leaders were arrested, released, and rearrested. They denounced "Clemenceau the Murderer" and stigmatized the ministry as a "government of assassins," but with improving economic conditions the tension declined somewhat in 1908.

Neither side really wanted open warfare. When *Le Temps* demanded that the government dissolve the *syndicats* Clemenceau reminded the Chamber of Deputies that, though the leaders might voice anarchistic aims, they represented 3000 unions which did not really endorse such views. "If you want to prosecute 3000 *syndicats*," he concluded, "it is not to me that you should address yourselves." [5] He knew that the French workers, despite the real hardships of the depression years, 1907–1908, were not in a genuinely rebellious mood. They trusted that their class solidarity and the justice of their cause would win respect for their rights.

This faith of the masses in moral pressure was strikingly demonstrated by the vine-growers in 1907. The spread of the vine parasite, Phylloxera,

[5] Sylvain Humbert, *Le Mouvement syndical* (Paris: Marcel Rivière, 1912), p. 67.

the competition from North African vineyards, and the decline of prices, threatened to ruin many thousands of peasants. They appealed to the government to modify tariffs and taxes, backing their requests by orderly mass demonstrations. On May 5, 80,000 peasants paraded at Narbonne; a week later 150,000 assembled at Béziers. Their leader was a simple soul, Marcellin Albert, hailed as the *rédempteur*, the *roi des gueux*. The parades, marked by exceptional restraint and sobriety, grew more impressive weekly; on June 9, 700,000 people gathered at Montpellier. Foreseeing that soon or late the ardor of these expectant throngs would explode in disorder Clemenceau pleaded vainly for a return to common sense. The demonstrations continued. It was an open defiance of the government's demands and reluctantly he ordered the leaders taken into custody. Immediately the mood of the demonstrators changed, their lofty exaltation crystallized into anger, erupted into violence. Local authorities telegraphed Paris that disorders were spreading from town to town, and more alarming still, that three hundred soldiers of the 17th Infantry had mutinied in sympathy with the agitators. In the Chamber of Deputies the extreme Right and the extreme Left combined to assail the government. Clemenceau defended his course of action crisply. He was in a combative mood.

On June 23, when his rowdier followers in the union of farm laborers were out of hand, pillaging and burning, Marcellin Albert struck a gesture at once noble, futile and pathetic. Under sentence of arrest he hastened to Paris for a personal appeal to Clemenceau, and was admitted, shabby, nervous and embarrassed, to the Ministry at the Place Beauvau. Asking nothing for himself, but pleading for the desperate farmers of the Midi who had entrusted their fate to his guidance, Albert finally broke into tears at Clemenceau's cold authority. He promised to return and counsel his followers to go back to work, pay their taxes, respect the law. Then, as he was penniless, he accepted the loan of a hundred francs, hastened to Montpellier to urge submission upon the other members of the strike committee, and, failing, surrendered himself to the Police. The government surmounted the crisis, restored order, and packed the foolish lads of the 17th Infantry off to Africa for punishment. But Clemenceau took no pride in the victory. More than ever politics seemed to him a shabby game in which the ambitious outgeneraled the honest and the cynical tricked the sincere. The methods whereby a minister kept in office were "an expense of spirit in a waste of shame" and he yearned for his free days in the opposition when his damns had no caution and his praise had no price.

In the religious controversy he likewise found himself edged into a compromise, successful in a political sense, though it seemed an evasion to his forthright mind. His first circular as Minister of Interior Affairs had been an order to the prefects to postpone the inventory of Church property wherever this step threatened to excite undue indignation. The tactful Briand, as Minister of Cults, eased the application of the law of December 9, 1905, separating Church and State, by a succession of graceful equivocations. The blundering efforts of the previous ministry proved that if the secular authorities took forceful possession of the sacred edifices, articles, vestments and relics, they would stir up dangerous resentments and riots in many pious parishes. Clemenceau summed up the situation in his irreverent but trenchant style with the laconic observation that a few candlesticks were not worth a human life. So, despite the uncompromising Papal Encyclical, *Gravissimi officii*, of August 10, 1906, which forbade the formation of cultural associations, Briand continued his policy of appeasement. Wherever local groups or committees would accept responsibility, the Church property was confided to them, but if the Catholics in a community forebore to organize an association the government permitted the continuation of religious worship on a *laissez faire* basis. This compromise, embodied in a legislative decree January 2, 1907, passed both chambers by large majorities and marked another triumph of conciliation for the Clemenceau Ministry. It calmed, insofar as it could be calmed, the feud between clericals and anticlericals which had embittered the quarrels between Right and Left in the Third Republic for over thirty years.[6]

His accession to power gave Clemenceau control over the War Department, that proud citadel of conservatism, dominated in fact until the Dreyfus revolution, and still largely dominated in spirit, by unreconstructed royalists, Catholics and aristocrats. In his first ministerial declaration he avowed the cabinet's firm intention to abolish military courts and substitute the guarantees of civil procedure. But when the hour came to strike he found his hand had grown numb. An army without discipline would be no better than a mob, a broken sword in the hand of the governing power, a lowered shield along the Rhine exposing the heart of France to the Teutonic thrust. The spread of strikes and disorders, the syndicalist

[6] The critical paragraph in the *Loi concernant l'exercice public des Cultes* reads as follows: "À défaut d'associations culturelles, les édifices affectés à l'exercice du culte, ainsi que les meubles les garnissant, continueront, sauf désaffectation dans les cas prévus par la loi du 9 décembre, 1905, à être laissés à la disposition des fidèles et des ministres du culte pour la practique de leur réligion" (*Bulletin des lois de la République Française*, XII Série, Premier Semestre de 1907, Paris: Imprimerie Nationale, 1907, No. 48,772, pp. 1366–1367).

propaganda inciting soldiers to mutiny, the revolt of the 17th Infantry, all taught how dangerous it would prove to tamper with military morale. The need, rather, was to quicken the spirit of discipline in the ranks and to improve the quality of the leadership. In 1907 Clemenceau endorsed an appointment which proved the broadening of his vision and did credit to his judgment. A new commandant was needed for the *École de Guerre*. One obvious choice was Ferdinand Foch, recently promoted general of brigade, author of two excellent treatises on the conduct of warfare, and widely respected by his fellow officers for his intelligence and strength of character. But Foch was a practising Catholic, a product of Jesuit schools, whose brother was a member of the Society of Jesus. Despite his talents, his rise, quite understandably, had been slow after 1900 in an army which was being "republicanized." Pressed to consider the general's qualifications, Clemenceau interviewed him twice in the summer of 1907, read his books, and decided to approve the appointment. He wanted a commandant at the head of the *École de Guerre* who would set the stamp of his character and intelligence on the republican officers of the future. In the thrust and parry of frank, uninhibited conversation he and Foch had taken one another's measure. It was an hour big with destiny for France.

Had the decision rested with him alone it is probable that Clemenceau, the anti-militarist, the critic of the high command, would have raised new revenues for the military machine. As foreign affairs claimed more of his time he grew alarmed at the precarious position of France. Russia, defeated in the Far East and shaken by revolution, had become less an ally than a liability, leaving German statesmen free to push their policies with impunity until the Russian power revived. Between 1901 and 1907 the estimated strength of the German standing army had increased from 604,000 to 629,000 men, while the French forces, because of a declining birth rate and the substitution of the two for the three year training period, had fallen from 574,000 to 559,000. By 1909 the Germans would have a mobile force of some 1,760,000 trained soldiers against the 1,300,000 combatants the Third Republic could put in line. The Reich, already spending 37 per cent of its revenue for armaments in 1906, was to increase the estimate one-fifth in the ensuing triennium, while France, which had allotted only 27 per cent of the national budget to defense in 1906, would be spending approximately the same proportion in 1909. This meant, in a Europe of dynamic and expanding states, a relative retrogression.[7]

But statistics could be juggled and told only half the story. In the

[7] These estimates are drawn from *The Statesman's Year Book*, 1906, 1907, 1908, 1909, and 1910. No government, of course, published the whole truth regarding its armaments.

quality of their training, staff work, equipment, health and morale the German corps were the most efficient in Europe. Clemenceau, haunted as always by his memories of 1870, watched the growing discrepancy of forces with gloomy apprehensions. But he remained the prisoner of an inelastic budget and a complacent Chamber, and in this as in so many other aspirations he had to curb his exasperation and resign himself to seek security for France through other expedients. This meant, as matters stood, to pursue more gingerly the foreign policies of Delcassé which he had himself attacked in 1905. To reëstablish a balance of power in Europe France must find stronger and more resolute allies.

For the parlous condition of the French navy Clemenceau felt less concern, though its relative decline was even more manifest. While Germany pushed resolutely ahead and usurped the position of second naval power of the world the French navy languished on a stationary budget. Its role, in the event of war, would be primarily defensive. Clemenceau placed considerable faith in submarines and pushed their construction so that France in 1909 possessed sixty-one undersea boats to Germany's four.[8] Of torpedo craft, likewise useful in a war of defense, France achieved by the same date a superiority of 331 to 47. But the list of capital ships told a different story. By launching the first *Dreadnought* in 1906, a heavily armored titan with twelve inch guns and a speed of over twenty knots, Britain had opened a new era in naval construction. In the four years which followed England built twenty capital ships, Germany sixteen, and France two. Most experts agreed that the command of the seas would depend upon these monitors of 18,000 tons and over, and the cheap and tardy naval program of the Clemenceau ministry becomes even more apparent when it is noted that, when the ministry fell in 1909, none of the six capital ships ordered in French yards in 1906 had been completed, while the Germans had launched ten laid down in 1907. France, with a naval budget only three-fourths that of Germany and one-third that of England, could not hold an equal place in the contest but should have made a better showing. Her deficiencies, moreover, were due to incompetence, confusion and political jobbery, as well as a niggardly conception of naval needs. There was a perennial shortage of naval supplies, ships lay in dock for months unfit for service, and the rate of repair and construction remained inexorably slow. Discontent among the mariners, and among the shipwrights in private and state employment, seems to have

[8] As early as 1901 Clemenceau had written a well reasoned and prophetic essay on the possibilities of the submarine (*Le Bloc*, April 14, 1901).

been the most serious obstacle and remedial legislation passed in 1907 and 1908 failed to modify it. These acts provided for better pay, shorter hours, and improved sanitary conditions on the ships, but stiffened the discipline and introduced a more rigid system of inspection. The evils, however, did not yield readily, and the will to push through the reform program with energy seems to have been singularly lacking.

Warnings of the coming storm which was to overturn the Clemenceau cabinet a year later rumbled through the Chamber in the autumn of 1908. The maladministration in the Ministry of Marine had been a scandal for years and was signalized after 1906 by a succession of naval disasters. Guns exploded, submarines sank with all hands, battleships burned, blew up or went aground with monotonous repetition. A committee of enquiry with the hardworking Delcassé as chairman dug into the evidence, and on October 19, 1908, Thomson, the Minister of Marine, was called upon to justify his department. He made a miserable and inconsequential defense. The revelations of neglect, incompetence and favoritism appeared so damning that Clemenceau saved his cabinet only by sacrificing the unlucky Thomson then and there. But Thomson's successor, Picard, found it impossible to remedy matters. In March, 1909, additional revelations on the moral and material disorganization in the Ministry of Marine brought further censure on the government, but the Chamber affirmed its waning confidence by 316 votes to 267.

Delcassé and Clemenceau were old antagonists,[9] and the former Minister of Foreign Affairs could be a dangerous, exact and pertinacious critic. In May, 1909, his committee returned to the attack with fresh evidence to show that the government had failed to carry out recommendations of the legislature passed two years earlier. Behind these persistent attacks lay the hostility of the colonial party in the Chamber of Deputies which was angered by Clemenceau's apparent indifference to the welfare of the French colonies and the navy that must defend them. Clemenceau could not plead ignorance as his excuse, for he had been chairman of a committee appointed in 1904 to institute reforms in the Ministry of Marine, and after

[9] The Clemenceau-Delcassé feud dated from 1894 when Clemenceau vainly sought Delcassé's influence to secure the reappointment of the Comte d'Aunay. D'Aunay had been French minister to Denmark, but Parisian journalists, including Clemenceau, obtained secret information on the Franco-Russian negotiations through a leak at the Copenhagen embassy and D'Aunay was blamed and dismissed. When Clemenceau became President of the Council of Ministers in 1906 he considered D'Aunay for the role of French ambassador to Germany but appointed Jules Cambon instead. D'Aunay he sent as French Minister to Switzerland.

1906, as President of the Council of Ministers, he could command all official sources of information on the defects of the fleet. But he still believed that the fate of France would be decided in Europe and that a centrifugal dispersal of wealth and armaments in ventures overseas was risky and wrongheaded strategy. On July 20, 1909, the critics renewed their interpellations on the navy, and Delcassé charged Clemenceau with failure to report conditions frankly when he had presided over the committee of enquiry in 1904. Clemenceau lost his temper and his parliamentary acumen. With venom in his voice he reminded the Chamber of the humiliation of 1905 when Delcassé had led France to the verge of war, a war the Republic was not prepared to fight, and Berlin had dictated Delcassé's removal and a conference on the Moroccan question. The deputies listened aghast to this public avowal of a French mortification: it was not *comme il faut* to speak of such matters. Moreover, to attack Delcassé personally did not invalidate his criticism; it was an unfair *riposte* and a breach of etiquette. A murmur of indignation swept the benches. Sarcastic and unabashed, Clemenceau repeated his charge that Delcassé had humiliated France. He seemed bent upon inviting a vote of censure, upon wringing it from an exasperated chamber, and the deputies complied. Confidence in the Ministry was denied by a vote of 212 to 176 and the cabinet fell.[10]

Like most French political crises the resignation of the Clemenceau Ministry, when patiently studied, can be traced to a number of interrelated causes. Naval affairs *had* been scandalously neglected, but that neglect had been tolerated for nearly ten years. A more serious, but unacknowledged, source of friction arose from the opposition of the great standing committees in the Senate and the Chamber which did not find Clemenceau pliable enough. The socialists resented his high-handed repression of strikes and his arrest of agitators and anarchists. The big business concerns, especially the French armament makers, thought their interests neglected. The budget project for 1910, which threatened to exceed forty billion francs, satisfied no one. The state purchase of the Western Railroad, undertaken to appease the Socialists, seemed a threat to private enterprise. The government had grown richer in promises as it grew

[10] For Delcassé's activities on the committee of enquiry on naval affairs the clearest account is Charles W. Porter, *The Career of Théophile Delcassé* (University of Pennsylvania thesis, Philadelphia, 1936), pp. 277–283. It is worth noting that when the vote of confidence in the Clemenceau ministry failed to pass nearly 200 deputies were absent or abstained from voting. See *Revue politique et parlementaire*, XVI (1909), 412.

poorer in performance and in trying to placate everybody it had ended by pleasing nobody. It is possible to gauge the rising discontent in the legislature by the number and tone of the interpellations, 293 already that session as Clemenceau protested a week before his fall.[11] Back of the dissatisfaction and pervading all political circles lay the conviction that French prestige had suffered a further decline. The Austrian annexation of Bosnia and Herzegovina in October, 1908, the failure of Russia to secure compensation, the threat to French influence and loans in Turkey and the Balkan states as the Austro-German influence spread, all this created a mood of discontent and pessimism in Paris. To survive, the cabinet needed to dispel this mood by some bold and successful stroke of foreign policy. It may be that Clemenceau planned such a *coup*—the evidence will be examined in the following chapter—but if so the plan miscarried.

It is not easy to formulate a judgment on the work of this first Clemenceau Ministry. The Department of Interior Affairs of which he retained the portfolio profited by a 25 per cent increase in its budget appropriations between 1906 and 1909. The police, public security, hospitals, prisons, public charities, hygiene, the press, departmental and communal personnel, all came under Clemenceau's jurisdiction, and all functioned without notorious scandal or inefficiency. But the operations of that vast administrative system of councils, departments, prefects, mayors and police officers could not be supervised by one man and Clemenceau's influence penetrated it as a series of energetic shocks, as a salutary fear of that irascible and arbitrary minister at the Place Beauvau, rather than as a direct intervention or personal touch. Moreover, as President of the Council of Ministers, Clemenceau spent more time and thought on the problems of foreign policy than the details of domestic administration.

A flood of anecdotes, most of them apocryphal, advertised his brusque and eccentric handling of his responsibilities. There can be no question that personal idiosyncrasies, whims, caprices, antipathies often colored his conduct of affairs and he delighted to profess trivial and petulant motives for grim and momentous decisions. But this was in part a pose, in part an expression of his vigorous sanity. Clemenceau would have agreed with Bergson on the creative role of humor in human relations. A crude but comic epithet could release new and dynamic ideas when debates had struck a deadlock, a jeer and an impudent gesture could break the spell of

[11] Adhémar Esmein, *Éléments de droit constitutionnel français et comparé*, 7th ed., 2 vols. (Paris, 1921), II, 463–464.

pompous argument. People are not ridiculous for what they are but for what they try to be, and Clemenceau's caustic manners seldom wounded honest and unaffected natures. But he loathed the longwinded phrases and hypocritical objections of the insincere and on such he warred without pity. No French statesman since Napoleon has excelled him in his gift of savage and intolerant relevance.

The cherished routine of his private life he guarded stubbornly against the claims of office, maintaining his selfish bachelor existence in the comfortable bourgeois flat hidden away behind a courtyard on the rue Franklin. The double study on the ground floor opened onto a rectangular, high-walled garden where he liked to pace up and down, invoking an inspiration for a speech or article. As the ideas came he would tramp inside to his desk to outline the project in his heavy script, turning with abrupt gesture to rustle through the litter of journals which accumulated like falling leaves, reaching for a reference work from the book-lined walls which he had come to know by touch as a peasant's bare soles know the dirt floor of his cottage.

Like all egocentric and independent workers he was jealous of his time and the order and arrangement of his days. Often before five in the morning the light would flash on over the huge horseshoe-shaped desk and the grey dawn would find him digging obdurately after the facts behind a pressing problem, sketching notes for a project to be debated in cabinet that afternoon, outlining arguments to refute a threatened interpellation in the Chamber. By the time his physical instructor arrived at eight to supervise his calisthenics he had completed what many men would consider a fair day's work. After a simple but adequate breakfast he would leave for the Place Beauvau, often on foot, his crushed hat with drooping brim jammed on his bald head, a loose top coat flapping about his short legs, a cane or umbrella hanging from his side pocket.

The careless dress, the cluttered study, the casual walk to work, the informal attitude towards his colleagues and subordinates (he had nicknames always witty and sometimes malicious for each of them) concealed a driving will, a widely informed and incisive mind, a profound and realistic grasp of his responsibilities. To work with him was an ordeal for he depleted those about him and charged himself with their exhausted energy. His crackling impatience with trivia, with pompous nonentities, with arid formulas, red tape and frozen systematology was the protest of an ardent spirit haunted by the flight of time and aching to achieve results. His career, especially the years in office, induced a sense of frustration to which he never resigned himself. There was so much to do, so little time to do it in, such illimitable opportunities for the betterment of human life, such colossal greed, such invincible sloth and complacency to be overcome. To convert others to urgently needed reforms, to make reason and intelligent charity prevail, remained his aim; the resort to force or compulsion always meant to Clemenceau a confession of failure. It is true that his eager and exasperated spirit constantly betrayed him into autocratic acts and arbitrary gestures, but few men have striven more conscientiously to persuade rather than to compel. His articles and books in a collected edition would run to a hundred volumes of vivid, luminous and convincing prose. Too insistent in tone much of it, too burdened with *il faut que*, too heavily sown with accusative cases, but in the light of history amazingly honest, clear-sighted and *just*. The style was the man and the faults of the style the faults of the man. But behind the barbed phrase, the impatient expletive, there is a passion for humanity, an outlawed affection that is nearer to anger than to tenderness. Some complexity of his nervous system, some early emotional frustration perhaps, had taught him to eschew all expressions of tenderness, to avoid them not merely as a form of self-betrayal but as a sort of self-treachery. He disclaimed his emotional obligations and hid his softer feelings behind a shield of protective ferocity. Such characters are common and generally popular in fiction. It is surprising that they are so frequently misunderstood in life.

To atone for his caustic criticism and arrogant moods Clemenceau practiced the more expensive courtesies. The visitor who escaped from an interview flaming with indignation would recollect as his temper cooled that the Tiger, though busy, had kept the appointment punctually, had prepared himself in advance to discuss the problem intelligently, had responded with an explicit, not an equivocal, *non*, and had offered an alternative project which on examination might not prove too objectionable. It was difficult to hate a man who, with secretaries waiting and ministers on the telephone, insisted on accompanying you to the door, and remembered to enquire if your son, the studious one, hated barrack life as much as ever, and might not be happier completing his military service at more congenial labor, in the cartographical bureau perhaps, or the quartermaster's office.

Such considerate gestures come with effortless grace to many politicians but with Clemenceau they were a deliberate act. Nothing came to him easily and effortlessly. His writing, his oratory, his interviews, even his diversions were activities hewn from the adamant day, blocked out by force of will against the encroaching walls of time. The writing period from five to eight in the morning was stolen from the night; he had trained himself to do with five hours of sleep. Exercise, dressing, breakfast, and the journey to his office separated this quarter of the day from the ten-thirty to twelve-thirty period, reserved for interviews, a check-up on the day's assignments, and brief dictation. Then back to the rue Franklin for lunch, a light meal of boiled eggs and a glass of water. After eating he relaxed for an hour; sprayed his rose bushes, perhaps, or read an article on the latest excavations in Crete, the current exhibition at the Louvre. At two he left for the Senate or Chamber to diagnose the drift of the debates, or to attend a cabinet meeting at the Élysée with the President of the Republic presiding, or to preside himself at a less formal session in one of the ministries. At five he sped back to his office to receive important officials, sign the mail, approve the day's decisions. Unless detained by some public function he dined at home after eight, then returned to the Ministry for a final session with his secretaries and subordinates which often lasted until midnight.

It is little use to ponder what satisfaction he wrung from such arduous living. He worked from an inward necessity as if life were an ache in the soul which must be drugged by labor. The exercise of power brought its own gratification no doubt: few men can resist the lure of authority. But it brought an added responsibility also to set things right. There were so many ancient injustices to reform; it had taken fourteen years to rectify the Dreyfus affair alone,[12] and time pressed. In his moments of depression all France seemed to Clemenceau a garden running to seeds and weeds. The beloved republic, the Attica of the modern world, was threatened on all fronts by jealous and aggressive neighbors, its fine culture exposed to internal decay and barbarian invasions. Clemenceau loved France, its people, its traditions, its culture, its countryside, but above all he loved its liberties, the respect for individuality, the tolerance of diverse opinions, the intellectual enthusiasm, the play of wit, the pursuit of knowledge. He saw this rare civilization threatened by the iron mood of industrialism, the inexorable march towards war. But he saw it as threatened even more certainly by faults and weaknesses inherent in French character and

[12] Dreyfus was finally exonerated by a decision of the *Cour de Cassation* in 1906, promoted to the rank of major, and named Chevalier in the Legion of Honor. Picquart, created general of brigade, became Minister of War in the first Clemenceau cabinet. A monument was erected to Scheurer-Kestner, and Zola's ashes were transported to the Panthéon.

French society, evils which, unchecked, would debase and destroy the finest civilization the world had known.

Many of these evils were apparent to other eyes besides his. "We know," Victor Sellas wrote in 1906, the year Clemenceau took office, "we know that although France is in the front rank of the nations in the moral influence which it exerts throughout the world, it is far from achieving an equivalent material influence. Its economic power is increasingly surpassed each year, in disturbing fashion, by England, by Germany, by the United States. The causes of this inferiority, when sought, are not difficult to uncover: alcoholism, depopulation, lack of initiative, inadequate general and professional training, agricultural, commercial and industrial red tape and routinism, ignorance of foreign languages, a disinclination to emigrate to the colonies or to visit foreign lands." [13]

All these defects and many more Clemenceau likewise deplored in French society, and because he loved France he could not refrain from scolding. He saw the Republic endangered, not by lack of natural endowment, of resources or opportunities, but by a lack of sufficient determination on the part of the people to make the effort demanded for survival and progress. France was declining through weakness of will. In his exaggerated display of energy and initiative he sought to set an example for his compatriots. He sought to supply what he considered a national deficiency from the reserves of his own tense and tempestuous nature.

[13] Victor Sellas, "Necessité d'une nouvelle adaptation sociale du service militaire," *Revue politique et parlementaire,* XIII (1906), 262–263.

CHAPTER VIII

PRESIDENT OF THE COUNCIL: FOREIGN AFFAIRS 1906–1909

. . . For France the danger of invasion is very real. We know that on the morrow of the outbreak of war between Germany and England, the German armies will invade France by way of Belgium, and that Germany will seek in France an indemnity for the losses likely to be suffered on the sea at the hands of the English.[1] CLEMENCEAU (1908)

WHEN the Sarrien Cabinet picked up the threads of French foreign policy in March, 1906, France was anxiously measuring her strength against Germany at the Algeciras Conference. A mood of uncertainty approaching panic had ruled the Quai d'Orsay since Delcassé's fall the previous June. Russia, crippled in the war with Japan, seemed about to dissolve in revolution. Britain, though friendly under the new Liberal Ministry, would promise nothing more than the diplomatic support provided for by the terms of the *Entente Cordiale* of 1904. More discouraging still, William II had cajoled the vacillating Czar, Nicholas II, into signing an accord at Björkoe in July, 1905, designed to unite Germany and Russia against England, and to draw France also into the German camp. The Björkoe pact was secret, but French diplomats gathered hints of its purport and their alarm deepened.

To Clemenceau's resourceful mind the French situation in 1906 seemed ripe with opportunities for a diplomat with initiative. Thanks to Delcassé's patient skill during his seven years at the Quai d'Orsay, France possessed private conventions with Spain and Italy which had eased the Mediterranean rivalries. The optimum course, Clemenceau decided, would be to wean Italy away from the Triple Alliance, and if possible draw Austria away from Germany. But these were distant hopes. The immediate prob-

[1] Henry Wickham Steed, *Through Thirty Years*, 2 vols. (Garden City: Doubleday, Page and Company, 1924), pp. 286–287. Clemenceau also repeated this remarkably clear-headed prophecy to Edward VII, to Sir Edward Goschen, British ambassador at Vienna, and to Izvolsky. See George P. Gooch and Harold W. V. Temperley, ed., *British Official Documents on the Origins of the War, 1898–1914*, VI, 157, and *Grosse Politik der Europäischen Kabinette*, XXVI, Pt. 1, p. 38.

lems concerned the best method of securing Russian support at Algeciras, thwarting the German demands over Morocco, and strengthening the *Entente* with Britain. If England and Russia could be persuaded to reconcile their rivalries in Asia, a *Triple Entente* might be organized to oppose a balance of power to the Triple Alliance. German strategy, Clemenceau appreciated with equal clarity, must aim at sowing dissension among France, Russia and Britain, for the Triple Entente of these three states, if consummated, would encircle the Central Powers.

At Saint Petersburg the Czar's government, undermined by debt, defeat, and revolution, was about to face the criticism of a popularly elected Duma which Nicholas II had been obliged to summon. Control of the state finances would be the crucial issue in the approaching contest between autocracy and parliamentarism. Czarist Russia had already borrowed some six milliards of francs on the Paris bourse and French bankers feared that further advances would be flinging good money after bad. But the French Foreign Office regarded the matter from another point of view. It was essential to fortify the Franco-Russian alliance, for it formed the corner stone of French foreign policy; the only matter in debate was the *quid pro quo* which might be exacted from Russia in return for new credit. Liberal-minded members of the Sarrien Cabinet might dislike the thought of strengthening the Czar's régime and robbing the Duma of its main advantage, but the cabinet as a whole placed French national security ahead of liberal sympathies. Even Clemenceau, who had never hesitated, as an independent journalist, to throw mud at Russian officialdom, hastened to assure the Russian ambassador that, as a minister, he would treat the Russian imperial régime with sympathy and confidence.[2]

So the Russian envoy, Count Kokovtsov, arriving in Paris at the end of March in no very hopeful mood, was delighted to find Poincaré at the Ministry of Finance most considerate and helpful. At the same time, however, Kokovtsov received an intimation that certain members of the cabinet opposed the loan, and he was advised to visit the Minister of Interior Affairs in particular. He hastened to the eighteenth-century hotel on the Place Beauvau where the ministry was housed. Clemenceau, barely settled in his new office, had doubtless anticipated the visit: he greeted the Russian brusquely and came straight to the point. There was the question whether, pending the organization of the Duma, the Czar's government

[2] *Un livre noir, diplomatie d'avant guerre d'après les documents des archives russes*, 3 vols. (Paris: Librairie du Travail, 1922–34), I, 15.

had authority to negotiate a loan at all. There was also the opposition of a powerful section of the French press to consider. For himself Clemenceau affirmed that he remained in doubt regarding the wisdom of further advances and must reserve his decision. Then, as Kokovtsov rose to go, he surprised the Russian statesman with a question that seemed almost an impertinence. "Why doesn't your emperor invite M. Miliukov to act as head of your government?" he enquired pointedly. "I believe this would be a good move both from the point of view of satisfying public opinion and from that of solving many problems." [3]

The nature of some of these problems became clearer to Kokovtsov in the days that followed. On April 7 the diplomats at Algeciras initialed a convention which decided the fate of Morocco. Only Austria had supported the German stand; the settlement, while affirming the independence of the Sultanate, opened the way for further French penetration and ultimate control. Russia had loyally supported the French stand, and the loan negotiations moved another step forward. But the bankers were still hesitant and the liberal journals hostile. Prodded delicately, Kokovtsov agreed that an extra commission should be paid over to the bankers to be distributed among the journalists. As Minister of Interior Affairs, Clemenceau had the press bureau under his supervision. There is no evidence that he intervened in the negotiations, but it is doubtful that he could have remained entirely ignorant of what took place. Kokovtsov was able shortly to assure his imperial master that the journals of the Left in Paris had ceased to criticize Russian affairs and that the journals of the Right were openly defending Russian autocracy against the revolutionary elements. By the end of April the Czar had two and a quarter milliard francs to draw upon and could afford to defy the Duma. Another link had been added to the golden chain uniting Paris and Saint Petersburg and to the iron ring slowly encircling the Central Powers.

For during these same days, while Kokovtsov bargained with the bankers and Poincaré pressed them to accommodate him as a patriotic duty, a second series of conferences, even more closely guarded, went forward at Paris. The Russian general Politzine and the French general Brun drew up by prearrangement a military convention which, after it had been formally approved by the two governments, became an integral part of

[3] Vladimir Nikolaevich Kokovtsov, *Out of My Past*, Hoover War Library Publication No. 6 (Stanford University Press, 1935), p. 117. Count Sergei Witte, the Russian statesman, takes most of the credit for the loan in his memoirs but shows even more clearly how definitely the French credit depended upon Russian support for France at Algeciras (*The Memoirs of Count Witte*, Garden City: Doubleday, Page and Company, 1921, pp. 285–315).

the treaty of alliance.[4] This revised military agreement named Germany specifically as the principal enemy; indicated more emphatically than the accord of 1899 that mutual defense against a German attack was the chief end of the Franco-Russian alliance; and provided that German mobilization would automatically entail Franco-Russian mobilization. Furthermore, the Russians were to furnish the French general staff with their plan of campaign, their secret data regarding German armaments, and other items of pertinent information. Final conversations regarding this pact were concluded by the generals on April 8. At a cost (to the loan subscribers) of a sum approximating half the annual budget, the French government had held its own at Algeciras, nullified the Kaiser's overtures to Russia and buried the Björkoe deal, and tightened the Franco-Russian accord with a close military compact. But it was a cynical mode of diplomacy which made liberal France the betrayer of the constitutional experiment in Russia; and the Duma, dissolved twice and finally emasculated, paid the price of French selfishness. Clemenceau, while acquiescing in the negotiations, viewed the settlement with wry contempt. Most French statesmen, Kokovtsov noted, believed it would be necessary for the Republic to choose between Russia and Great Britain as an ally. But Clemenceau, obdurate as always, clung to the conviction that it would be possible to win Russia *and* Britain. To this ideal he now directed his energies.

Many years earlier, in 1891, he had visited London to explore, unofficially, the possibilities of an Anglo-French alliance. Believing, apparently, that the Liberal Unionist group then held the real balance of power in English politics, he sought an interview with Joseph Chamberlain on July 16. The offer he had been empowered to make by an influential element in the French Chamber of Deputies was a free hand for England in Egypt if, in return, the British government would grant France moral support in her diplomatic isolation. The Triple Alliance had just been renewed and the need of a counter-alliance to balance it appeared more imperative than ever. But the moment was not auspicious for a Franco-British *rapprochement*. Chamberlain himself had pro-German sympathies, and the Conservative Prime Minister, Lord Salisbury, to whom he relayed the French proposal, regarded the Latins as "dying nations" and rejected the overture curtly. Before the end of the summer of 1891 the Freycinet Cabinet of that day had cast the die for an alliance with Russia,

[4] Aleksandr G. Shliapnikov, ed., *Les Alliés contre la Russie* (Paris: Delpeuch, 1926), pp. 15–16, 36–45.

and Clemenceau reluctantly acknowledged defeat. Yet he continued to hope for a change of sentiment in British governing circles. "I still believe," he wrote in October, "that the advent of Gladstone to power would promise to accomplish immediately what Salisbury refused — the *entente cordiale* of the two peoples."[5] His hope was unfounded, but the phrase *entente cordiale*, later to become so popular, is a tribute to his diplomatic sense. He had gauged correctly the British dislike of strict formulas and rigid compacts. Even when a later British government forsook the position of "splendid isolation" it resisted to the day of hostilities the French desire for a specific treaty of alliance.

By 1904 the change of sentiment at London, which Clemenceau had anticipated, came about. Queen Victoria had died in 1901, Salisbury in 1903. Edward VII, strongly pro-French in his sympathies, helped to promote and to popularize an *entente cordiale* with France. The new understanding weathered the crisis of the Russo-Japanese War, when France's ally, Russia, fought England's ally, Japan; and at the close of 1905, with the Conference of Algeciras impending, the Rouvier Cabinet proposed that the French and British general staffs should implement the *entente* by a military convention. In January and February, 1906, the British War Office drew up in detail a project for disembarking 100,000 men at French and Belgian ports within two weeks if war came. The discussions remained verbal for the most part, but British, French, and Belgian officers collaborated in working out the problems that would arise in transporting, feeding, and billeting the British force, and they shared information on their own plans of mobilization. The diplomats still insisted that full freedom of action had been reserved by the respective governments, and the French cabinet remained in doubt how far it could depend upon the British assurances. In Germany, however, the hard-headed Von Moltke, chief of the German Staff, accepted it as self-evident that, if France and Germany came to war, Belgium would be drawn in on the French side and England would dispatch an armed force to the continent.

Distrust of England died slowly in French political circles. As Clemenceau's influence in the Sarrien Cabinet continued to mount in the summer of 1906, his Anglophile sentiments alarmed friends of the Russian alliance and advocates of French colonial expansion. They feared that French loans to Russia (one fourth of all French foreign investments), the French colonial empire, and the great structure of French Catholic missions

[5] James Louis Garvin, *The Life of Joseph Chamberlain*, 3 vols. (London: Macmillan, 1932–34), II, 457–462.

abroad would all be sacrificed to British pressure. "Clemenceau is the proconsul of the English king, charged with the administration of his province of the Gauls," declared a former foreign minister, Gustave Flourens, in a vicious attack.[6] But Clemenceau held his course. Though the British still resisted coyly, he considered them committed to aid France with arms and he counted upon the aggressiveness and the maladroit diplomacy of the Germans to cement the *Entente*. Nor, in the outcome, was he mistaken. The rapid development of the German fleet, coupled with German trade rivalry, burdened the British taxpayer, curtailed the Liberal program of social reform, and roiled British sensibilities.

By the close of 1906 the British had set their international course, and by the close of 1907 they had confirmed it. But their ambiguous attitude, their desire to commit their ally without being committed themselves, exhausted Clemenceau's patience. In March, 1907, while confined to his bed with grippe, he brooded over the situation, and in April he decided on a quick visit to London. Lord Roberts and Winston Churchill were urging army expansion upon the hesitant Liberals, and the time seemed opportune to consolidate the Anglo-French pact on military coöperation. Clemenceau directed his main arguments at Haldane, British Secretary of State for War, and impressed him but failed to change his opinion. Haldane found his visitor a dour political fighter, surprisingly well informed, and firmly convinced that Britain would need a conscript army if war came. He tried to explain that such a scheme was impossible in England, that the navy was already a staggering burden, that no nation could afford both a first-class army and a first-class fleet. Clemenceau remained unconvinced: Germany was disproving the argument even while they talked. But he saw no point in pressing the comparison too sharply and he and Haldane parted with sincere expressions of mutual respect.

Interviews with Asquith and Campbell-Bannerman provided a still sharper disappointment. In bargaining Clemenceau consistently demanded more than he hoped or expected to win, and his consternation at British evasiveness may have been partly an affectation. But he had good grounds for mortification. He tried to convince the British Prime Minister that German influence was spreading at an alarming pace in Denmark, Holland, and Belgium. Campbell-Bannerman remained unimpressed. He urged the need for a strong British expeditionary force which

[6] Gustave Flourens, *La France conquise: Edouard VII et Clemenceau* (Paris: Garnier Frères, 1906), p. 127.

could cross the Channel promptly to block an invasion of the Low Countries. Campbell-Bannerman expressed grave doubts whether British public opinion would sanction the dispatch of an army to the continent. As the Prime Minister was chairman of the Committee on Imperial Defence it seemed incredible that he could be ignorant of the plans worked out by the British, French, and Belgian staff officers a year earlier.[7] Clemenceau returned to Paris in a glum mood and asked the British ambassador, Sir Francis Bertie, for a clarification. The French general staff had revised their plan of 1903 in 1906. It was imperative for them to know if they could depend upon British military and naval support in a war with Germany. Had England changed her attitude? Such a reversal would make a disastrous impression upon his cabinet colleagues and he had thought it better, pending an explanation, to withhold from them the substance of his talks in London.

At the British capital the Foreign Minister, Sir Edward Grey, talked with the French ambassador, Paul Cambon, and sought to dispel the painful impression created by Campbell-Bannerman's frankness. This was not easy without formally disavowing the Prime Minister's remarks. Lord Fitzmaurice, Under-Secretary for Foreign Affairs, raised the critical question: "Has the French Government, through their general staff, or otherwise, got in their possession any record justifying, or which might seem to justify, M. Clemenceau's assertion about the employment of 115,000 British troops in Belgium under certain eventualities in agreement with them?"[8] Grey hoped not, but he could not be perfectly sure, and the military conversations *had* been remarkably explicit. In the end it seemed best to imply that Clemenceau must have drawn a false deduction from Campbell-Bannerman's observations. The French could rest assured that, in the event of war, there would be no limitation on the use of British naval and military forces and that these forces would be employed in whatever manner promised to be most effective. This affirmation did not constitute a formal commitment but Clemenceau had to be satisfied with it. Italy as well as Germany had taken alarm at rumors that the French fleet would be massed in the Mediterranean in the event of war, while the British guarded the North Sea. For the moment it seemed prudent not

[7] John Ecclesfield Tyler, *The British Army and the Continent, 1904–1914* (London: E. Arnold and Company, 1938), p. 76. The progress of the Anglo-Belgian staff conversations, initiated in January, 1906, has been traced by Carl Hosse, *Die englisch-belgischen Aufmarschpläne gegen Deutschland vor dem Weltkriege* (Zurich: Amalthea-Verlag, 1930), pp. 39 ff.

[8] *British Documents on the Origins of the War*, VI, 27.

to place any more emphasis on Anglo-French plans for coöperation. Clemenceau's impetuosity had ruffled the dovecotes of European diplomacy and jeopardized the prospects of the Second Hague Peace Conference which was to assemble in June. The Germans in particular feared to accept a reduction in armaments when the net of diplomacy was being woven so closely about them. The Conference, not surprisingly, proved a failure, save for some minor agreements prohibiting matters considered of no moment, as, for example, the launching of explosives from aircraft.

The hesitant attitude of the British ministers regarding the Anglo-French military conversations is understandable for they knew that the German government was alarmed and suspicious. At the close of 1906 Clemenceau had been asked in the French Chamber whether an Anglo-French pact had been concluded. He replied blandly that he had not been in office long enough to read all the treaties in the archives of the Foreign Office but he had the general impression that no specific convention of that nature existed. Such a denial gave the rumor a semi-official validity. In January the German ambassador in London asked Haldane unequivocally whether England and France had concluded a military convention. Haldane said no, not to his knowledge, though it was possible that a British staff officer and a French staff officer might have talked informally without notifying him. As the Germans, through unofficial channels, had gathered many details of the 1906 conversations, including the proposed size, composition, and area of operations of the projected expeditionary force, such evasions — *grossartige Lüge* the Kaiser called them bluntly — hardly soothed the ruffled German susceptibilities.[9]

After a year as President of the Council of Ministers Clemenceau had good reason to feel satisfied with the drift of French foreign policy. The last obstacles to a *Triple Entente* dissolved in the summer of 1907. The revised form of the Franco-Russian military pact of 1906, which specified Germany as the enemy, robbed it of its earlier anti-British character, but vestiges of this previous inspiration remained and Clemenceau had not revealed its exact form to his friends across the Channel. It seemed advisable first to promote an Anglo-Russian accord and to that aim he dedicated all the considerable resources of French diplomacy.

From the day his ministry was accredited, October 25, 1906, he spurred on the Anglo-Russian *rapprochement*; it was indeed the object of his first official activities. He had dined with the Russian Foreign Minister, Izvolsky, the previous evening, breakfasted with the Russian ambassador

[9] *Grosse Politik der Europäischen Kabinette*, XXI, Pt. 2, pp. 468–470.

two days later, conferred with the British ambassador the same morning, and impressed upon each the importance of a prompt alignment of the three Powers. The British were friendly to the idea, the more so, perhaps, because they hoped to learn the exact bearing of the Franco-Russian alliance and the purport of the French loans (Russian railway thrusts at Persia and India, financed by French capital, were a perpetual nightmare to them). When, after the usual bargaining and dissembling, Britain and Russia finally concluded agreements regulating their interests in Tibet, Afghanistan and Persia (August 31, 1907), Sir Edward Grey instructed Sir Francis Bertie in Paris to inform Clemenceau personally of the terms. Clemenceau promised to respect the confidence; but he seized the first opportunity which offered to felicitate the Russian ambassador on the settlement for it was part of his method to make each partner conscious how intimate his relations were with the other. "Russia," he declared, "in signing an accord with England, and with Japan, has rendered a great service to France, which had been deeply grieved at the temporary enfeeblement of Russia in international politics."[10] He might have added that France had also rendered a service to Russia by predisposing Japan to be friendly (loans again), and was prepared to oblige Russia with further credits if these were needed. They were. By 1914 Russian flotations on the Paris bourse exceeded twelve milliard francs, one-fourth of French foreign investments, and although the Russian government retired each bond issue as it fell due the terms of the refunding grew steadily more ruinous.

By 1908 the Triple Entente (though British diplomats deprecated the use of the term) had become an actuality and Edward VII was one of its most active exponents. German diplomatic overtures were falling back like spears flung against the stars, while the Entente leaders met, conferred, and separated at frequent intervals, weaving their tenuous projects, their web of half-uttered agreements. In April Clemenceau visited London for the funeral of Campbell-Bannerman, dined with Asquith, and had long talks with Morley and Sir Edward Grey on the need for strengthening the British army. A few weeks later President Fallières paid a state visit and was banqueted at Buckingham Palace. In June the British sovereigns met the Czar and Czarina at Reval, and on August 22 Edward VII, Clemenceau and Izvolsky conferred in Marienbad. Two days later Clemenceau saw Izvolsky again, at Karlsbad, and talked very gloomily of the danger of war between England and Germany. He feared that Germany would immediately fall upon France and attempt to dispose of the French armies

[10] Shliapnikov, *Les Alliés contre la Russie*, p. 18.

in a lightning campaign; and that England, safe behind her sea wall, would let the Germans exhaust their strength on the battlefields of Europe while the British gathered in their trade and colonies.

Was Clemenceau inviting similar confidences from Izvolsky regarding *perfide Albion*? In this diplomatic sparring none of the Entente statesmen spoke his whole mind, and each was prepared to entertain German propositions on the side. Thus Izvolsky poured out Clemenceau's complaints (which had their echoes in Russia) to the Austrian foreign minister, Aehrenthal, a few weeks later. The Entente, so ran the rumor in Berlin and Vienna, was not too *cordiale* and might be split by adroit pressure. Aehrenthal flattered Izvolsky, told him that Austria meditated the annexation of Bosnia and Herzegovina, and promised to support the opening of the Straits to Russia in return. This "Buchlau bargain" seemed to the Austrian minister a promising day's work, for he strongly doubted that Britain would agree to opening the Straits and British opposition could not fail to estrange the Russians.

The closing months of 1908 brought a thorough testing of the Entente where its joints were weakest. France and Germany clashed again over Morocco. On September 25 the German consul at Casablanca attempted to aid the escape of six deserters from the French foreign legion, creating a sharp altercation over the status of French police authority in the Sultanate. Fortunately neither William II nor Clemenceau believed the issue worth a conflict and it led to an agreement, concluded February 9, 1909, whereby France promised to protect German economic interests in Morocco and Germany recognized the French responsibility to preserve peace and order there. Morocco remained technically an independent state, however, despite French penetration, and this clause disappointed French imperialists, who conceived that Clemenceau had sacrificed colonial interests and favored German economic infiltration. The British also regarded the convention with suspicion. While congratulating the Quai d'Orsay that the problem of the deserters had been referred to the Hague Court, and that the incident had led to a clarification of the Moroccan question, the diplomats at London asked themselves whether Clemenceau had not double-crossed them and prepared the ground for a Franco-German economic condominium in Morocco. They were not accustomed to such independence on the part of their Gallic partner.

But the Casablanca negotiations were completely overshadowed in importance by the Balkan crisis which followed the Austrian *coup* of October 7. The Young Turk revolution in the summer of 1908 had excited the nationalist hopes of the submerged Balkan peoples and Aehrenthal decided to act swiftly. Izvolsky, as well as Clemenceau and Sir Edward Grey, was taken by surprise. He had counted upon further negotiations or a conference; instead Aehrenthal presented Europe with the announcement of the annexation as a *fait accompli*; and at the same moment Bulgaria announced her independence, clearly acting in concert with the Austrian stroke. Izvolsky found that his demands for the opening of the Straits fell on deaf ears. Grey was cool and Clemenceau indifferent when he asked their support, a natural reward for his attempt to play both sides. Germany stood behind Austria; Serbia mobilized and appealed to Russia to aid the Balkan Slavs; but Russia dared not risk a war and had to swallow the humiliation. Yet the strain told. Concurrently with the collapse of Anglo-German naval conversations, and with the Franco-German tension over Morocco, the reverberations of the Bosnian *coup* brought war one step nearer. Clemenceau's gloomy apprehensions arose from his realistic grasp of the dangers threatening European peace. No other statesman had a quicker apprehension or wider contacts.

Though French and British leaders remained cool to Izvolsky's grievances at the manner in which Aehrenthal had outwitted him, they recognized the Austrian *coup* as a severe reverse for the Entente. The Pan-Slav movement in the Balkans had received a check, Russia a humiliation, and the Balkan peoples a warning. All the Powers were fishing assiduously in those troubled waters but Austria alone had profited. The diplomatic principle of reciprocal compensation required that England, France and Russia gain advantages in equal degree or accept a loss of prestige. German diplomacy had become paramount at Constantinople and the Austro-German *Drang nach Osten* threatened Saloniki and Bagdad.

The rivalry between the Triple Alliance and the Triple Entente had tended by 1908 to become a personal duel between William II and Edward VII. The Kaiser saw his uncle's Machiavellian hand in every intrigue, and Edward, despite his royal and gracious manners, made little effort to conceal the dislike which he felt for his nephew. Towards Clemenceau the Kaiser nurtured less resentment but his vanity urged him to a trial of skill with the veteran French parliamentarian when the opportunity offered.

All the Great Powers were playing favorites among the Balkan nations: Austria had aided Bulgaria to independence, Russia supported Serbia, Britain had long upheld the integrity of the Turkish Empire, and France, or at least Clemenceau, chose somewhat unwisely to champion the cause of the Greeks. He hoped to see the modern Hellenes revive the claims of Byzantium if not the culture of Athens, and he counted in return upon the benefits of Greek friendship for France in the Near East, orders for ships and guns, the use of Greek bases for the French fleet, opportunities for French officers to train the Greek forces.

In 1907 King George of Greece visited Paris to seek financial aid, arms and professional assistance in building up his military and naval forces. He pointed out that the British failure to support Denmark had turned the Baltic Sea into a German lake, and he implied that the eastern Mediterranean must soon be over-shadowed by Austro-German influence unless Greece received generous assistance from the Entente. As the French fleet was concentrating more and more definitely in the Mediterranean, Greek bases in return for arms and loans provided the foundations for a bargain and Clemenceau made it clear that he was disposed to help. But the English remained cool to the project. The Under-Secretary for Foreign Affairs called Sir Edward Grey's attention to the negotiations in November, 1907. "The French Government, or at any rate M. Clemenceau, are strongly pro-Hellene — the latter gentleman being almost Byronic in his enthusiasm for this abject race, and a friendly attitude on our part would be agreeable to him." [11] The friendly attitude failed to develop. British statesmen saw no adequate advantage in fanning Greek ambitions; such a course would offend the Turks, antagonize Mohammedans throughout the Empire, and increase the agitation for independence already stirring the people of Malta and Cyprus, islands the British had no inclination to liberate.

The situation of Crete was the critical issue on which the Greek government weighed the worth of Entente friendship. Britain, France, Russia and Italy had exercised a protectorate over the Cretans since 1898, restraining the island population from uniting with Greece. In 1908 Clemenceau, who had visited Crete and knew the sentiment of the population, suggested to the Greek minister at Paris that the moment might soon be ripe for annexation.[12] The course involved risk, for the Young Turks at Constantinople insisted that they would resist the step by force of arms. Clemenceau sought to secure the consent of the other protecting Powers, Britain, Russia and Italy, to withdraw the mixed garrison and leave the Cretans free to follow their inclination for union, but he failed to carry

[11] *British Documents on the Origins of the War*, VIII, 47.

[12] Édouard Driault and Michel Lhéritier, *Histoire diplomatique de la Grèce de 1821 à nos jours*, 5 vols. (Paris: *Les Presses Universitaires de la France*, 1925–26), IV, 572.

his point and he held the resistance at London responsible for his failure. By the opening of 1909 he had grown sharply impatient with his British colleagues. "There is a cleft in the *Entente*," he warned the London *Times*' correspondent in February, "and care must be taken that it does not widen." [13] A week later the British received a lesson on what that cleft might lead to, for France and Germany completed their agreement on Moroccan affairs, defining French police powers and German economic interests in that country.

France, however, lacking British aid, dared not encourage the Greeks to the point of war with Turkey. Clemenceau's hopes of making Greece the *point d'appui* of French power in the eastern Mediterranean miscarried, for the Greek king turned to Germany and Austria instead. William II, aware of the French designs, developed a sudden enthusiasm for Greek scenery which lured him on royal yachting trips to Corfu, where he conferred with King George and professed his sympathy for Greek aspirations. Promises of arms from Krupp consoled the Hellenic cabinet for munitions ordered in France which never left Marseilles. The cartoonists seized the chance to portray the Kaiser as Faust wooing Helen, and the French discovered that Greece was capable of pursuing an independent course.

The position of the protecting Powers, and the role of the French and British statesmen in particular, had become distinctly embarrassing by the spring of 1909. They were holding Crete in the hope of exacting compensation but dared not acknowledge such an aim; their irresolute policy had antagonized Turkey without winning Greece, and their tardy decision to withdraw their forces from the island on July 27 but refuse the Cretans union with Greece satisfied no one. The Greek king, aware that his own role squinted at duplicity, insisted that Clemenceau had failed to keep his promises. Greek army officers, disgusted with the royal conduct of affairs, upset the cabinet on July 19, announced far-reaching reforms, and proposed that a German general be called in to reorganize the Greek army. It marked a further reverse for the Entente, crowning a year of waning influence in the Balkan theatre, and Parisian politicians, reading the news in their morning journals on July 20, recognized it as a personal defeat for Clemenceau. Crete was to be evacuated at the end of the week without compensation; the French loans to Greece had failed to assure Hellenic loyalty or markets; the mission of a French admiral to build up the Greek

[13] *British Documents on the Origins of the War*, VII, 133.

fleet had miscarried; and the munitions ordered for Greece from Schneider-Creusot had not been delivered.

A despatch forwarded to Sir Edward Grey on July 24, 1909, by the British minister at Berne furnishes an epilogue to the Greek fiasco. He had dined, he wrote, with Stephen Pichon, French Minister for Foreign Affairs, on July 19. "His Excellency," the British envoy observed, "stated that he was going to Paris that night in order to answer some questions that were to be asked in the Chambers, especially respecting Greece. These questions were never asked as on the following day the Clemenceau government fell most unexpectedly." [14]

French ministries often appear to fall unexpectedly, but those behind the scenes can usually hear the creaking of the clockwork as the fated hour approaches. In the summer of 1909 dissatisfaction with the handling of domestic problems, disgust at repeated evidence of chaos in the marine, impatience over a further reverse in foreign policy, all combined to provoke a crisis. Clemenceau's petulant attack on Delcassé on July 20 struck the spark for a prepared explosion. For back of the more easily discernible causes of discontent it is possible to detect the pressure of powerful economic forces. Rivalry between British and French armament firms, between Vickers and Schneider, had grown acute, and the French interests held their government responsible for lost orders. Spanish naval needs, Greek armaments, Moroccan mines and railroads, above all the vast Russian naval and military program that was to be financed from French credits, all these fruitful fields had been invaded by Vickers, Krupp, and Skoda to the disadvantage of the French manufacturers.

It is possible, too, that Clemenceau had dipped more deeply into Greek affairs than it would have been politic to acknowledge. He surrendered his portfolio like a schoolboy offered an unanticipated holiday and remarked gleefully to his crestfallen colleagues that, having overturned so many previous ministries, he had ended by wrecking his own. Perhaps he was relieved that the cabinet had fallen so unexpectedly and the threatened interpellations, "especially respecting Greece," would not have to be answered.

[14] *British Documents on the Origins of the War*, IX, 27.

CHAPTER IX

IN OPPOSITION
1909–1914

. . . Ceux qui, voyant le mal, s'y resignent ou s'en font les complices, sont les ouvriers d'une oeuvre mauvaise et je les combattrai de toute la force qui m'est laissée. Les questions de personne ne me sont rien. Je ne demande rien de la République que la liberté de dire ma pensée, toute ma pensée. Et je continuerai de la dire dans l'intérêt de mon pays.[1] CLEMENCEAU

THE sudden release on July 20, 1909, from the formidable burdens of the premiership brought Clemenceau an intoxicating sense of freedom. A literary friend, André Maurel, who had noted in him during the three years at the ministry a growing moroseness, a quickened irritability, found him, in the days after his cabinet fell, restored to a mood of youth and buoyancy. "I never witnessed an outburst of joy so sincere, so gleeful," Maurel recalled, "as when he signed before me, Place Beauvau, the decree which named Briand president of the council in his stead."[2] The suggestion that he might shortly be called to head another cabinet he brushed aside with a gesture. "In France the conscript serves only one period," he replied lightly. It is evidence of his high spirits that he forgot the most important qualification: unless there should be a war.

It is easy to believe that Clemenceau found a malicious pleasure in bequeathing to the suave and politic Briand the heritage of domestic difficulties which had accumulated. Briand the socialist, the erstwhile advocate of the general strike, faced the ironic duty a year later of breaking a general strike of the railway workers. He succeeded (and became anathema to his ancient associates) by calling the strikers to the colors and then ordering them back to work as soldiers, a manoeuvre which Clemenceau with all his resourcefulness could not have improved upon. But Briand had the engaging personality required to carry through such an autocratic act with the best possible grace, while Clemenceau's flinty

[1] Georges Clemenceau, *La France devant l'Allemagne* (Paris: Payot, 1918), p. 64. From *L'Homme libre* of July 4, 1913.

[2] André Maurel, *Six Écrivains de la Guerre* (Paris: Renaissance du livre, 1917), p. 21.

manners might have provided the spark needed for a serious conflagration. "Briand, whom I know well, is the readiest promiser and the most evasive of men," a friend observed without malice. "With Clemenceau you get at least a refusal and that is something."[3] Briand's facility at compromise, his patient and prodigious labors on behalf of peaceful solutions, were to win him the Nobel Prize twenty years later. But Clemenceau had come to distrust a colleague so adept at making friends, so skillful at disarming enemies. Disagreements had arisen between him and Briand, and between him and Caillaux, which weakened the prestige of the cabinet and helped to destroy its unity.[4]

The dissolution of his cabinet made Clemenceau's annual holiday in Karlsbad in 1909 a particularly welcome relaxation. His brother Paul had married an Austrian girl, Sofie Szeps, daughter of the influential Viennese journalist, Moritz Szeps, and he had many friends in Viennese circles. His sister-in-law, Berta, who came to Karlsbad on August 10, found him looking worn and aged but in excellent spirits. He was surrounded by newspapers which he explained with a sweep of his arm. "Now I will become a journalist again. Now I am free once more. Now I can laugh and swear at other people's stupidities again instead of perpetrating stupidities myself."[5]

But escape from political claims could not be won so easily. Two days later came an invitation to lunch with Edward VII at Marienbad which he could not well refuse. The two aging statesmen (both had been born in 1841 and were almost seventy) compared their impressions once again on the drift of international affairs, both agreed that the Bosnian crisis had driven the Central Powers into closer concert, while Britain, France and Russia had failed to unite their policies effectively. Edward spoke with regret of earlier, less urgent days, of the happier future which might have faced Europe if the Archduke Rudolf of Austria, who died so tragically at Mayerling in 1889, and the liberal-minded Frederick III, who reigned a scant hundred days in 1888, had survived to direct the policies at

[3] Jeanne Maurice Pouquet, *Le Salon de Madame Arman de Caillevet* (Paris: Hachette, 1926), p. 238.

[4] In particular the case of a Parisian financier, Rochette, arrested in 1908 for misappropriation of funds. Clemenceau's enemies asserted that he had Rochette arrested without due authorization and without informing Briand, then Minister of Justice. Briand affirmed before a committee of enquiry in 1914 that Rochette had been arrested legally. See Georges Suarez, *Briand*, 4 vols. (Paris: Plon, 1936–38), II, 344. Rochette had powerful political friends, including Caillaux. Briand retained Caillaux in the reconstructed cabinet after Clemenceau resigned.

[5] Berta Szeps Zuckerkandl, *My Life and History* (New York: Knopf, 1939), p. 204.

Vienna and Berlin. Both Edward and Clemenceau had come to respect and in their worldly ways to trust one another, both enjoyed their yearly rendezvous at Austrian spas, and both realized that there would not be many more of them. When the following August came, Marienbad and Karlsbad lacked two prominent visitors. Edward was dead; and Clemenceau was lecturing in South America.

Edward had been spared the horror of that Armageddon which his prescient fears foresaw and a loyal empire mourned him as Edward the Peacemaker. "He did the best he could," was Clemenceau's more realistic epitaph. But even Clemenceau, released from the anxieties of office, had come to wonder if his own sense of the imminence of war had been exaggerated. Many observers as well-informed and keen-witted as he believed that the prospects of peace were improving. Hans Delbrück, writing in the *Preussische Jahrbücher* early in 1909, ventured the opinion that Frenchmen had laid aside the dream of revenge against Germany and were not disposed to back Britain in aggressive moves. For France, Delbrück pointed out, had become the banker of Europe, and the wealth of millions of small investors depended upon loans to Turkey, the Balkan states, and even to Austria. A general conflict would involve heavy financial losses for the French.[6] A few months later, André Tardieu, summing up the condition of Franco-German relations for readers of the *Revue des deux mondes*, found them much improved. He expressed a hope that the amicable settlement of disputes and the growing intellectual and cultural reciprocity which had marked the triennium of the Clemenceau Ministry might continue.[7]

Clemenceau wondered whether diplomats, like doctors, because they faced a succession of crises, might come to see the world as sicker than it was. But some stubborn sense of reality within him insisted that 1908 had been a rehearsal for a tragedy upon which the curtain might rise at any time. A general war had been averted only because Russia was still weak and unprepared; because France did not feel directly menaced by events in the Balkans; because Britain had not faced the certainty that, if German diplomacy became paramount at Constantinople, Bagdad and Saloniki would fall to the Central Powers. In 1908 British diplomats still hoped to regain their influence at Constantinople and to preserve the Turkish Empire, or else to divide it on profitable terms. The French sought to protect

[6] Hans Delbrück, *Preussische Jahrbucher*, CXXXIV (January 1909), 176–177.

[7] André Tardieu, "France et Allemagne," *Revue des deux mondes*, LII (Paris, July 1, 1909), 65–98.

their credits to Russia, Turkey, Serbia and Greece. The Russians believed the hour at hand when the Straits would be opened to their warships through a conference rather than a conflict. But Austria seized Bosnia and Herzegovina without yielding compensation to the other Powers and without promoting any stable solution of the Balkan tension. War had not flamed across Europe in 1908 primarily because Russia was still too weak to fight. To Clemenceau, with his inside knowledge of events, this truth stood out starkly. Next year, or the year after, when Russia was stronger and the Entente more resolute, a crisis would occur which could not be resolved by bluff or by appeasement.

His fear remained no less real because it was half-intuitive. Behind the play of politics he had come to recognize the iron drive of economic forces which he never fully understood. He saw issues with the eye of the journalist or dramatist, conflicts personified. When he fought collectivism he fought Jaurès; when he curbed a strike he appealed to the good sense of the average worker or arrested the leaders of the *Confédération Générale du Travail.* When he negotiated an international accord he reasoned with the diplomats responsible, with Chamberlain, or Haldane, or Edward VII, with Grey, Izvolsky, Bülow. But twentieth-century class warfare had become more and more a matter of long range strife between *syndicats* and corporations in which lawyers were more important than pickets and credit than courage, and both sides were hostile to state interference. In a similar fashion international rivalries had become a matter of loans, monopolies, concessions, of economic penetration, interlocking directorates and international pools of armament patents. With his nineteenth-century mind Clemenceau never clearly grasped the effect of these transitions. He remained in his essential training a Jacobin idealist, blind to the truth that the industrial revolution had invalidated his political philosophy before it had been fairly tried. In the nineteenth century men had died on the barricades for the right to vote. In the twentieth they were dying for the right to work, for the right to a living wage. The machinery of parliamentarism and conventional diplomacy with which Clemenceau worked was half-archaic, and he had little knowledge or mastery of the newer instruments of power politics.

This lack of training in economic problems forced Clemenceau while in power to leave the national finances in other hands and helps to explain the wide latitude which he allowed Caillaux. For three years Caillaux dressed the budget, paring expenses, conciliating the legislative committees, converting bond issues and meeting the interest charges on the national debt, charges which had mounted until they devoured one-third of the revenue. The army, the navy, education and the social services all suffered from inadequate appropriations, but Clemenceau acquiesced in the solutions worked out, for with all his acuteness of mind, his reverence for realities, he shrank from the labor of mastering the logic of large scale accounting. Unconsciously, perhaps, he resented the fiscal prescience which enabled a Poincaré or a Caillaux to penetrate the arcana of economics. His feuds with both of them were exacerbated by jealousy, by the forced recognition that they excelled him in a field of first importance to the statesman.

In a worthier sense his jealousy and suspicion might be attributed to the fear of being deceived, the dread every responsible person must feel of lending himself, with the best intentions, to the mistaken designs of others. "I have known my share of happiness and grief," he affirmed more than once, "but above all else, of deception." [8] This distrust of collaboration as an unworthy compromise even persuaded him to refuse membership in the *Académie Française*: as one of the Forty Immortals he felt that he would have to abandon a part of himself.[9] His acceptance of cabinet office, his descent into the arena of practical politics, had been an abdication, how much of an abdication he realized only when he was free to be his arbitrary self once more. This loud insistence upon a complete personal autonomy may have been in part a pose, in part an emotional necessity. But at least he maintained it with courage and consistency. In his battles with tongue and pen he saw himself, not without justice, as a cleric in Julien Benda's sense of the term, one with Spinoza, Voltaire and Zola, with all lovers of truth and honesty who have dared to plead unpopular causes, defying the timid voice of prudence and the tough voice of authority, speaking out their judgments in obedience to some imperial note within themselves.

The years from 1909 to 1914 formed in many respects the calmest and most genial period of Clemenceau's life. As his financial position improved he cleared off most of his indebtedness. At Bernouville, near Gisors, a couple of hours' drive from Paris, he purchased a white, rose-hung cottage, furnished it with his best loved books, bric-a-brac and souvenirs, and escaped there with a few chosen friends when he wished to relax over a weekend. Sometimes his son Michel, or his son-in-law

[8] Jean Jules Henry Mordacq, *Clemenceau au soir de sa vie, 1920–1929*, 2 vols. (Paris: Plon, 1933), II, 57.

[9] Georges Suarez, *Clemenceau*, 2 vols. (Paris: Les Éditions de France, 1932), II, 134–135.

Jacquemaire, accompanied him. Gustave Geffroy drove out from Paris to recall old days on *La Justice* thirty years before; Claude Monet came over from Giverny to admire the cottage with a painter's eye. Clemenceau amused himself, like any retired bourgeois of limited means, with plans for redecorating the rooms, rearranging the furniture, replanting the garden. The quiet village of a few hundred souls soothed his impetuous spirit and he played with the thought of writing another novel, not a problem novel full of psychology and social significance like *Les Plus Forts*, but a love story. It seemed as if the Tiger, almost seventy, had grown a little weary and begun to sheathe his claws. His health was none too good; a disorder of the liver often gave his complexion a yellowish tinge; and an enlargement of the prostate gland caused him considerable discomfort.

Leisure, fatigue, ill-health, a gentler mood, these should have made Clemenceau more tolerant of tenderness, should have reunited him to his estranged wife had their temperaments permitted a reconciliation. She had apparently taken the initiative at least once during his term at the Ministry of Interior Affairs and called at the Place Beauvau. Four years had elapsed since their previous meeting but he received her with unrelenting frigidity and insisted that his secretaries remain in the room. The discussion rapidly degenerated into a dialogue of bitter reproaches which lasted two hours and settled nothing.[10] Psychologists, no doubt, could provide a clue to Clemenceau's intractable attitude, his persistent repudiation of emotional obligations. Even towards his daughters he was unusually curt and gruff; and when his son Michel was summoned for military training he kept him on a small and strict allowance and insisted that, despite the youth's uncertain health, he should be granted no favors or luxuries. But this show of severity hid a father's natural concern, as the letters he wrote almost daily to a friend in Nancy bear witness. He was watching over Michel by proxy, contrasting his son's letters with a first-hand account of conditions, and his seeming heartlessness was meant to be for both of them an imposed discipline. He thought Michel complained too much, that he needed to inure himself to the rigors of barrack life and to improve his sense of humor. But he followed the route marches of the recruits on his map, and he shivered when the temperature dropped. "It must be devilishly cold at Nancy. This is no picnic for the little soldiers."[11]

[10] Georges Louis, *Les Carnets de Georges Louis* (Paris: Rieder, 1926), I, 44–45.
[11] Suarez, *Clemenceau*, II, 14.

After less than a year of relative relaxation and ampler leisure Clemenceau became restless for the smoke of battle, for some new opponent to attack, some deadline to meet. The summer of 1910 brought the flattering opportunity to lecture on Democracy in the Argentine Republic, Brazil and Uruguay, and he seized the chance eagerly, sailing from Genoa in June. The two weeks' voyage, the novelty and beauty of the South American scenes, the cordial and deferential welcome extended to him as a leading statesman and journalist of the Old World, warmed Clemenceau's cynical nature, and his comments on the New World republics, their culture, politics, products and problems, reveal him in an observant, enthusiastic, holiday temper. Europe was enslaved to her past, her historic soil poisoned by two thousand years of remembered strife, her people dowered with inextinguishable feuds and prejudices. But in the New World, despite racial problems, Clemenceau believed that democracy had taken healthier root and he hymned its praises with a new confidence.

This recovered vitality of spirit made the lecture tour a brilliant success, and the stimulus of organizing his thoughts for the platform fired his literary ambitions. He returned with notes for a book on South American problems, which appeared in French and English the following year,[12] and with the concept of a more grandiose project germinating in his mind. This was to be a work in several volumes which would trace the evolution of the democratic ideal from the earliest times, considering it from the sociological, the philosophical and the scientific, as well as the historical point of view. As outlined, this monumental treatise promised to rank with Montesquieu's *Esprit des Lois* or Voltaire's *Essai sur les Moeurs*, and Clemenceau continued to collect material for it during 1911 and 1912.

For over fifty years his thoughts had quested after the rectifying principle in life and society. As a medical student he had been led, from his interest in mentally disordered patients, to ponder the larger problems of social maladjustment in general. Later, as a journalist, politician and diplomat he had observed the elements of conflict and cohesion working in society and he had striven to identify the forces which made for disorganization and violence, the principles which promoted order and harmony. The titles assigned his literary efforts are frequently suggestive of this search: *La Justice*, *La Mêlée sociale*, *L'Iniquité*, *Justice militaire*, *L'Homme libre*; and his thoughts constantly leapt from individual cases

[12] Georges Clemenceau, *Notes de voyage dans l'Amérique du Sud, Argentine, Uruguay, Brésil* (Paris: Hachette, 1911); *South America Today* (New York: Putnam, 1911).

to the larger issues they prefigured, problems of law, morality, social coöperation, *solidarité*. As he grew older he grew more skeptical that the disharmonies and antagonisms dividing classes and nations could be greatly ameliorated. Authority and liberty, he agreed, were metaphysical opposites which *ought* to find their reconciliation in useful social activity. The democratic way of life was ideally the best because it promised the maximum of freedom for the individual and the minimum of coercion, but it assumed that the individuals would be able and willing to acquit themselves voluntarily of their responsibilities towards society.

Modern democracies, Clemenceau concluded, while manifesting an increasing bureaucratic efficiency, had been marred by parliamentary incompetence. In other words they remained weakest at that point where individuals, instead of following an established pattern of activity, were invited to improvise and apply a common solution voluntarily. It was possible to win one man by honest argument, and, having persuaded him, to retain his loyal coöperation. But to make reason and equity prevail in a disparate group, a crowd, a mob, that was another matter. Passions, prejudices, all the forces of unreason constantly warred against the just solution. So long as men were prepared to take up arms in defense of their convictions or possessions there would be other men willing to slay them. Up to the present, Clemenceau submitted realistically, to prevent war men had evolved only one practical line of approach, arbitration, which derived its validity from sanctions, which rested upon . . . war.[13]

The notes on South America and the projected treatise on democracy did not suffice for Clemenceau's indefatigable pen. It seemed as if he must empty his inkwell daily (he shunned fountain pens) on some topic of timely import. With a group of young associates he embarked upon a new journalistic venture. *L'Homme libre* did not appeal to the masses and the editions seldom ran beyond a few thousand copies, but there was no politician in Paris who did not read it.[14] With all his ancient fire Clemenceau once more deflated reputations and lanced political abscesses, refuted the arguments of his fellow columnists and parliamentarians, dissected the policies of the cabinet, and disinterred from moribund committees issues which had been shelved instead of solved. His motto, as in his first journalistic initiation in America half-a-century before, was still: A Question is never settled until it is settled right.

[13] Léon Abensour, "Un grand projet de G. Clemenceau," *Grand revue*, CXXXI (1930), 529–550.

[14] *Les Carnets de Georges Louis*, II, 60.

The new activities had recharged his energies, but the inflammation in his prostate gland continued and early in 1912 he decided to submit to an operation. At the hospital chosen he received special care and attention from the sisters of charity who served as nurses, Sister Théoneste in particular ministering to the needs of her formidable patient with a serenity and skill which speeded his recovery. Clemenceau retained a lively sense of gratitude for the excellent routine, the reassuring mood and calm competence that surrounded him during his days of convalescence, and he found conversation with the sisters pleasant and enlightening. "We discussed everything," he recalled, "with complete freedom and without a suspicion of offense, and perhaps we all gained a deeper spirit of tolerance and good will towards those who held opinions not our own. They did not alter theirs nor I mine, but we agreed that it is not necessary to hate one another because of opposing sentiments on the insoluble question of human destiny. I am very proud to think that, should my friends in the rue Bizet have need of a service which it is in my power to render them, they will do me the honor of asking it of me." [15]

Clemenceau required all his new serenity and vigor for the shades of approaching war already darkened the European skies. Between France and Germany the Moroccan question had excited a new crisis in 1911. The German Foreign Office, pricked on by German business firms, manifested its dissatisfaction with the construction the French had placed upon the accord of 1909. In May, 1911, a French force occupied Fez. A few weeks later a cabinet change brought the presumably pliant Caillaux to the head of the ministry at Paris, and the German Foreign Minister, Kiderlen-Wächter, insisted upon the Bismarckian gesture of sending a gunboat to Agadir to protect German interests. "You have bought your freedom of action in Morocco from Spain, England, and even from Italy," the French ambassador was informed curtly, "and you have ignored us. You should have conferred with us before going to Fez." [16]

Through July the threat of war hung heavily over Europe; but Morocco was not worth a general conflagration and a compromise emerged. Caillaux negotiated directly and secretly with Berlin, over the head of his inexperienced Minister of Foreign Affairs, De Selves, and the French ambassador, Jules Cambon. In the agreement officially communicated the Germans recognized French political control of Morocco but exacted in

[15] Suarez, *Clemenceau*, II, 148.

[16] *Documents diplomatiques françaises: Affaires de Maroc, VI (1910–1912)*, No. 455. For the convention which followed the Agadir crisis, see pp. 625–635.

compensation 100,000 square miles of the French Congo, a not unreasonable compromise, as the French also received a small area near Lake Chad, so that the whole deal could have been represented as a simple and mutual rectification of frontiers. The French Chamber and Senate ratified the convention, but De Selves, or possibly Jules Cambon (who had been appointed to the Berlin post by Clemenceau), let the latter know of Caillaux' extra-diplomatic intercourse with Berlin. Summoned before a senate commission, Caillaux denied that there had been any political or financial discussions outside official channels. Clemenceau turned upon De Selves. "Is the Minister of Foreign Affairs able to confirm this statement?" De Selves begged leave not to answer and handed in his resignation after the meeting. Unable to reconstruct his cabinet in the face of the general distrust Caillaux himself resigned two days later. His eagerness to reach a general accord with Germany on colonial matters seemed to ardent French patriots too humble and conciliatory, and Clemenceau, stigmatizing the convention as a Trojan Horse, refused to vote for its acceptance.

As the case of Caillaux illustrated, European diplomacy had become more and more a façade behind which rival economic groups were locked in a devious, shifting struggle for profits. As Europe descended towards the abyss of war fear drove the peoples to approve fantastic funds for armaments, and when the threat of a neighbor's war machine failed to excite the expected response an inspired press whipped up the necessary hysteria. In this campaign of deliberate incitement Clemenceau took a lively share, and responsibility for intensifying the war fever cannot be lifted from his shoulders. His motives, there seems no reason to doubt, were unselfish and patriotic, though he must have known that the billions voted for war on the eve of 1914 excited a frantic scramble among all the armament firms of Europe. The connections between the munitions makers, the press, public opinion and government orders can not be traced with any completeness, but illuminating incidents have been reconstructed which reveal, like lightning flashes, the dark and fateful road down which the nations marched to the mounting thunder of the anvil chorus.

The half-legendary figure of Basil Zaharoff has come to symbolize the power of the international armament maker and Clemenceau's relations with him have been the subject of considerable speculation. In 1907 Zaharoff, already associated with Vickers Ltd., the British firm, and with Loewe-Gontard in Germany, opened a Paris office on the rue Hoche and sought a place on the board of the Schneider-Creusot interests in France.

Seconding the government efforts to improve the navy, he endowed a home for seamen, a gesture for which, on the recommendation of the Minister of Marine, he was appointed a Chevalier of the Legion of Honor. Through the purchase of a harmless non-political paper, *Quotidiens Illustrés* he secured secret control of a second journal, *Excelsior*, which served as a lever for moving public opinion when it was necessary to employ the technique of "incitement." The fact that Zaharoff's career in the field of French finance, armaments and journalism began during the first Clemenceau ministry proves nothing beyond coincidence. In the decade which followed, however, he advanced from Chevalier to Grand Officer of the Legion of Honor; won a seat on the board of the Banque de France; acquired control of the principality of Monaco by a secret convention in 1918 (which Clemenceau negotiated); and founded a French affiliate, Vickers Française, with Michel Clemenceau on the board of directors. Such incidents have been accumulated to prove that Clemenceau sponsored the career of Zaharoff as earlier he had sponsored that of Cornélius Herz, and it is true that most of Zaharoff's official honors came to him during the first and second Clemenceau ministries.[17] The evidence, as evidence, proves nothing more than Clemenceau's desire to win the services of an indispensable agent for the arming of the Republic, and there can be little doubt that Zaharoff's aid contributed in no small measure to the success of the Entente preparations for war.

As the relative strength of the Triple Alliance and the Triple Entente grew more nearly equal the competition in arms grew more keen. By 1912 Russia was pressing ahead with vast military reforms, and the Third (and thoroughly tamed) Duma voted the equivalent of half-a-billion dollars for a new fleet. The money was to be spent in Russia, however, a condition which compelled foreign firms to send their specialists to the Czar's empire and to construct the necessary docks and arsenals there as national enterprises. In the scramble for orders which ensued Vickers Ltd. secured the lion's share of the contracts, to the chagrin of French manufacturers.

This extensive Russian program threatened not only Austria and Germany; it alarmed even more the smaller states of the Near East, Rumania and Turkey in particular. Entente diplomacy had recovered the initiative since the reverses of 1908 and 1909. In Greece a French military mission

[17] Robert Neumann, *Zaharoff*, translated from the German by R. T. Clark (New York: Knopf, 1935), 111–113, 260; Philip Noel-Baker, *The Private Manufacture of Armaments* (New York: Oxford University Press, 1937), p. 247.

and a British naval mission received authority to reorganize the Hellenic forces and to purchase supplies. At Constantinople the pro-German sentiment cooled somewhat after 1912, when Italy seized Tripoli: it was felt in Turkish government circles that a word from Berlin could have restrained the Italians and the word had not been spoken. The Balkan Wars of 1912 and 1913 provided a further lesson for the Turks. Krupp, Skoda, Schneider and Vickers had all taken a hand in equipping the Balkan states, and the joint attack which these states made upon Turkey defeated the German-trained Ottoman troops. The battles and sieges provided a practical test of new military arms and methods, and the outcome, on the whole, seemed a triumph for Entente gold, steel, and strategy. This proved especially true in the Second Balkan War of 1913, when Bulgaria, the "Little Prussia" of the Balkans, incited by Austrian encouragement, attacked her late allies, Serbia and Greece, over the division of the Turkish spoils. Bulgaria suffered a swift defeat, and it required all the art of Austrian diplomacy, backed by German might, to curb the victorious Serbs and block the creation of a Greater Serbia with access to the Adriatic Sea.

For the Turks the lesson had been sharp and severe. German friendship had failed to save them from defeat in Tripoli or from the loss of almost all their provinces in Europe. The Russian naval preparations on the Black Sea constituted a growing menace from which the German fleet could offer no protection. "Zaharoff thinks it will take three or four years to build armored cruisers on the Black Sea in sufficient strength to overawe Turkey," the financial attaché of the Russian embassy at Paris wrote in 1913.[18] The Turks regarded the danger as more imminent and decided to take immediate steps to meet the Russian threat: they turned for aid to France and Britain, well knowing that the western Powers were almost as antagonistic to Russian as to German control of Constantinople. On October 28, 1913, the German Foreign Office learned with consternation that the British had won a concession from the Porte to build and equip all Turkish ships for a period of thirty years, while French firms were to receive 75 per cent of Turkish army contracts. The financial burden of this armament expansion would be met in part by a bond issue of 500,000,000 francs to be floated on the Paris bourse.[19]

A friendly Turkey, which would open the Dardanelles to the Entente

[18] Noel-Baker, *The Private Manufacture of Armaments*, pp. 349–350.

[19] Bernard Menne, *Blood and Steel: the Rise of the House of Krupp* (New York: Lee Furman, Inc., 1938), pp. 310–312.

fleets, might well prove the decisive factor in a general European War, and it appeared as if the French and British had scored a brilliant diplomatic triumph. Britain, by lending technical aid and advice for the development of the Russian and Greek navies, had brought the Porte to terms, secured to Vickers lucrative orders for Turkish (as well as Greek and Russian) naval supplies, and threatened the Berlin to Bagdad railway project (a German venture) at its most vital link, Constantinople. For the Central Powers the threat of encirclement was becoming a grim reality. The German response may be read in part from the army bills of 1911, 1912 and 1913, which raised the total of effectives from 623,000 to 820,000 men on active service. Announcement of the German increases, publicized by the Parisian press, hastened the French into a program of army expansion and the restoration of the three-year training period. These reforms, it was estimated, would raise the total of French effectives to 750,000 by 1914.

As politician and journalist Clemenceau never ceased to reiterate throughout these years that the whole blame for the increasing burden of arms, and for the restoration of the three-year period, lay squarely on the shoulders of the German militarists. "One must be deliberately blind," he wrote in *L'Homme libre*, May 21, 1913, "not to see that the (German) lust for power, the impact of which makes Europe tremble each day, has fixed as its policy the extermination of France. If the catastrophe is inevitable we must steel ourselves to meet it with all our strength."[20] Eloquently, indefatigably and relentlessly he fought, refuted and ridiculed the proposals of the Socialists and pacifists that friendly conferences between well disposed French and German groups might yet evolve a formula for the reduction of armaments and the arbitration of disputes. When delegates from the two nations assembled at Berne with this aim in view he promised the failure of their deliberations in advance. "What too many of these people here still do not wish to realize," he wrote, "is that Germany, entirely organized for violence, cannot escape if she would — and certainly reveals no desire to escape — from the fatality of further harvests of violence."

On July 14, 1914, the last Bastille Day before the storm broke, Clemenceau delivered in the Senate a crushing denunciation against the Minister of War for the lack of adequate preparation of all types of military matériel. The next day he followed up his attack with an article

[20] Georges Clemenceau, *Discours de Guerre* (Paris: Plon, 1934), p. 2, from *L'Homme libre*, May 21, 1913.

calculated to shock and alarm his readers. "What have they accomplished, during half-a-century of peace, all these noble patriots to whom the organization of our military forces has been entrusted? France has provided the men. With what sort of equipment have they been furnished? If the arms they are to bear prove inferior to those they must encounter (a thing beyond excuse when the nation has poured out its gold without stint) you hear already the cry of 1870: 'We are betrayed!' It is eternally with me, the terrible despair of those heroes, armed with nothing but their valor, who died, mowed down by a merciless rain of lead, without being able even to exchange blow for blow." [21]

Two weeks later Europe was at war and Clemenceau's long campaign for more adequate armaments had its vindication. This was going to be "no picnic for the little soldiers." On July 31 a fanatical patriot assassinated Jean Jaurès because the great tribune had once dared to plead for Franco-German friendship and a socialist international. Clemenceau paid an honest tribute to his great rival. "It was the fate of Jaurès to preach the brotherhood of nations and to believe with such unswerving faith in this noble conception that he was not daunted by the brutal reality of the facts." [22] He might have added that on the day Jaurès died, Basil Zaharoff, who likewise was not daunted by the brutal reality of the facts, was raised to the rank of Commander in the Legion of Honor "for exceptional services to the Republic." [23]

[21] Clemenceau, *Discours de Guerre*, p. 38, from *L'Homme libre*, July 15, 1914.
[22] Clemenceau, *Discours de Guerre*, p. 48, from *L'Homme libre*, August 2, 1914.
[23] Noel-Baker, *The Private Manufacture of Armaments*, p. 138.

CHAPTER X

MAN IN CHAINS
1914–1917

Si la terre pouvait dire, elle nous raconterait tous ces magnifiques recommencements d'histoire dont elle palpite encore, et que nous embaumons froidement en des pages sans vie. Une fatalité veut qu'elle se dérobe à nous dans les gouffres sans fond d'une gestation infinie. Elle se tait, mais le peu que nous savons de ce qui fut suffit à nous élever au-dessus de nous-mêmes, à nous faire une vie supérieure à nôtre vie, en nous rattachant à la grande chaîne, de fer et d'or mêlés, comme un anneau fragile, mais durable encore, entre les choses qui furent et des choses qui, par nous, auront été.[1]

CLEMENCEAU

THE first clangors of war went to Clemenceau's head like a mighty music. His brain rang with echoing phrases which his pen could not capture fast enough, so that at times they grew too stupendous and incoherent to record. All his life the fever of combat had burned in his blood and the mounting diapason of a world in arms transformed him momentarily into a poet. He made his daily article a mirror of the soul of France in her tragic hour, polishing and repolishing his prose that it might reflect more faithfully the burning images of a nation wounded almost to death. In those first desperate weeks, while the Teutonic tide flowed relentlessly towards Paris, he wrote and rewrote like one who had made a vow that no epic action should escape his pen, no least share of the agony remain unrecorded.

The conflict unleashed in August, 1914, stilled the feuds of French political life in the *union sacrée* and brought for the moment a similar integration to Clemenceau's disharmonic spirit. Wherever he turned he rejoiced to find all his countrymen joined in unity and strength.

From the blind confusion of factional strife the Frenchman has emerged in this hour all of a piece throughout, stronger, more resolute, silent, smiling, his eyes bright with an invincible fire which affirms that the legend of France shall not fail. . . . It is that mysterious hour when something comes to birth in us which burns out the

[1] Georges Clemenceau, *La France devant l'Allemagne* (Paris: Payot, 1918), pp. 272–273. Reprinted from *L'Homme Enchaîné*, October 2, 1915.

Max Pohly, from BLACK STAR

A glimpse of the Tiger in a jovial mood.

dross and clears the way for the casting of a metal which neither steel nor diamond can scratch. And when, some day, after superhuman efforts, all these souls, fatigued with heroism, meet again under the vast blue vault of a regenerated fatherland, it must be that of so many hearts which were sundered a soul of France will forge itself, and the discords which are a condition of life will dissolve, fast fused in a bond of solidarity so closely knit that nothing will have power to shatter it.[2]

Behind the little soldier in the trenches, mud-stained, grumbling, and heroic, Clemenceau envisaged the French countryside, beautified by toil, for which the *poilu* was laying down his life.

From the sea to the mountains, it transpierces him with an intense spirit of dedication, a passion which embraces all the tributes of a soil now prodigal, now niggardly, all the lively dreams cradled by the hearthside, all the hopes of heaven which, even if deceptive, have none the less guided the soul on its march towards the stars, a march in which the journey, perhaps, is better than the goal. From the cloudy horizons of the ocean, from the translucent blue of the inland lakes which fashion the soul for high endeavor, from the jagged peaks of the Pyrenees and the Alps, from radiant valleys with their flashing streams and bountiful harvests, he has journeyed here to fall with his face to the invader. An invincible force has conducted him to this place, where the pitiless determination even of those who love him has decreed that he is to honor to the death a sacrifice which is beyond love.[3]

To see his fellow Frenchmen, faced with their great hour, rise to the stature demanded by the epic tragedy, charged Clemenceau's heart with a pride that was almost unendurable. He had often feared, and expressed the fear, that during the decades of peace under the Third Republic the French character had deteriorated. Now, looking backward, he felt rebuked for his doubts, and it was clear to him that even in flaccid years such episodes as the Dreyfus conflict should have convinced him that France still bred heroes.

It [peace] had inspired, of all types of civic courage, one of the loftiest forms of nobility, that wherein a citizen is called upon to take, in the silence of his room and without witnesses, a decision upon which all the happiness or misery of the future depends. The man who deliberately sacrifices all his social advantages of the moment, even the welfare of those dearest to him, in obedience to his conscience, is a hero whose courage cannot be surpassed. But it may be equalled.

For there remains the ideal of military courage, inviolate in its beauty and its austerity. Is it not the greatest sacrifice of all to give oneself completely to a noble cause? And how could the sacrifice be more complete than when it is offered in the

[2] Clemenceau, *La France devant l'Allemagne*, p. 124.

[3] Clemenceau, *La France devant l'Allemagne*, p. 272. It is worth noting that Clemenceau pictures the conscript as a peasant, not as a clerk or factory worker, and that he eulogizes rural, not urban, France.

flower of youth, when all the senses respond with trembling initiative to the radiant procession of hopes whose secret the adolescent does not yet possess. He believes, he aspires, he anticipates. Whatever life may bring him, this is a sacred moment, the more beautiful in its promises because it still lacks the deficits of reality. Everything awakens, everything sings, everything beckons to life. And all this dream of fragile beauty, more precious than the untested truth of things, the young man will be asked to fling into the abyss because a summons more imperative than all others has so decreed.[4]

It troubled Clemenceau that the vastness of the tragedy, the anonymity of the collective effort, depersonalized the hero and bleached the individual action of its valorous worth. "Man, in this tragic ensemble, is no more than a lost atom," he lamented. His visits to the front convinced him, against his heart's lyric protest, that in war as in industry the machine was the master.

We crossed the fields and soon rejoined the [battery of] Seventy-fives, whose fire had quickened. But where one had expected to find the tumult and the shouting of combat one found mute gunners, moving like automatons. On all the immense plain, overshadowed by the wings of death, one saw nothing, comprehended nothing. The gun shrugged its shoulders as if in play and a tiny white puff of shrapnel appeared for an instant. The voice of the Seventy-five is a lovely thing, it speaks with a gay, decisive accent, like the snap of a wind-whipped flag. But all around one senses the presence of an implacable energy, converging from every side, maturing its dark purposes in secret like Fate in a classic drama, in order to make the consummation the more overwhelming when it is revealed.[5]

The victory on the Marne assured Paris a respite; but Clemenceau did not share the over-confidence of some French generals who assumed that the German retreat would continue and the end of the war was in sight. With the transition to trench warfare and the horrible carnage which accompanied each attempt to break the enemy lines his anger mounted against the military specialists who had failed to foresee and prepare for this type of warfare. Before winter closed down the foe had dug his trenches from Switzerland to the North Sea, and fortified them so strongly with barbed wire and machine gun nests that nothing less than high explosive shells could blast him out of them. The French and British lacked heavy artillery and high explosive and their supply of machine guns was utterly inadequate. Someone had blundered.

As a member of the Senate Committee on the Army Clemenceau enjoyed the privilege of prying into military affairs and he rapidly made

[4] Clemenceau, *La France devant l'Allemagne*, pp. 174–175.
[5] Clemenceau, *La France devant l'Allemagne*, p. 287.

himself a terror to the generals and the Minister of War. His fight, like that waged by Lloyd George in England, to break through the entrenched conservatism of the military caste had something heroic about it: it was a tense, interlocked warfare of attrition as unrelenting as the daily death-grip on the Western Front. The grim and terrible truth that thousands of Frenchmen were being marched to death day after day against positions impregnable to unsupported infantry was a truth too horrible for publication. Yet it seemed as if nothing short of widespread publicity and the subsequent chorus of wrath would restrain the general staff from perpetuating these holocausts indefinitely. "The danger of speaking out and the danger of remaining silent," Clemenceau confessed, "balanced itself agonizingly in our minds."[6]

To marshal public opinion, keep it on the *qui vive*, yet withhold the full evidence of official incompetence so that he might retain the threat of exposure as a trump card to compel reforms, this was a game at which none could surpass Clemenceau and no other French politician was in a better position to play it. He constituted himself a *liaison officier* between a driven bureaucracy and a desperate public. Hints to his readers that he knew much more than the censor allowed him to utter; threats to the bureaucrats that he would publicize their mistakes and stupidities unless they hastened the remedy: such remained his formula from 1914 to 1917. If French democratic institutions survived and functioned, if the French people endured the losses, horrors and defeats of war for four years and still supported the government and the army, Clemenceau's protean labors contributed as much as the efforts of one individual can contribute to this result and to the ultimate victory. In the darkest hours of the struggle he still dared to defend parliamentary democracy as a system in which the virtues outweighed the flagrant deficits and disadvantages.

> Parliamentarism, with all its faults — and they are innumerable — has great virtues. It is perfectible, more so than royalism. I believe that Parliament is the greatest organism ever invented for committing political blunders, but they have the great advantage of being reparable, and this because the country has the will to do it.[7]

Despite such professions of faith, however, he recognized clearly and coldly that in war a government which cannot learn quickly and reform itself promptly is doomed, and in France both the parliament and the army command were slow to learn. "The evil," he wrote, "can be summed

[6] Georges Clemenceau, *La Leçon de la Russie* (Paris: Floury, 1915), p. 68.
[7] *Journal Officiel: Sénat: Débats parlementaires*, session of July 22, 1917, p. 756.

up in a word: the omnipotent anarchy of an irresponsible bureaucracy."[8] Bureaucratic machinery was indispensable; without it there could be no effective administration or social organization; but the machine must remain controllable and perfectible. Particularly in wartime it was necessary to guard against the autonomy of the bureaucrats.

> Those who make the preparations for war are already designated to conduct it, and if the course of operations brings to light faults more or less serious—as happened with the development of our excellent light artillery as well as in the creation of our heavy artillery—it is a dire undertaking to effect a change. A bureaucracy which conceives itself to be infallible, if by an unlucky chance it controls the censorship, will hold as an enemy of the commonwealth anyone who advocates the swift reform necessary to save the nation.[9]

As he was forbidden to point his moral directly, Clemenceau lashed the French bureaucrats, military theorists, and munition makers over the shoulders of their Russian counterparts. The collapse of the early Russian offensive revealed defects of preparation and leadership in the Czar's army which astounded and dismayed the Duma. Day after day Clemenceau reported the rank and scandalous details which the Duma investigations brought to light, basing his information on neutral sources—the *Journal de Genève*, the *Gazette de Lausanne*—and then pointed out mildly that the Duma committee had concluded that Russia was probably no worse prepared than France or Great Britain. The one truth which emerged starkly in every country was that the generals and the politicians would pass the blame back and forth glibly, while the infantry paid with their lives for the cannon which had not been cast, the machine guns which were never delivered, the shells with defective fuses, the grenades which failed to arrive. Nor did they suffer less dearly from the ideological rigidity of theorists who fought their battles on paper, and ordered infantry advances across quivering quagmires and through impenetrable thickets which would have been all but impassable even without an enemy to defend them.

By the end of September, 1914, Clemenceau's competent and caustic criticism goaded the censor into suppressing *L'Homme Libre*: the journal reappeared the following day as *L'Homme Enchaîné*. The new title was more than a jibe at official restraint; it was a rebuke to all citizens in all ranks who were chained by habit, by sloth, by selfishness, by privilege. In a democracy, Clemenceau warned, the citizen enjoys the maximum liberty

[8] Georges Clemenceau, *La Leçon de la Russie* (Paris: Floury, 1915), p. 36.
[9] Clemenceau, *La Leçon de la Russie*, p. 52.

so that he may voluntarily perform his maximum duty. But "Liberty does not make man an infallible god," he observed pointedly.[10] The liberation and rehabilitation of France demanded the submission of all to an inflexible discipline, the synthesis of all energies, all efforts, all wills in one dynamic drive. The immediate problem, in France, in Russia, in Britain, was to inject a new spirit and impetus into the national administration, to compel and carry through by the irresistible pressure of a united public opinion the necessary reconstruction and reform.

> In the national organization there is, by definition, a will superior to the bureaucracy. It resides in the government. The government has only to say: *I will*, and having said it, to act. In theory, you observe, nothing is more simple. The chief difficulty is that most of these governments see only through the eyes of the administration, hear only with its ears, judge only according to its faculties. Is it not the chief merit of a bureaucracy, in the opinion of many people, that it thinks, wills and acts without putting the minister to further inconvenience than that of attaching his signature? If the men who are nominally and believe themselves to be actually in power, but whose first concern is to abandon their authority to an irresponsible bureaucracy, had taken the reins of control in firm hands, we would never have known the evils of bureaucracy, because the bureaucracy, restricted to the limits of its functions, would have been a servant insead of a master.[11]

As a member of the Senate Committee on the Army and the Committee on Foreign Affairs Clemenceau could evaluate the time and energy lost through departmental friction, jealousy, rivalry, conflict of powers, and stolid, unimaginative, case-hardened conservatism. Those who sought, for reasons sound or mischievous, to delay or discourage any measure or project enjoyed a thousand opportunities to do so. Those who endeavored, honestly and earnestly, to push the war effort, faced a thousand obstacles which wore out their energies. It seemed easier to find soldiers who would die for France than to find workmen who would forego the right to strike, civil servants who would relinquish their little brief authority that bureaus might be merged, or officers who would forget their seniority and their *amour propre* and serve in units or submit to orders they disliked. Man was still in chains, chains of routine thinking, of professional privilege, of social pride. Only in the front-line trenches among the poilus facing death with weary fatalism did Clemenceau find the *union sacrée* to which all Frenchmen paid lip service. In contrast to these doomed battalions the citizens behind the lines seemed to him to pass much of their time in hypocritical pretenses, in silly bombast and attitudinizing. Some-

[10] Clemenceau, *La Leçon de la Russie*, p. 34.

[11] Clemenceau, *La Leçon de la Russie*, p. 53.

where in his complex make-up he carried a touchstone which detected the spurious in mankind, and more than ever it infuriated him to see insolent and incompetent men in office disposing of the lives and labors of the patient, the industrious, the humble.

In the civilian administration, in the army command, the personnel remained prisoners of a dilatory but sacrosanct routine elaborated in the pre-war era. Changes of ministry increased the confusion without resolving the problems or reducing the inertia. The occasion called for a unification of authority, the polarizing of all wills in one direction, the focussing of all energies in one general effort, but the government proved unequal to the task. The Viviani cabinet, in office when war came, was reshuffled in August, 1914, and finally yielded place to Briand's fifth ministry a year later. Briand likewise patched and repatched but could not retain the confidence of the Chamber and in March, 1917, Alexandre Ribot organized a cabinet. Overwhelmed by the mounting disasters of that black year the Ribot ministry fell in September and Paul Painlevé accepted office but was overthrown within two months. These ministerial crises were the outward and visible signs of the hidden conflicts between the general staff and the civilian cabinet, between various ministers and the powerful parliamentary committees, between public opinion and censorship, between capital and labor. As the war dragged along these opposing elements tended to align themselves in two national camps. Those grimly set to endure the *guerre à outrance* rallied behind Clemenceau. Those who believed it possible to make an honorable peace before France was bled white found their leader and their spokesman in Joseph Caillaux.

That French democracy survived the crises of 1914–1918 must surprise a later generation which has seen democratic regimes succumb before milder ordeals. The transition from peace to war always strains and sometimes wrecks a constitutional government. From August 4 to December 22, 1914, France was ruled by executive decree: parliament had abdicated. The staff at army headquarters enjoyed complete autonomy in military matters. This provisional state of affairs — a *de facto* dictatorship — might have marked the end of the Third Republic had it continued too long, but it was modified by the end of the year. Parliament resumed its sessions and commenced its slow fight to win back control over the executive and the army command, retracing, as it were in brief, the history of French political evolution from 1871 to 1914. This struggle remained an undercover war, the issues being too delicate for public declamation. The most effective instruments of the legislature proved to be its permanent committees, particularly the Senate Committee on the Army which Clemenceau directed with skill and vigor. After 1915 the Chambers sometimes met in secret session to press vital interpellations, and the fight to subordinate the army chiefs to civilian control was continued more energetically. The power of summary trial and judgment granted the extraordinary *cours martiales* in September, 1914, was withdrawn in September, 1916, and the competence of the ordinary military courts restricted. Joffre, whose popularity made him an asset and a liability to the government, was created a Marshal of France at the beginning of 1917, but removed from the supreme command. The central problem, however, the relationship between the Ministry of War and the army command, continued to defy solution. In the outcome a dual control emerged. The Minister of War and a "Chief of the General Staff" responsible to the minister were to decide the broad lines of strategy and correlate them with the political situation. The Commander-in-chief of the French armies was to execute them. The chief defect of this arrangement was its ambiguity; personal relations could make or mar it; and the task of coördinating the efforts of the French armies with the plans of their British, Italian and Russian allies had not been clarified.[12]

There was a lesson to be learned from all this concentration, dispersion, and reassignment of authority, and Clemenceau never tired of preaching it. Organization was not everything. The men in power must be dominated by a spirit of unity, a common will to sink all rivalries and work together for victory. The implements of government, considered merely as machinery, were confusing, imperfect, archaic. War cabinets foundered, were refloated, and foundered again as frequently as in peace time. Ministries were created, split, merged, their functions allocated elsewhere, their control arbitrarily extended or curtailed at the whim of each new president of the council. The high command of the army, within its own broad sphere of operations, exercised similar independence and erected bureaus which duplicated the functions of existing civilian organs. This tinkering with old administrative machinery and inventing new could not assure victory any more than hiring an office, a staff and a printing press assured a good newspaper. And when the experiment failed, hiring a second staff and press, and moving them in on top of the first, seldom improved

[12] Pierre Renouvin, *The Forms of War Government in France*, Economic and Social History of the World War, General Editor, James T. Shotwell (New Haven: Yale University Press, 1927), pp. 84–89.

matters. The rival organs, boards and commissions set up by the civil power and the military power, by different ministers or different corps, often fought one another more insistently than they fought the foe, each withholding its findings, guarding its privileges, and disparaging the achievements of its rivals.

A similar spirit of secrecy, suspicion and overt opposition sapped the effective collaboration of the Allied governments in their joint war effort. As a member of the Senate Committee on Foreign Affairs Clemenceau could follow the shifting pattern of diplomatic bargaining whereby each of the Allies sought to protect its assets and enlarge its share of the spoils. Before the war Jaurès complained that France became a party to five secret treaties between 1902 and 1911, the terms of which the Foreign Office refused to divulge to the Chambers. After the outbreak of hostilities this secret diplomacy continued more cryptically and more arbitrarily. The Treaty of London (April 26, 1915) which lured Italy into the war on the side of the Allies contained grandiose promises of Austrian territory, part of the Adriatic littoral already pledged to Serbia, a share of Asia Minor and compensation in Africa. Russia, by an accord of May 18, 1915, received the title deeds to Constantinople and the Straits. The Sykes-Picot Agreement of May 16, 1916, promised Russia further gains south of the Caucasus, while assigning Syria and Lebanon to France and Mesopotamia to Britain. Despite the promises of reciprocal compensation embodied in the Treaty of London, Italy was ignored in this new deal, and when the Italians learned of it they demanded their share. A further convention was therefore framed (April 17, 1917) vaguely assigning Adalia, Smyrna and Konia to Italy, provided that Russia assented. This evasive compact was known as the Treaty of Saint-Jean de Maurienne. More constructive and more immediately relevant than these territorial allotments was an accord (September 5, 1914) whereby Britain, France and Russia pledged themselves to make no separate peace with the Central Powers, an accord to which Italy and Japan adhered a year later.

Clemenceau's cynical realism throughout the war and after must be judged against this half-hidden background of power politics. He did not believe in, and would not permit himself to be seduced by, the dream that a brave new world would emerge from the melting pot, peopled by a regenerated humanity under ideal leadership. Rather, he anticipated a sterner and more relentless struggle for existence in which France must find herself increasingly crippled by the fact that she was, in point of population and birth-rate, the weakest of the Great Powers. He shared the belief of all patriotic Frenchmen that in defending herself France was defending the finest ideals of European civilization, but he did not believe it prudent to rely upon international generosity to assure the French people reparation for their sacrifices unless they emerged from the war with the strength and determination to demand it. Herein he showed himself too old to unlearn the lessons of a lifetime. In domestic politics one might, occasionally, find a handful of high-minded citizens willing to sacrifice themselves unselfishly for truth and justice, as in the Dreyfus Affair. But all his experience of international rivalry convinced him that there would be little help forthcoming and little justice shown at the peace table to those participants who lacked the skill and energy to recoup their own losses, press their own claims, and collect their own compensation.

It seems apparent that even during the most idealistic phase of the war, after the proclamation of President Wilson's Fourteen Points, a majority of the French people shared Clemenceau's realistic reading of the situation. Certainly, if votes are a test, a majority of French parliamentarians supported his conclusions. To trust one's Allies, farther than one could enforce the bargain, was precarious; to trust one's enemies was suicide. Peace without victory would be a betrayal of the living and a dishonor to the dead. Only the Socialists openly refused their assent to that single-minded prosecution of the war which he demanded. In 1917, when the bloody repulse of Nivelle's spring offensive had reduced whole French divisions to mutiny; when the weakening of Russia assured Germany a numerical superiority on the Western Front; when the disaster at Caporetto had made Italy a liability instead of an asset; and the submarine campaign threatened to break British mastery of the seas, all the most determined, most patriotic and most heroic elements of the French population rallied behind the seventy-six year old veteran, who demanded an end to defeatism and a prosecution of the war to the last franc and the last man and the last ditch.

What France required in 1917 was not a new strategic formula, nor a slogan, nor even a symbol: it was a supreme effort of will. Clemenceau recognized this, and recognized the precise moment to put himself forward as the spokesman of all that was uncompromising and combative and self-sacrificing in the heart of the French nation. His discourse on anti-patriotism, pronounced before the Senate on July 22, 1917, was a bugle call reforming the ranks on a stricken field. From a people who saw no light ahead, a people who had lost faith in victory, a people in whom the will to endure had been numbed by the appalling casualties, by the growing confusion, by hope deferred, by a subtle and subsidized conspiracy of defeatism, he demanded one crowning effort.

> The final months [he proclaimed], the final weeks of the war, it has been said, will probably be the hardest. Here is a thought for us to ponder while we gird ourselves for the test which awaits us. The Japanese say that the victor is he who can believe for a quarter of an hour longer than his opponent that he will be the victor. Very well. We must sustain these final months, these final weeks, in the same manner that we faced the first days of the war.[13]

In the same courageous spirit, he might have added by way of clarification, not precisely in the same manner. For his whole address breathed a demand for repressive action against strikers, saboteurs, defeatists, antipatriots in the ranks of labor, whom he accused of weakening the will to fight and crippling the war drive of the French people. On the outbreak of hostilities in 1914 the cabinet had meditated the arrest of some 6,000 such potential dissidents whose names were on record with the Minister of the Interior in the famous "Carnet B." Most of them had been left at liberty, however, through the tolerant policy of the minister, Louis Malvy. But the list of disloyal utterances, incitements to resistance, and correspondence with enemy agents, which Clemenceau had compiled and now charged against syndicalist leaders and other agitators, persuaded the senators the time had come to end such forbearance. Malvy's reluctance to arrest agitators and aliens suddenly resembled, not tolerance, but treason. Clemenceau's famous address spurred the secret police to furious activity, an activity which did not cease even with victory. The widening investigation involved not only Malvy but Caillaux, while lesser agents, convicted of communicating with the enemy and spreading defeatist propaganda, were imprisoned or shot.

How the masses of the French people responded to his appeal and supported his administration with grim and heroic fortitude forms a proud but stark and terrible page in French history. For France had already suffered proportionally heavier casualties than any other major combatant, and the decision which placed Clemenceau in power ordained another year of slaughter. Whether a better, a less vindictive, a more equal peace could have been negotiated in 1917 is a question which now can never be resolved. But the extra year of fighting, which raised the French casualty lists to 1,400,000 killed and twice as many wounded in more or less crippling fashion, destroyed something in the physical stamina

[13] *Journal Officiel: Sénat: Débats parlementaires*, session of July 22, 1917, pp. 751–768. The address was printed in pamphlet form by the Librairie Payot and sold for 50 centimes.

as well as in the physical reserves of the nation. Sacrifices so exacting, emotions so long sustained, so cruelly stimulated, do not cease with the cannon fire. Frenchmen, returning to their homes after the armistice, were to demand more than victory, more than a liberated fatherland, more than the recovery of Alsace-Lorraine. They were to demand revenge against Germany and reparations for their losses, and they would have been either more or less than human if they had failed to do so. The dead, 1,400,000 of them, the living dead, at least 500,000 more, mutilated, crippled, blinded, mentally deranged, all these were to the French people innocent victims of Teutonic treachery, barbarity and lust for power. In the devastated provinces, too, the property damage was a direct consequence, in French eyes, of German hatred, of a calculated intent to ruin and destroy French life and culture. For the mines flooded, wells destroyed, fruit and shade trees cut down, factories blasted, schools, libraries, hospitals, churches bombed and gutted, farms burned, cattle slaughtered, for all these things and for four years' agony beyond record or measurement the French people were to demand payment.

An invaded nation does not spin sophistries regarding the responsibility for a war or entertain two views concerning the identity of the aggressor. The question is resolved by an indisputable brute fact, the presence of the enemy within its borders, the miseries of a captive population, the curfew, the confiscations, the compulsory labor, the searches, the seizure of hostages, the summary executions. That the French people, in 1919, who had suffered two Prussian invasions within living memory, should demand reprisals and guarantees was inevitable. The remarkable thing about their demands was not the amount or the nature of them; rather it was the patience, the restraint, the forbearance which the French showed in compromising their claims. Or rather, in leaving Clemenceau to compound the claims for them. For they trusted Clemenceau in 1919 as they had trusted him in 1917 and 1918. They put their hopes for the peace in his hands because they knew and had faith in his spirit, his character, his methods, they shared his cynicism and his realism, they revered his pertinacity and his courage, and they believed that he loved France.

Like the apotheosis of Woodrow Wilson as the Prophet of Humanity, the exaltation of Georges Clemenceau into *Père la Victoire* and the effect it exerted on events belongs to the *imponderabilia* of history. He became, almost overnight, a living legend, an avatar of the indomitable soul of France, which had surmounted defeat and survived destruction and passed through the valley of death. What his example meant to the French people in 1917–1918 no show of hands, no parliamentary vote, no journalistic bombast can convey. Legends such as Clemenceau's are "such stuff as dreams are made on" and a record of some of the dreams haunting the sleep of the average Frenchman in November, 1917, helps to explain the strength and the foundations of the national will. Here is a typical illustration:

> I dreamed that the disasters and treacheries had multiplied for our Allies and especially for us until the moment arrived when France saw herself facing hopeless defeat. No more money, no more friends, no more soldiers. . . . We were compelled, with death in our hearts, to surrender the country forever.
>
> The Chamber held a final session. . . . By 500 votes the decree passed that every Frenchman had permission, from that moment, to desert the fatherland and go to live where he chose, if he could not bear to remain during an enemy occupation which there was no means of resisting. After this vote the silence of death reigned. Men wrung their hands, strangling their sobs. Suddenly Clemenceau, once more President of the Council of Ministers, reared himself up in the tribune and declaimed:
>
> "You have passed your decree. Very well. I will say my last word: here it is. The country grants permission to desert, good! But the first Frenchman who seeks to set foot outside of France will have to reckon with me, for I—I shall never permit it."
>
> This redemption of dignity, which proved that at the moment of dying we still had a resolute government, gave us joy in spite of everything.[14]

It would seem, in a time of trial and tension, that the mysterious forces which rally the masses in support of a party or a policy are the product of a mood rather than a motive. Among specific groups, however, especially in the political and business circles, political support is a matter of the head rather than the heart, a course deliberately adopted because it promises gain or avoids loss. Thus Clemenceau's prosecution of the "defeatists" was, in one aspect, a search for a national scapegoat. It deflected attention from the army generals who had blundered, from the profiteers grown rich on war contracts, from the *embusqués* or slackers filling snug posts in superfluous bureaus. Clemenceau in power meant to the popular mind the end of privilege and favoritism, a more prompt recognition of merit, a more just equalization of the war burden. That, to the powerful interests which dictated politics, was his main asset. For the bankers, the manufacturers, the armament makers, did not fear that Clemenceau in power would threaten their profits. They had looked ahead and seen French government orders and subsidies, larger and more lucrative than ever, underwritten by American credit. In 1917 the wealthy classes in

[14] Marguerite Combes, *Le Rêve de la Personnalité* (Paris: Bouvin et Cie, 1932), p. 89.

France envisaged, as an alternative to Clemenceau, a government of the Socialists, a negotiated peace, confiscation of war profits and great fortunes, repudiation of government bonds, an inexorable drift towards Marxism such as they saw taking place in Russia. So France must be whipped up to a new effort, the war must continue, and the Socialists and Syndicalists must be discredited as defeatists and anti-patriots. A Clemenceau ministry marked an end to the *union sacrée*, an end to Socialist representation in the cabinet, an end to the various *pourparlers* looking to a negotiated peace. The Tiger had received, and knew that he had received, a mandate to save France not only from Prussianism but from Bolshevism. It was this tacit understanding which assured him his majority of the Center and the Right. It dictated his round-up of labor agitators and repression of strikes. It compelled a public repudiation of the secret peace overtures which previous cabinets had more or less officially entertained. It made France more than ever the spearhead of Allied opposition to the Central Powers.

Had the advocates of a "white peace" raised Caillaux [15] to office in the summer of 1917 it is not inconceivable that the war might have ended in a stalemate truce before the close of the year. Two events in 1917 set the stage for the crescendo of 1918 and the Carthaginian peace of 1919: the entry of the United States into the war in April and the erection of the Clemenceau Ministry in November. Clemenceau's personal influence and responsibility for the outcome of the war and the nature of the peace is as great, perhaps greater, than that of any other statesman of the time. But given his role, his character, his history, it is almost unthinkable that he could have pursued a different course. He was elected to make war and he made war: he made it with the aid of any and all groups which would support his policies, the wealthy, the bondholders, the profiteers, the munition makers, with nationalists of the *Action Française*, with militarists and clericals, with a million public officials who feared the new broom of a Socialist administration. But first and foremost he made it with the support of millions of grim and disillusioned and exhausted

[15] Caillaux ranked himself with Jaurès as a victim of French chauvinism. He insisted that the Clemenceau dictatorship was an instrument of the *Action Française* and similar groups, which sought to monopolize the "sacred flame" of revenge against Germany. The conviction Caillaux nursed, that it was possible for France and Germany to reach an understanding, to achieve a negotiated instead of a dictated peace, did not in itself constitute treason or even defeatism. After the war Clemenceau himself came to feel somewhat ashamed of his attacks on his opponent and his share in Caillaux' imprisonment. See Joseph Caillaux, *Mes prisons* (Paris: Aux éditions de la Sirène, 1921), pp. 50–68.

Frenchmen and French women who accepted his word and believed with him that victory on the battlefield, no matter how high the cost, was indispensable for the salvation of France.[16]

[16] In secret negotiations the individual responsibility of the statesman in power may be very great; his personal preferences or prejudices may decide the success or failure of the overture. The part played by Clemenceau, Poincaré, Ribot, and other French nationalists in discouraging efforts at a negotiated peace in 1917 and 1918 may be studied to advantage in such recent works as Kent Forster, *The Failures of Peace* (Philadelphia: University of Pennsylvania Press, 1941); Ebba Dahlin, *French and German Public Opinion on Declared War Aims 1914–1918* (Stanford University Press, 1933); and Frank P. Chambers, *The War behind the War, 1914–1918* (New York: Harcourt, Brace and Company, 1939).

CHAPTER XI

PREFACE TO RETREAT

November, 1917–March, 1918

Mais tout de même il y avait une loi qui dominait tout cela et qui de cette incohérence faisait sortir une espèce de raison efficace.[1] CLEMENCEAU

THE ministry of Paul Painlevé, after two months in office, fell with little warning on November 13, 1917. Only a few shrewd and trusted politicians of the Right and Center knew that Poincaré and Clemenceau had recently composed their differences and that the President of the Republic was prepared to call on Clemenceau to form a new cabinet devoted wholeheartedly to the prosecution of the war. It is never easy to trace the undercurrents in French politics which bring a new ministry to the surface, but it is certain that Clemenceau had been warned and was waiting for the call.

For some weeks he had been seeking out and lining up the men he wanted as associates. Stephen Pichon returned to the Foreign Office. Georges Leygues, who likewise had served in the 1906–1909 ministry, took the Department of Marine. The new cabinet was not, like the earlier, to be a roster of famous names, for this time Clemenceau needed and sought hardworking, efficient, and responsible subordinates who would grasp and prosecute his policies. Louis-Lucien Klotz remained in charge of Finances; Jules Pams headed the Ministry of the Interior; Albert Claveille, Public Works; Étienne Clementel, Commerce; Henri Simon, Colonies; Pierre Colliard, Labor; Victor Boret, Agriculture; Louis Laferre, Public Instruction; Louis Nail, Justice; Charles Jonnart (and later Albert Lebrun), Blockade and Liberated Areas; and Louis Loucheur (one of the most able and energetic men in the group), Armaments and Aviation. Clemenceau himself took the critical post of War Minister.

In addition to the fourteen ministers there were ten undersecretaries appointed to supervise vital sub-branches of administration, and Clemenceau sometimes leaned on such agents more heavily than on the ministers

[1] Jean Martet, *Le Silence de M. Clemenceau* (Paris, Albin Michel, 1929), p. 157.

themselves. For he was in office with a single purpose, ruthlessly pursued: to win the war and consecrate the victory by a successful peace. In pursuit of that aim he seized his instruments as occasion required, seized them with rough and ready grasp as an angry carpenter seizes convenient tools, because they are near at hand and possess cutting edges. Frequently the edges proved too soft for the job. "Pams, Nail, Pichon," he recalled in after years, ". . . Nice fellows! They had only one fault. They were too decent. They weren't made for war. . . ."[2]

At seventy-six Clemenceau retained a nervous drive, an electric energy and capacity for work which often reduced his younger colleagues to exhaustion. In 1917 as in 1907 he began his day at five in the morning, wrote and studied until seven-thirty, took half-an-hour's calisthenics, and had breakfasted and reached the Ministry of War on the rue Saint-Dominique before nine. There he received his secretaries, and consulted Pichon for foreign affairs and General Alby, his liaison officer with the High Command, for the military situation. The tireless, omniscient and indispensable Mandel reported on the domestic situation and summarized the day's news. After dictating notes and telegrams evoked by these reports, Clemenceau left for a session with the ministry or with the smaller war cabinet, returning at midday. This was the hour he reserved for callers too important to relegate to a subordinate; but he depended upon the tactful Jules Jeanneney (who headed his *Président du Conseil* secretariat) to reduce their number and curtail their interviews. After half-an-hour, if he was fortunate, he could slip away to the rue Franklin for his frugal lunch and a little repose; but by two he was back and met further callers and delegations until three. The remainder of the afternoon found him in the Chamber or Senate, sampling the debates, but he returned to his office about five-thirty to sign despatches. Then, save on days of special pressure or emergency, he relaxed for an hour and chatted with the circle of his more intimate assistants who formed a privileged "cabinet of reference." Jeanneney, Édouard Ignace (who watched over military justice and public order), Raux (Prefect of Police), Mandel and Mordacq were in almost constant attendance; and in 1919 André Tardieu, Jules Cambon and Nicolas Piétri joined the group. Jean Martet, Clemenceau's personal secretary, ventured in and out, soliciting his momentary attention for details of correspondence too urgent to postpone until the morrow. After eight some members of his family, his brothers and their wives, his children and grandchildren, might visit for a short period to entertain and distract him. Their presence provided a casual domestic note at the

[2] Jean Martet, *Clemenceau* (London, 1930), p. 33.

end of a crowded day, after which he returned to his bachelor home, dined quietly, and went to bed.[3]

Each French minister on assuming office appoints an office staff to assist him. The secretariat which served Clemenceau in his duties as President of the Council of Ministers was efficiently managed by Jules Jeanneney. As Minister of War he required a second staff, and to head this war department secretariat he chose a logical, loyal and intelligent general, Jean Jules Henri Mordacq, who advised him on matters of military administration. Discipline had declined dangerously in the French armies during 1917, though Pétain labored magnificently to repair the loss of nerve which followed Nivelle's disastrous April offensive. With Pétain's permission, and Mordacq to manipulate the changes, Clemenceau purged the army divisions of colonels, brigadier generals and generals too old or too inept for active service, promoted younger officers, and quickened the spirit of discipline in the ranks by an intelligent distribution of penalties, rewards, furloughs and decorations. Nor did civilian officials escape a scrutiny and a culling over. He demoted or retired a number of prefects and sub-prefects who had been lax in curbing defeatist propaganda, and this ruthless purge had a salutary effect throughout the *départements*.

The French people, not for the first time in their history, had thrown themselves into the arms of a strong man, and they were relieved that he did not shrink from the responsibilities of government, or dilute his authority by ill-timed reverence for legal and constitutional forms. Though Clemenceau would never concede any admiration for Napoleon his own temper and methods of managing men owed more than he knew to the tradition set by the Corsican, and to the energetic dictatorship of the Committee of Public Safety. He lacked Napoleon's genius for organization and never found a fair opportunity to employ such talents for administrative improvisation as he did possess. He was not called to office in 1917 with a mandate to reform French institutions. He was chosen because, in his previous ministry, he had shown courage in repressing strikes and sabotage, because he symbolized French hostility towards Germany, because he spoke English and had been one of the architects of the Entente Cordiale, because he had lived in the United States and might prove *persona grata* to the people of that great sister republic without whose aid France could not fight on. His specific task was to cement relations with London and Washington, to keep the Western Front the center

[3] Jean Jules Henri Mordacq, *Le Ministre Clemenceau*, 4 vols. (Paris: Plon, 1930–31), I, 26–28.

of the Allied war effort; and to establish, if possible, a unified command of the Allied forces in France under the direction of the French general staff. It was essential to this last aim that he should knit more closely the civil and military institutions in France, but without allowing the army to penetrate and overshadow the sphere of parliamentary control. Measured by these demands, he was to make his two years in office a triumph of successful achievements, a record which demonstrates his sense of responsibility, his political acumen, and his loyalty to the constitutional republic. The subsequent course of French history has shown that the forces he had to combat in preserving the republic were more real and more powerful than most contemporary critics comprehended. The masses of the French people, while understanding little of the tactics he employed or the need for them, accorded him an intuitive respect for the honesty of his aim, the intensity of his endeavor. They took him to their hearts with an affection almost feudal, conceiving him as an eccentric, peppery, autocratic country squire, driving his tenants mercilessly in an hour of disaster, but comprehending and sharing their sufferings, and sparing himself even less than he spared them.

There can be no doubt that American aid in money and matériel at the close of 1917 contributed even more decisively than Clemenceau's reforms to the revival of French morale. While the United States was still neutral the French government had borrowed some $700,000,000 from American banks. In the twenty months which followed, from April, 1917 to November, 1918, the United States Treasury quintupled this sum, advancing $2,985,000,000 at a lower rate of interest. "Without means of payment in dollars," André Tardieu later admitted, ". . . the Allies would have been beaten before the end of 1917."[4] Coupled with a domestic loan for 10,000,000,000 francs, opened for subscription the week after Clemenceau organized his ministry, this golden flood speeded up the lagging wheels of French war production. Manufacturers, traders and producers knew that these credits would be used to subsidize war contracts, and that the cabinet, not parliament, would determine the disbursal. To render the new loan of November, 1917, even more attractive to investors, the bonds (issued at 68.60 and bearing interest at 4 per cent) were declared acceptable in payment of the war profits tax.[5] Clemenceau could afford to court the

[4] André Tardieu, *France and America: Some Experiences in Coöperation* (Boston: Houghton Mifflin, 1927), pp. 227–230.

[5] Henri Truchy, *Les Finances de guerre de la France* (Paris: Les Presses Universitaires de la France, 1926), pp. 118–124, 85–87.

great corporations and business circles for he had a clear majority in the Chamber without the votes of the Socialists.

In the military sphere Clemenceau recognized in advance that his most serious problem was the establishment of closer and more effective working arrangements between the Cabinet and the General Staff. To promote this he prepared, in rough and ready fashion, to utilize, repatch or scrap the existing organs and personnel, but he was convinced that personal relations were the important factor and the mechanism of contact a secondary affair. Under his predecessors the *political* direction of military policy had been entrusted to a reduced "War Cabinet" of six members, the ministers of the Navy, Foreign Affairs, Armament, Blockade, Finance and War. Between this War Cabinet and the General Staff a cool distrust reigned with each side jealously guarding its power and resisting encroachments. Clemenceau insisted on a closer contact and a franker exchange of information, but he assuaged military sensitivities with an assurance that the War Cabinet was concerned with the political implications of the fighting and decisions in matters of tactics would be left to the staff and to field headquarters.

The situation, when Clemenceau took charge, was further complicated by the illogical organization of the military command itself. Pétain had been appointed Commander-in-chief of the French armies, and Foch Chief of the General Staff. But their powers were not clearly defined and both controlled and expanded their own hierarchy of departments, bureaus, schools, commissions and offices which evolved substantially into two general staffs, one in the field and one in the interior. This anomalous state of affairs was not resolved until March, 1918, when the two staff organizations were merged under Pétain's direction, while Foch became generalissimo of the Allied armies with his own corps of assistants, advisers and *liaison officiers*. In the interval the task of conciliating and coördinating the divergent views and activities of the War Cabinet, the Staff College under Foch and the field staff under Pétain, devolved upon Clemenceau, with Mordacq and Alby as his *aides*.[6]

A second problem of military coördination, vaster, more urgent, and far more difficult to resolve, claimed Clemenceau's attention at the same time. From his predecessor, Paul Painlevé, he had inherited a half-hatched project for a Supreme War Council of the Allied Powers. It was to be a super-cabinet, composed of the British, French and Italian premiers each

[6] Pierre Renouvin, *The Forms of War Government in France* (New Haven: Yale University Press, 1927), pp. 95–97.

assisted by a military adviser. This plan proposed a *political* council to effect *military* coördination and control war strategy, and it won little applause from the parliaments, the press or the general staffs. It had, however, the formal approval of the American government. Both the British and French were bidding eagerly for American approval, courting the American leaders in Europe, Pershing, House and Bliss, in an effort to carry through their national programs with American assistance. Clemenceau presented the French case to House and Bliss on November 25, 1917, a few days after he assumed office. With Pétain standing by to back up his figures, he summarized the French sacrifices as 2,600,000 men killed, wounded, incapacitated or prisoners. He insisted that France had only 1,100,000 men to hold a front of 500 kilometers, while the British, with 1,200,000 effectives, occupied only 105 kilometers. These figures seemed to leave little room for doubt as to which Ally deserved aid first, though they ignored the natural advantages, strength or vulnerability of the segments of the front line held by French and British divisions respectively. Turning next to the question of a unified command, Clemenceau declared that the French were in hearty accord with the Americans in believing such unity essential to Allied success, and he suggested that an executive board, composed of the chiefs of staff of the French, British, American and Italian armies, should be entrusted with the direction of military strategy.

Eager to forward this policy, Colonel House assured Clemenceau that it would have the approval of Woodrow Wilson, and he proposed that he should take it upon himself to urge the plan upon the British Prime Minister, Lloyd George, who was expected in Paris the following day. Clemenceau assented, watched House depart, and raised his hands in a characteristic gesture of admiration. He liked this "highly civilized gentleman from the wilds of Texas" but he had no faith that House would win Lloyd George to the project. He was right. Lloyd George, who was waging a bitter fight with the Imperial General Staff on his own home front, insisted that the *civilian* members of the Supreme War Council must retain control and vetoed an executive board composed of the chiefs of staff. When House returned to announce his failure, Clemenceau greeted the news with a sardonic smile. "It vitiates the entire plan," he affirmed with weary disgust. "What I shall do is to put in a second or third rate man instead of Foch, and let the thing drift where it will. . . ."[7]

[7] Edward M. House, *The Intimate Papers of Colonel House*, arranged by Charles Seymour, 4 vols. (Boston: Houghton Mifflin, 1926–1928), III, 262.

But he was better than his word. He appointed the astute and capable Weygand as French military adviser. The Supreme War Council continued in existence, organized on the Lloyd George formula, drifting where it would while the British Prime Minister fought a stiff duel with his general staff for control of British war strategy.

At the beginning of January, 1918, Clemenceau listed the military problems which he considered most urgent for the New Year. He wanted the six French and five British divisions, which had been despatched to Italy the previous autumn after the Italian rout at Caporetto, returned to the Western Front to form an army of reserve. He wanted the Allied expeditionary force stationed at Saloniki to make its presence felt, and had already (December 10) supplanted Sarrail, the French general in command, by the more confident Guillaumat. He wanted the British and French commanders-in-chief, Sir Douglas Haig and Henri Pétain, still inclined to theories of attack and mobile warfare, to prepare defenses in depth on the Western Front against the certainty of a German offensive in the spring. Above all, he wanted the Allied Governments to face honestly the question of unity of command and the equitable distribution of manpower. To Pershing, Bliss and House he reiterated the importance of speeding up American reinforcements. With Sir Henry Wilson, military adviser to the British Cabinet, and Lord Milner, Under-Secretary for War, he pleaded in vain for more British troops in France, pointing out that the British had dispersed one third of their effectives in minor theatres of conflict, chiefly in the Near East. The French still regarded the Mediterranean lands as their particular sphere of enterprise, and it galled them that, while they dared not spare the forces to carve up the Turkish Empire, the British were doing it for them and would undoubtedly retain most of the gains.

On January 30 the Supreme War Council opened a three day session in Paris. Clemenceau presided, and the British military representative, Sir William Robertson, recorded a warm tribute to his skill and energy. "He had a tactful, but none the less masterful, way of getting through the business on hand, and I can recollect many instances when he succeeded in extracting a decision and bringing to an end the discussion of thorny questions which threatened to be both abortive and interminable."[8] General Tasker H. Bliss, present as Chief of Staff of the army of the United States, likewise appreciated Clemenceau's direct and logical approach to

[8] Sir William Robertson, *From Private to Field Marshal* (London: Constable, 1921), p. 292.

the problems confronting the conference.[9] The military representatives had united before the meeting and drafted a plan for the creation of an army of reserve on the Western Front. Clemenceau therefore opened the debate by asking pertinently: (1) Shall we constitute a General Reserve? (2) Shall it be a Reserve for the whole front from the North Sea to the Adriatic? (3) How shall it be composed? (4) Who shall command it? After considerable discussion the Council voted to adopt in principle the proposal to create an Army of Reserve. When formed, it was to be entrusted to the direction of an Executive Committee composed of the military representatives of France, Great Britain, Italy, the United States and Belgium, with General Foch as president.

Though approved in council the plan failed in operation. Sir William Robertson, denied the dual rôle of Chief of the Imperial General Staff and British representative on the Executive Committee, resigned in a huff. Sir Douglas Haig could not spare any divisions from the British Expeditionary Force for an Army of Reserve. General Pétain, French Commander-in-Chief, likewise resisted the detachment of a part of his forces; and the Italian command refused even to sanction the return of the French and British divisions then serving in Italy. In his memoirs Lloyd George intimates that Clemenceau, jealous of Foch, encouraged Haig and Pétain in their resistance. But the plan for an Army of Reserve also met with considerable opposition, as Lloyd George admits, from the British Imperial General Staff. The Staff would not willingly yield authority over part of the British forces to a civilian council of prime ministers, nor to a committee of military experts if this committee was subject to Foch's control.[10] Though Lloyd George replaced the recalcitrant Robertson by the more conciliatory Sir Henry Wilson, the opposition of the British military clique still blocked the plan for a Reserve, until defeat demonstrated the risk of such divided councils in the face of a resolute foe with the inside lines and unified control of all his available forces.

Undiscouraged by the attitude of the military leaders, Clemenceau labored during January and February, 1918, to assemble at the Ministry of War an adequate body of information on the strength, composition, equipment and supply services of the various Allied forces, and the preparations made to reinforce the Western Front. The French, British

[9] Tasker H. Bliss, "The Evolution of the Unified Command," *Foreign Affairs*, I (December 15, 1922), 1–30.

[10] David Lloyd George, *War Memoirs*, 6 vols. (Boston: Little Brown & Co., 1933–1937), V, 285–362.

and American commanders agreed to permit General August Roques, as special investigator for the French ministry, to make a survey of their several sectors and report his conclusions to Clemenceau. In return for their courtesy they were to be furnished with copies of Roques' report and recommendations. This was a step towards unity of criticism if not unity of direction. But the Allied commanders, after three years of war, were still far from achieving a true spirit of trust and coöperation. Each wanted to win the war on his own section of the front; each had attempted ambitious offensives with his own limited resources and on his own initiative; and each had failed in sanguinary fashion. The members of the American mission, studying the situation for President Wilson at first hand, reported their conviction that a military crisis might be expected not later than the spring of 1918. "This crisis is largely due to lack of military coördination, lack of unity of control on the part of the Allied forces in the field. The lack of unity of control results from military jealousy and suspicion as to ultimate national aims." [11]

The weak link in the control of a modern army is the contact between the civilian cabinet at home and the army commander in the field. This is especially true when the army is an expeditionary force. Clemenceau fully understood the difficulties Lloyd George faced in his determination to retain control over Haig's movements. But French interests demanded unity of direction for the Allied forces on the Western Front. This unified command must be exercised by a French general, but the general must not thereby come to possess powers which would make him a threat to the cabinet at Paris. In his heart Clemenceau did not trust his Allies or his own generals. A mobilized army, domestic, allied or enemy, encamped on the land constituted a supreme threat to civil institutions, or so it seemed to him, and the history of France afforded grounds for his apprehensions. Control of the British divisions in France presented a test case, the more significant because it would furnish a precedent for the relations between the French government and the American Expeditionary Force. In a war which might last for years the American forces could become in time the most powerful army on the Western Front. Unified command, exercised by a French general, who might thereby find opportunity to balance the British and American forces against one another and keep France mistress in her own house, seemed to Clemenceau no more than far-sighted insurance.

It was possible, of course, that the American Expeditionary Force might

[11] Tasker H. Bliss, "The Evolution of the Unified Command," *Foreign Affairs*, I, 9–10.

not become an integrated unit. In his appeals to House, Bliss and Pershing that they hasten over American troops Clemenceau urged that the American companies and regiments should be fed into experienced French divisions, and take the field under French command. In this way they could acquire their front-line training under the wisest and safest auspices, and the creation of a unified American Expeditionary Force might be postponed to a later time. The British, who were equally anxious to reinforce their depleted units with American infantry, insisted to Pershing that his men would be happier learning battle conditions from comrades who spoke the same language.[12] Pershing, who foresaw the difficulty he would encounter when the time came (if it ever came) to reclaim his dispersed companies, and the impracticability of trying to train regimental and divisional officers if he lacked regiments and divisions for them to command, refused his consent to this amalgam. In an effort to force his hand, Clemenceau resorted to a manoeuvre which might easily have created distrust and resentment between the American Commander-in-chief and the Secretary of War, Newton D. Baker. In a telegram to Washington Clemenceau implied that Pershing was acting in an obstinate and obstructive manner at variance with the understanding worked out by the American and French governments, and he proposed that the general's resistance should be over-ridden by direct orders from Baker or from President Wilson.[13]

Perhaps he hoped that Baker and Wilson, as civilians, would welcome an opportunity to reprimand an over-independent military leader. If so, his calculations miscarried. Pershing received assurances that he was still free to decide the matter on his own responsibility, and he worked out a compromise. He agreed that newly arrived American regiments should have a short period of training with French divisions in a quiet sector; but he continued to insist stubbornly that unified American divisions and corps should be organized at the earliest practicable moment.

As spring approached General Erich von Ludendorff, now the master mind at German staff headquarters, completed his plans for the all-or-

[12] This competition between the French and British to secure American aid had been going on since the beginning of the war, and it grew sharper as American intervention became more probable. In March, 1917, the French government despatched Joffre and Viviani to the United States to win American sympathy, whereupon the British rushed Balfour over on a swifter ship. E. L. Spears, *Prelude to Victory* (London: Jonathan Cape, 1939), p. 512. Pershing endeavored, not without success, to play the British and French against one another in his fight for an independent American Expeditionary Force.

[13] John J. Pershing, *My Experiences in the World War*, 2 vols. (New York: Stokes, 1931), I, 271–276.

nothing gamble which was, he hoped, to end the war before American aid could turn the scale. Clemenceau agreed with Foch and Mordacq that to parry the German initiative a fluid and disposable reserve would be desperately needed. None had yet been created. An eleventh hour session of the Supreme War Council, held in London on March 14–15, found and left the situation still at a deadlock. Haig and Pétain still opposed the suggestion of the Council and of the Executive Committee of military advisers that some divisions be spared for a reserve. The Council thereupon despatched a representative to Italian Headquarters to propose the establishment of a reserve nucleus formed from Italian troops. The Italian reply reached Paris on March 20. It was a refusal.

The following morning at 4 A.M. the Germans opened a terrible barrage from Croisilles to La Fère: in two days they had shattered the British Fifth Army, sent it reeling back in fragments, and driven a wedge through the Allied defenses at the junction of the French and British sectors. Clemenceau, motoring to Pétain's headquarters at Compiègne on March 23, demanded a frank account of the disaster. All available sources of intelligence agreed that the Fifth Army had collapsed and held out little hope that it could maintain further resistance. If the widening breach could not be closed by French reserves the British would fall back on the Channel ports leaving the French no choice, Pétain prophesied pessimistically, but to recoil on Paris. "After a talk like that," Clemenceau confessed to Mordacq on the drive back, "you've got to have a soul of steel to keep your confidence."[14] He knew that Paris had been filled with panic since morning, when the shells from the German long range cannon first astonished the capital. The roads out of the city were crowded with refugees, an exodus reminiscent of 1914, and the government was preparing to flee to Tours.

On the fourth day of the offensive Haig swallowed his pride and appealed to the French for help. It was the moment that Clemenceau had been waiting for, the moment when he could present his demands and have them honored. To Lord Milner, who had been sent post haste from London, he insisted that important decisions must be taken at once: he had called a meeting of French and British leaders at Compiègne for the afternoon of March 25. By five o'clock he had Poincaré, Foch and Milner at Pétain's headquarters, but Haig and Wilson failed to appear. Foch insisted that the critical issue at the moment was to save Amiens; the loss of that vital railway junction would sever the British and French

[14] Mordacq, *Le Ministère Clemenceau*, I, 228.

lines beyond repair; but a common decision on policy was impossible without the presence of the British commander to concur in it. Clemenceau therefore proposed that the group re-assemble the following afternoon (March 26) at Dury, if Haig would favor the meeting with his attendance, and this the British commander promised to do if the rendezvous could be changed to Doullens. It was Clemenceau's hour and he could afford to be patient, for that same afternoon Weygand, Foch's right-hand man, had received a note from Haig in the latter's own handwriting, confessing that the British Army must abandon Amiens and "fight its way slowly back covering the Channel ports." [15] Had the fatalistic mood which dominated Haig and Pétain prevailed at this moment a retreat from Dunkirk might have occurred in 1918 instead of 1940. But Foch's steel composure stilled the panic. "Common sense indicates that when the enemy wishes to begin making a hole, you do not make it wider. You close it, or you try to close it," he insisted to Poincaré and Clemenceau.[16] And Clemenceau, who had almost resigned himself to accept Pétain's dark prophecies, took fresh heart.

The historic session at Doullens opened at noon on March 26, when Poincaré, Foch, Pétain, Milner, Wilson, Haig and Clemenceau gathered in the *mairie*. Haig looked worn and grim; he was compromised by defeat and equivocation for he denied before Milner that he had planned to abandon Amiens and retreat to the Channel. He insisted, however, that he could not be confident of holding south of the Somme without aid, and for that reason he had transferred the remnants of the Fifth Army to Pétain's command. Pétain responded that the Fifth Army had practically ceased to exist; that he had despatched all the French reserves that he could spare to save Amiens, and that Haig should do the same. To this Haig replied that he had no more reserves, and a chilly silence descended upon the group, broken by the rhythmic tramp of British troops filing past the *mairie* in phlegmatic retreat. Wilson snorted. Foch drummed softly on the table. Clemenceau regarded Milner thoughtfully until the Englishman met his glance, rose to his feet, and beckoned him aside. Could not the British and French governments entrust the coördination of the armies to Foch, Milner suggested. Clemenceau thought that they could; the problem was to find a formula which would placate the vanity of the generals. If Milner would approach Haig, he would reason with Pétain. Their acquiescence secured, Clemenceau seated himself at

[15] Lloyd George, *War Memoirs,* V, 388.
[16] Lloyd George, *War Memoirs,* V, 389.

the table and drafted in five lines the arrangement which they had been seeking for five months.

> General Foch is charged by the British and French governments with coördinating the action of the Allied armies on the Western Front. To this end he will come to an understanding with the commanders-in-chief who are requested to furnish him with all necessary information.[17]

The meeting broke up at two. Haig hastened back to his threatened army in a bleak mood. But the French delegates, their confidence reviving, adjourned to a nearby hotel for a cheerful lunch. But Clemenceau's satisfaction was tinged with envy. "Well," he threw at Foch as they sat down, "you have got the place you wanted so badly."[18] He was thinking, perhaps, of the previous evening, when Milner had sent Wilson to suggest that he himself should take on the role of military coördinator with Foch as his chief of staff. He declined perforce, and in after years he ridiculed the idea that he could ever seriously have entertained such a notion. "I'd even had a uniform already designed—and the most gorgeous cap," he agreed mockingly when asked if he had coveted the post of generalissimo.[19] But he was too human, and too much a Frenchman, not to envy the magic of a soldier's fame. And too much of a politician not to distrust it.

In hours of crisis the battle front drew him irresistibly. He could not stay away from that shifting line where the surge of the German effort broke on the dikes of Allied resistance. On the afternoon of March 28 he was back at Foch's headquarters, temporarily located in a typical French farm house hidden among trees near Clermont-sur-Oise. No echo of war disturbed the pastoral charm; the armies had outranged their artillery or exhausted their ammunition; and it was difficult to believe that a desperate battle was raging a few miles from that soft lawn where a blossoming cherry tree shed its snow. Indoors, Foch, Pétain and Clemenceau leaned their heads over the maps, marking the infiltrations of the advancing German tide, while couriers came and went, and the metallic voice of the field telephone relayed its cold statistics. This was war; and as Clemenceau watched Foch shaping order from chaos with swift, calculated decisions and resolute orders, he felt a glow of generous enthusiasm for the steel nerves of the little Gascon whom he knew to be as weary as he was

[17] Mordacq, *Le Ministère Clemenceau*, I, 222–236.

[18] Ferdinand Foch, *The Memoirs of Marshal Foch* (Garden City: Doubleday, Doran, 1931), p. 264.

[19] Jean Martet, *Clemenceau* (London, 1930), p. 197n.

himself, and whose head he had seen, in brief minutes of reprieve, nodding over the illimitable charts.

Suddenly there was an interruption. General Pershing had arrived to speak with General Foch. Clemenceau and Pétain stepped out onto the lawn, but they had scarcely crossed it when Foch rushed Pershing over to them, urging him, with Gallic effervescence, to repeat his announcement. Pershing, his French limited but adequate, explained that he came to offer Foch all the American troops at his disposal. The offer was accepted on the spot; the First Division of the A. E. F., then holding a defensive position in Lorraine, was ordered to Picardy, while the remaining four American divisions then in France left to relieve French units in quiet sectors. The spontaneity and generosity of Pershing's act went to Clemenceau's heart; driving back to Paris in the rain, amid the tragic wreckage of war which clogged the roads behind Montdidier, his spirits rose above the confusion, the suffering files of the wounded, the gutted homes dotting the stricken landscape. He insisted that the Germans had shot their bolt, that here they would advance no further. He was right. At German headquarters Ludendorff had recognized the stiffening of the Allied lines and was reluctantly abandoning his hopes of changing the battle to a war of movement for which he had trained his reserves.

That night, for the first time in a week, Clemenceau slept undisturbed. The next day he strode through the corridors of the Chamber of Deputies where a hundred dangerous rumors had gathered credence as the dark days passed until the mounting fear and discontent threatened to wreck the ministry. At his appearance the hopeful, the fearful, the news-hungry crowded about him, noting his squared shoulders, his sardonic smile, his eyes as hard as agates. "Oh, yes," he conceded, when asked if the front had cracked. "There were breaks, plenty of breaches. They could have walked right through. They didn't dare risk it, the fools. Then I summoned Foch and I said to him: 'A little pasting up here, some more there. After that, we will assemble reserves. . . .' "[20] Undoubtedly the boastful tone of the interview has been exaggerated by the journalist reporting it. But such displays of insouciance were in the Clemenceau tradition.

A few minutes later he was speeding towards Montdidier. Likewise in the Clemenceau tradition, and not the best Clemenceau tradition, was his deliberate courting of danger during these anxious days. He refused to enter the air raid shelters during an *alerte*. He stood unnecessa-

[20] Lucien Graux, *Les Fausses nouvelles de la grande guerre*, 6 vols. (Paris: L'Édition Française Illustrée, 1919), V, 334.

rily long under the tottering arch of the Church of Saint Gervais, where seventy-five worshippers had been killed on March 29 by the long range cannon. At the front he exposed himself so ostentatiously to shell and machine gun fire that even Mordacq, usually the most flattering of Boswells, felt ashamed of what he rightly called his chief's *coquetterie*.[21]

Perhaps Clemenceau was ashamed of living while so many brave men died. His thoughts, on days of crisis, turned to the common soldiers, suffering as always the penalties of their leaders' miscalculations, stemming with their bodies the breaches in the broken dike, that France might survive. In their self-abnegation, their humble acceptance of exhausting labor and omnipresent death, he found some sort of anodyne for his own feverish self-contempt. After his outbursts of prodigious exertion he sometimes slipped into moods of despair in which he fled from himself in disgust. His bravado before the journalists, his malicious jibes at discomfited rivals and humiliated generals, were projections of this inward conflict: he identified himself with the defeated and scorned his own pleasure over a hollow success. He could take no enduring satisfaction in his own labors because he could never feel certain in his heart whether his efforts were inspired by an honest sense of duty and zeal for France or by love of his own self-importance.

With the poilus he could escape from such disturbing doubts which, like a hair-shirt forever itching his mind, were themselves a product of his pride and egoism. In the trenches he found something which all his life he had secretly revered, something which shamed his cynicism and silenced his self-contempt, a spirit of anonymous service faithful unto death. They haunted his mind, those humble sons of France, standing at their stations while the heavens fell, their faces grey and their eyes fixed and dilated, like figures in an El Greco painting who have seen the Apocalypse.

On the firing line [he wrote] a pipe or an insouciant cigarette conceals the individuality of a face. All the life in it becomes concentrated in the eyes which reflect things that cannot be discussed without profaning them. The lips are those of youth or age, pouting and retracting under a shadowy moustache or a bristle of grey whiskers. But the flame of the eyes, sunk in their dark orbits, burns with calm intensity as they focus themselves upon the unknown, that unknown which no longer has the power to astonish them. These are our soldiers of the Year II, who follow, as in the Bible, a pillar of fire. . . .[22]

[21] Mordacq, *Le Ministère Clemenceau*, I, 250–252.

[22] Graux, *Les Fausses nouvelles de la grande guerre*, V, 338.

CHAPTER XII

THE TEST

April–July, 1918

On vivait au pire de la tourmente.[1]
CLEMENCEAU

IN LAUNCHING their smashing offensive of March, 1918, the German high command counted confidently upon cracking the Franco-British lines and forcing a mass capitulation in open fighting. This triumph was denied them through Foch's resolution and the tenacity of the Allied soldiers. They had also counted upon breaking French morale behind the lines, and this aim, though it came equally close to success, was frustrated by the stoicism of the French people and the audacity of Clemenceau.

Ludendorff anticipated Hitler by twenty years in that calculated combination of a lightning offensive synchronized with an assault on the enemy's nerve centers, the whole designed to shatter his morale and paralyze his initiative during the vital hours required for a *coup de grâce*. Thus, the German drive against the British Fifth Army was timed to open before dawn on March 21. The following night, March 22, French headquarters at Compiègne were bombed heavily and repeatedly by relays of German planes and the staff driven to seek a new refuge when they should have been concentrating on incoming reports. At nine in the morning of March 23 (the day news of a German break-through circulated in Paris) "Big Bertha" began to shell the city at fifteen-minute intervals. This sequence of shocks proved almost too much for war-strung Parisian nerves: half-a-million people fled the capital during the following week and the government agencies collected their files and prepared to leave at a moment's notice. But Clemenceau's resolution rallied the cabinet and quelled the plans for evacuation while Foch's determination arrested the confusion at military headquarters. On the battlefield there was defeat

[1] Georges Clemenceau, *Grandeur et misère d'une victoire* (Paris: Plon, 1930), p. ii.

and withdrawal but not irretrievable disaster; in Paris there was deep anxiety and depression but no general panic.

The Germans recognized Clemenceau's value as a pillar of French confidence. On March 11 their raiders bombed the Ministry of War where his labors kept him most of the day, and the attack on Compiègne missed him by only a few hours. But his movements were too mercurial to make him a target easy to locate. In politics, however, it is sometimes more effective to destroy the reputation than the man, and in April Clemenceau had to face a new attack which found him vulnerable. On the second of the month the Austrian foreign minister, Count Czernin, announced before the Vienna Municipal Council that, before the Germans began their new offensive, the French were already so war-weary they had appealed to Austria for peace. The statement, which speedily found its way into the Parisian press, struck French readers with double force. That the Clemenceau cabinet, which had pledged itself to uncompromising war, which had proscribed the defeatists and arrested Caillaux himself the previous January, should have opened secret peace negotiations seemed incredible. "Clemenceau . . . is not the man to dally with peace proposals," the British ambassador, Sir Francis Bertie, noted firmly in his diary.[2] But the pebble Czernin had tossed into the pool of Parisian politics set up a widening circle of ripples. People reminded themselves that the President of the Council of Ministers had a brother, Albert, who had been hired to defend one of the alleged enemy agents.[3] He had another brother, Paul, who had married a Viennese girl. His own visits to Austrian spas, in the days before 1914, were recalled, and his connections, journalistic and otherwise, in the Austrian capital. Perhaps, after all, Czernin had some basis for his claim. Parisian reporters, tracing Clemenceau to Beauvais where he was dining with Foch on April 6, begged by telephone for some comment on the charge. They got it. "Count Czernin," Clemenceau barked back categorically, "has lied."

The facts were not quite so unequivocal. Tentative negotiations, more or less serious and more or less reputable, had been initiated by Austrian and French agencies from the first year of the war.[4] There had even been

[2] Francis L., Viscount Bertie of Thame, *Diary, 1914–1918*, 2 vols. (London: Hodder and Stoughton, 1924), II, 215.

[3] *Journal Officiel: Débats: Chambre des Députés*, Session of March 8, 1918, p. 849.

[4] They may be studied in Kent Forster, *The Failures of Peace* (Philadelphia: University of Pennsylvania Press, 1941) and in James Brown Scott, ed., *Official Statements of War Aims and Peace Proposals* (Washington: Carnegie Endowment for International Peace, 1921), pp. 298–336.

unofficial and ineffective meetings in Switzerland during 1917 between Madame Paul Clemenceau and her sister, Berta Szeps Zuckerkandl.[5] More important, and much more compromising (for the Austro-Hungarian monarchy), was a contact established by the Emperor Charles and his Bourbon wife, the Empress Zita, with the brothers of the Empress, the princes Sixtus and Xavier of Bourbon. Prince Sixtus, who regarded himself as French, but was excluded from service in the French army, had enlisted in a Belgian artillery regiment. In 1917, after talking privately with Poincaré, he obtained an interview with Charles and Czernin. When he returned to France he carried an autograph letter from Charles, assenting to most of the suggestions raised, and acknowledging "the just claims of France to Alsace-Lorraine." But the Kaiser and the German Chancellor, Bethmann-Hollweg, would not respond to Austrian hints that peace should be sought along this line; while, on the Allied side, though Lloyd George was admitted to the secret discussions and endorsed them, Italian suspicions were aroused. The Austrian territory promised to Italy under the Treaty of London stood in the way of a separate accord between the western Powers and Austria. By June, 1917, the Sixtus negotiations were stalled.

Two months later, however, an agent of Count Czernin, Count Nicholaus Revertera, opened conversations with his relative, Count Abel Armand, a major on the French general staff. Whoever authorized Armand's mission (the Quai d'Orsay guards its secrets well) clearly sought to split Austria from Germany, tempting the Austrian government with an offer of Poland, Bavaria and Silesia. Germany, in addition to losing Bavaria and Silesia, was to surrender Belgium, Alsace-Lorraine, the Left Bank of the Rhine and German Poland, and to pay reparations for all damage inflicted by her armies and submarines. Apparently Czernin weighed these proposals but he regarded them as too severe (!) to communicate to Berlin. Clemenceau undoubtedly knew something of the conversations; he may even have drafted the proposals; but if so he can have had no least illusion that the Germans would consider them. His intention, no doubt, was to learn what he could of the enemy's state of mind, tempt him to make indiscreet commitments, and then undermine his confidence by offering terms which only a smashing Allied victory could render conceivable.

Nevertheless, Czernin's public announcement that peace parleys had been undertaken at all came at an awkward moment for the harassed

[5] Berta Szeps Zuckerkandl, *My Life and History* (New York: Knopf, 1939), pp. 223–248.

French government. With the public in a fearful and suspicious mood, Clemenceau dared not leave the challenge of the Austrian foreign minister unanswered. He had, moreover, at his disposal the opportunity to make a stunning *riposte*, for the Emperor Charles, in the letter which he had entrusted to Prince Sixtus the previous March, had promised to support "by all means and using all my personal influence with my allies, the just French claims to Alsace-Lorraine."[6] The Sixtus correspondence had been carried on under a solemn pledge of secrecy, but Clemenceau argued that Czernin's attack freed him from conditions undertaken by his predecessors in office, and on April 14 he gave Charles' letter to the press. Czernin, alarmed and discomfited, declared it a forgery; Charles attempted a lame and humiliating equivocation. The Austro-Hungarian peoples, shocked at the revelations and the sorry role of their emperor, lost faith in their leaders, and the Germans could no longer trust their wavering ally. Clemenceau had shown once more that he was a dangerous man to attack and that he was no less capable than in his old duelling days of making a prompt and ruthless retaliation. His manoeuvre reversed the effect of Czernin's disclosure and forced the latter to resign on April 15, while Charles sought to placate his German ally with promises of Austrian divisions on the Western Front.

By mid-April it was evident that for the moment the joint military and diplomatic offensive undertaken by the Central Powers had not only failed to achieve its aims, it had consolidated Allied resistance. Ludendorff gave the Franco-British armies a generalissimo; Czernin gave Clemenceau a new lease on his quasi-dictatorship. Once initiated, the unified command took rapid form. With the concurrence of the American government and the reluctant acquiescence of the British military party, Foch's somewhat anomalous authority over the Allied forces was defined and redefined until on April 14, three weeks after the Doullens conference, he assumed the specific title "Commander-in-chief of the Allied Armies." By persistent pressure, patient study, and a swift *coup* when events permitted, Foch and Clemenceau had asserted a military leadership for France which was a fair recognition of French military prestige and sacrifice. The American forces on the continent had likewise been placed under the unified command by a formal agreement. On April 3, at Beauvais, Pershing and Bliss joined Clemenceau, Lloyd George, Foch, Pétain, Haig and Henry Wilson in drawing up a new document which established, as Bliss

[6] R. B. Mowat, *A History of European Diplomacy*, 3 vols. (London: Longmans, Green & Co., 1927), III, 96–111.

noted, "the nearest approach to unified command that, in expressed terms, was ever made."[7]

General Foch is authorized by the British, French and American governments to coördinate the action of the Allied armies on the Western Front. All the powers necessary for the effective realization of this purpose are conferred upon him. With this end in view the British, French and American governments confide to General Foch the strategic direction of military operations.

The Commanders-in-chief of the British, French and American armies shall exercise in full degree the tactical conduct of their armies. Each Commander-in-chief shall have the right to appeal to his government if, in his opinion, his army finds itself in danger through any instruction received from General Foch.[8]

The new generalissimo issued his first orders the same day, proposing minor Anglo-French attacks to ease the pressure on the Somme. To Clemenceau, as Minister of War, he suggested the despatch of a telegram to General Guillaumat at Saloniki urging a continuous activity in that quarter such as might keep the Central Powers apprehensive of an advance in the Balkans. This, Foch and Clemenceau hoped, would persuade the Germans to retain extra forces in the east, forces which they might otherwise transfer to France and further increase their numerical advantage on the Western Front.

Spending half his time at headquarters or in dashing up and down the lines, receiving despatches and dictating instructions *en route*, Clemenceau almost forgot that he had a political front to defend. His scorn for protracted discussion, his taste for authority, for energetic decisions, for prompt action, grew stronger during the emergency and made him more irascible than ever with querulous and obstructive legislators. For weeks during April and May he refused to answer questions, although pertinent interpellations on the conduct of military and diplomatic affairs accumulated on the desk of the presiding officer in the Chamber. The Socialist leaders fumed and fretted in impotent anger, their indignation muffled by the censorship, their parliamentary manoeuvres baulked by the bland refusal which met all their attempts to peer behind the wall of official secrecy.

The rancors which he made so little effort to assuage were to outlast Clemenceau's popularity and tinge his final years with indissoluble bitterness. But for the moment his thick-skinned indifference to criticism in-

[7] Tasker H. Bliss, "The Evolution of the Unified Command," *Foreign Affairs*, I (December 1922), 28–29.

[8] Jean Jules Henri Mordacq, *Le Ministère Clemenceau*, 4 vols. (Paris: Plon, 1930–31), II, 267.

sulated him against the courtesies which must otherwise have wasted much of his time. He still insisted upon preserving parliamentary forms, but he steadily reduced parliamentary influence, adducing arguments for his course which often savored of sophistry and infuriated his opponents. Interpellations on the military situation he turned aside with the excuse that any revelations would supply useful information to the enemy. When the Socialists asked for a secret session at which such matters might be aired he responded that secret sessions were a denial of democracy which guaranteed the electors the right to know how their representatives spoke and voted in the legislature. A stronger argument, and one which the saner elements in the Chamber appreciated, was the fact that secret sessions were anything but secret, and the debates held *in camerâ* in 1916 had been public knowledge within twenty-four hours.

There still remained, as critical organs of the legislative power, the permanent committees, especially the Committee on Military Affairs of the Senate on which Clemenceau had himself served with such vigor and distinction. When the need arose to quiet excessive apprehensions he faced these critical bodies and put up the best defense he could. The ordeal invariably irritated and exhausted him, but a sustaining vote by the committee, when the news of it circulated through the Chamber, disarmed all but the most recalcitrant opponents of the government. All attempts to unseat the Clemenceau cabinet by a vote of no confidence failed signally. At its strongest (January 15, 1918, the day after the arrest of Joseph Caillaux) the opposition could muster only 143 votes against 368 for the ministry.

To withhold information on military movements and diplomatic overtures might be defended, especially in war time, by the ancient principle *salus populi suprema lex esto*. But Clemenceau felt more vulnerable when the legislators assailed him on juridical or financial issues. He feared in particular that the fate of his cabinet might hang in the balance when the "defeatists" were brought to trial. An acquittal for Caillaux and Malvy would have been a rebuke to the government for the high-handed exercise it had made of its war powers, the intrusive censorship, arbitrary arrests, and secret investigations. It would also have vindicated, or seemed to vindicate, that section of the French parliament and the French public which believed in the possibility of a reasonable negotiated peace, without annexations or indemnities on either side. But official pressure, supplementing the war fever and suspicion, left the accused little chance to clear themselves. Bolo, an obscure enemy agent, was convicted in February and shot April 17. The deputies Caillaux, Malvy, Loustalot and Charles Humbert, stripped of their parliamentary immunity, received varying sentences of imprisonment or exile; and three journalists accused of spreading enemy propaganda through a popular newspaper, the *Bonnet Rouge*, were convicted by a military tribunal. This severity silenced many would-be critics in journalistic and parliamentary circles, for it was known that Clemenceau had secured access to the police *dossiers*, and conscience made cowards of many malcontents who might otherwise have assailed a régime less ready and less ruthless in striking back.

A similar hesitation restrained the Socialists who yearned to assail the Clemenceau government for its tolerance of financial frauds and excess business profits. In February, 1918, Clemenceau had demanded and received the power to legislate by decree in the whole domain of French economic life. Thereafter no effective means existed by which the Socialists and other critics could discover and control the war expenditures. They suspected with reason that profiteers were reaping a golden harvest; but when the government called for new credits they dared not vote against the war budgets and face the damning accusation of disloyalty. The cabinet counted with success upon the same fear to silence opposition when it ordered the transfer of strikers of military age to the trenches.

There is some reason to suspect, however, that the sword of patriotic justice which Clemenceau wielded had a sharp edge for the workers but a blunt edge for the capitalists. The week Bolo was shot a group of French industrialists, who had sold cyanide and carbides to Germany through Switzerland, were acquitted with the tacit approval of the ministry.[9] And Clemenceau's enigmatic friend, Basil Zaharoff, who was building up a fabulous fortune from war industries, though accused of furnishing supplies, from Spanish bases, to German submarines in the Mediterranean, was never brought into court although the government investigated the charges.[10] The profits and industries of war create their own logic, and the capital invested in them casts its vote, in subtle and incommunicable ways, for the *guerre à outrance*. When, in this, it sustains the will of the embattled nation, it reaps the rewards of its service.

The French people, aware that secret groups, selfish motives, and sinister influences might be prolonging the war, still believed that France could not sheathe the sword without victory. Duty to the dead demanded further sacrifices from the living. "Those who have fallen," Clemenceau

[9] Francis Delaisi, "Corruption in Armaments," *Living Age*, September 1931.

[10] George Seldes, *Iron, Blood and Profits* (New York: Harper and Brothers, 1934), p. 185.

reminded the Chamber of Deputies, "have not died in vain for they found a way to glorify the history of France. It remains for the living to set a crown upon the magnificent labors of the dead." The only crown which would not dishonor such heroic sacrifices, he insisted, was a complete victory, and victory was certain if the Allies could hold out for a few more weeks. "American aid will decide the outcome of this war,"[11] he promised at the beginning of June; and the French people, accepting this assurance, prepared to see the class of 1920 called to service while the American legions were girding on their armor.

American aid in money, materials and manpower was flowing across the Atlantic in a stream which promised to reach decisive proportions by 1919. But as Clemenceau warned, the Germans had in the interval a surplus of a million men, released from the Russian front, which they could hurl against the French lines so desperately thinned by three years of slaughter. Britain could not or would not greatly strengthen its expeditionary force, although, as Lloyd George later confessed, the French *dead* almost equalled the British total of killed, wounded and missing, and Great Britain had a larger population from which to draw. For the moment, therefore, the French saw nothing to do but dig in and hold on. Even the Socialists must now recognize, Clemenceau observed grimly, that to negotiate a peace with Germany was for the lamb to lie down with the lion. The Russians had discovered this at Brest-Litovsk.

The jibe was, as Clemenceau intended it to be, a telling thrust. The French Socialists had placed great hopes in the declaration of the German Reichstag (passed July 19, 1917, by 212 votes to 126) that it favored a peace of lasting understanding without forced acquisition of territory or political, economic or financial exactions. The crushing terms which the German militarists imposed upon Russia in 1918, detaching the Ukraine, Lithuania, Estonia, Livonia, Courland, Finland and Russian Poland, left the Allies no illusions regarding the terms they might expect if they, too, laid down their arms in defeat. Even President Wilson, who had published his Fourteen Points in January, modified his attitude three months later, and declared that to crush the German militarists the Allies must use force, force to the utmost, force without stint or limit. Clemenceau's iron will and Jacobin dictatorship kept the French people keyed to the strain of the last gamble only because they believed it could prove a winning gamble, because they were convinced that American aid would turn the scale in time. Pétain, a cautious calculator, summarized the situation in

[11] *Journal Officiel: Chambre des Députés: Débats*, Session of June 4, 1918, p. 1616.

two sentences. "If we can hold on until the end of June our situation will be excellent. In July we can resume the offensive; after that victory will be ours." [12]

So Foch and Ludendorff prepared to fight it out, Foch with inadequate reserves but almost unlimited credit, Ludendorff with eighty-two reserve divisions which dwindled and dissolved as he flung them repeatedly against the elastic Allied defenses. Clemenceau's duty during this duel of giants in the spring and summer of 1918 was the maintenance of French civilian morale and he discharged it well. He possessed the invaluable form of intuition which penetrates an opponent's mind and mood. He knew that the Germans were war-weary and undernourished. He knew that there had been serious strikes in Berlin. He knew that reports of American aid, so heartening to the Allies, would have an equal and opposite impact upon the disheartened people across the Rhine. Magnified to astronomical figures in the propaganda leaflets rained upon the German cities, this aid would win its first victory in the German mind, sapping the will to fight on until suddenly the German spirit broke. He knew that when two opponents are equally weary hope and will power decide the issue, and he vowed that France should not fail for lack of will. Ludendorff, in his memoirs, recognized Clemenceau's achievement and paid him higher praise than he accorded Foch. "Clemenceau knew what he wanted. His policy was a war policy; he suppressed every sign of peace agitation and strengthened the spirit of his country. His proceedings against Caillaux showed clearly what we were to expect of him." [13]

Yet there were hours when even Clemenceau's spirit failed as he watched the infernal auction and measured the price of victory in terms of human life. The problem of manpower drove other thoughts from his mind. He could not armor himself against statistics as the generals had learned to do: these dying men were Frenchmen, with farms or shops they had wanted to go back to, with families waiting in some darkened cottage down a well remembered road or decorous house at the corner of a quaint medieval street. The conviction haunted him that he ought to find better means to spare them, that he ought to exact more aid from Britain, from Italy, from the United States, that France might be spared these last bright drops of irrecoverable blood. Though he restrained his bitter-

[12] Liddell Hart, *A History of the World War, 1914–1918* (Boston: Little Brown & Co., 1935), p. 536.

[13] Erich von Ludendorff, *My War Memories, 1914–1918*, 2 vols. (London: Hutchinson & Co., 1919), II, 513.

ness in public, his colleagues were shocked at his savage comments over the delay in feeding American infantry and machine gunners into the front lines. Pershing's dogged determination to build up an independent American expeditionary force seemed to Clemenceau an act of insubordination. For to him the unified command meant that Foch controlled the Allied armies in France and he, as French Minister of War, controlled Foch. The facts would not admit of such an interpretation and in the end it became necessary for Poincaré, as President of the Republic, to support Foch when the latter refused to "command" Pershing's obedience. As Commander-in-chief of the Allied Armies, Poincaré pointed out, Foch was responsible not only to the French Government but to the British and American Governments as well. Thus in the test Clemenceau found that the Unified Command, instead of bringing military affairs on the Western Front more directly under his supervision, actually divided and diluted his authority, a consummation he could not bring himself to acknowledge or accept.

From the United States he demanded, as was his habit, at least twice as much as he hoped to obtain. When his requisitions were met, he quadrupled them, reacting with a greater exigence like a spoiled child towards an indulgent parent. As each emergency arose in the affairs of France, a shipping crisis, an oil scarcity, a coal deficiency, a food shortage, he turned towards Washington as if Columbia were a fairy godmother who could wave a golden wand and solve the problem. In June, 1918, he asked President Wilson for $100,000,000 in gold as if the possibility of a refusal had not crossed his mind. And Pershing has recorded a revealing comment which escaped him at the session of the Supreme War Council on June 2. "M. Clemenceau reverted to the shortage of available men in the United States, saying he had thought our resources inexhaustible. . . ."[14]

It must be remembered, in his defense, that he had to fight, and knew he had to fight, a sharp duel with the British if he were to secure for France a fair proportion of American supplies and men. Fear that the British might divert the reinforcements from across the Atlantic towards distant imperial objectives of their own was never far from his mind, and he sought a means to pool and audit the American consignments so that he might feel confident that France received her full share. On April 18, 1918, he and Pershing discussed the advantages in organization which

[14] John J. Pershing, *My Experiences in the World War*, 2 vols. (New York: Stokes, 1931), II, 74.

would result from pooling all the war *matériel* intended for the Allies. He approved the project which Pershing had drawn up and he appointed M. Louis Loucheur, his energetic Minister of Munitions, to coöperate with Colonel Charles G. Dawes, General Purchasing Agent of the American Expeditionary Force.[15] When invited to collaborate, Lloyd George also approved of the project, in principle, though he apparently suspected that the French were trying to steal a march. A preliminary discussion by American, French, British and Italian representatives, held May 6, promptly evoked the old, obstructive spirit of military-civilian rivalry and inter-Allied distrust, a mood so persistent the French had coined a word for it: *alliophobie*. Further examination of the proposal was relegated to a second conference scheduled for May 14, but the British reverted to their exasperating tactics of delay and failed to appear. Despite their absence, Clemenceau, as chairman of the session, submitted a memorandum creating the Inter-Allied Board to coördinate the services of supply. But the question of the degree of civilian control complicated the program. Pershing and Dawes insisted upon a *military* Board of Allied Supply, and on May 22 Clemenceau yielded, signing with Pershing a succinct agreement for the creation of a board composed of representatives from each of the Allied armies. The board was to control, regulate and allot all military supplies and military utilities.

But this centralization of authority, this "Unified Command" for the Services of Supply, which appealed to and was ardently desired by the military minds, could not be realized in its entirety. Though the British reluctantly assented to it as a *fait accompli*, and the Board was formally organized in June, the French modified their attitude and accepted its jurisdiction only in the advanced zone of military activities, the zone in the rear remaining under the direction of the civil authorities. Apparently French industrial and commercial circles had taken alarm at the prospect of a strict military control which might prove insusceptible to their influence, and Clemenceau had to temporize with them. But he could not evade the fact that as American aid increased, becoming more munificent and more indispensable, American wishes and American methods would resolve all issues. In August he acknowledged the growing economic dependence of France by an agreement that henceforth all French purchases of whatever nature, made in the United States, would be effected through the mediation of and under the control of the War Industries

[15] Charles G. D. Dawes, *A Journal of the Great War*, 2 vols. (Boston: Houghton Mifflin Co., 1921), pp. 84–88.

Keystone View Co.

Clemenceau on one of his unheralded visits to the Western Front.

Board at Washington.[16] This centralization of authority, which made speculation in war supplies difficult and private monopolies impossible, was not altogether popular in France, but it saved the government from exploitation.

As a purchasing agent bidding for American manpower Clemenceau proved less successful for there the British stole a march on him. The pressure, often indirect, but steady and relentless, which he brought to bear on Pershing, only toughened the latter's determination to retain control of his regiments. Clemenceau's grim drive for cannon fodder antagonized the American commander; and at Washington and London British diplomacy scored against the French pressure. By offering extra marine tonnage the British won approval for the shipment of six American divisions in May, 1918, all of which, with Pershing's reluctant consent, were to be brigaded with British divisions to learn their final lessons under battle conditions.

It was apparent that the British were using all their advantages: they could find extra tonnage when it was a matter of transporting American regiments to feed into their expeditionary force, but they interposed difficulties when Pershing sought artillery, signal corps, and auxiliary troops for an independent American army. This, however, was a game at which two could play, and Clemenceau, who knew that Pershing was eager to develop an American air force but lacked planes, wooed him with the promise of French warplanes provided the Americans would furnish the raw material for building more. London, not to be outdone, countered with a proposal to furnish British aircraft for American operations, an offer which their factories were in a more favorable position to fulfill. But Pershing, a little disillusioned by such calculating "coöperation," let the matter rest for the moment.

This inter-Allied contest, in which he felt that he was losing too many tricks, exasperated Clemenceau's nerves, and he prepared to preside at the session of the Supreme War Council, which met on June 2, with bitterness in his heart. He had just learned of the option on 120,000 American troops shipped in May, an option which the British had secured behind his back. He wanted to know why half these reinforcements should not be assigned to French divisions, or failing that, whether the Americans would furnish 120,000 men in June to be brigaded with the French. Pershing declined to commit himself or his government on this point.

[16] Étienne Clémentel, *La France et la politique économique interalliée* (Paris: Presses Universitaires de la France, 1931), p. 283.

After an acrimonious debate, Clemenceau was forced to recognize the British option on the May contingents and to postpone the allotment of the June reinforcements until a later meeting. He did, however, wring from Lloyd George the promise that Britain would furnish more ships to expedite the transfer of American infantry and supplies.

Having taken Pershing's measure and discovered the limit of his concessions, Clemenceau turned his attack on the British, perhaps with the intention of discrediting them in Pershing's opinion. Why was it, he and Foch demanded, that the Germans, with a population of 68,000,000, were able to maintain 204 divisions in the field, while the British, with 46,000,000 inhabitants, could only furnish 43 divisions? At this point, to Pershing's surprise, both sides began citing widely varying estimates on the number and strength of the Allied divisions in active service, and it became apparent that "the numbers were variously stated according to which side was speaking."[17] Clemenceau seemed to realize suddenly the unfavorable impression which such wrangling made on Pershing, for he left Foch to press the French point of view and withdrew from the discussion. Foch and the British war minister, Lord Milner, then drew up a plan calling for the despatch of 500,000 American troops in June and July, priority to be given to 210,000 combatant troops. At the same time Clemenceau persuaded Lloyd George and Orlando to sign a cablegram to President Wilson, urging the shipment of 300,000 American soldiers a month "with a view to establishing a total American force of 100 divisions at as early a date as this can possibly be done." As an American division, with its services, numbered some 40,000 men, this proposal would mean an expeditionary force approaching 4,000,000.

> We are satisfied [the cable concluded] that General Foch, who is conducting the present campaign with consummate ability, and on whose military judgment we continue to place the most absolute reliance, is not over-estimating the needs of the case. . . .[18]

During this wrangling and disjointed session of June 2, as Pershing observed, Clemenceau's attention frequently wandered from the discussion. He had a battle of his own to fight on the political front, a battle which reached its climax the following day in the Chamber of Deputies. For France was standing at bay once again, enduring the full fury of a second German drive which had commenced on May 27, and a crisis had

[17] Pershing, *My Experiences in the World War*, II, 77.
[18] Pershing, *My Experiences in the World War*, II, 80.

developed more desperate and discouraging than the March disaster two months earlier. Only Clemenceau was in a position fully to comprehend and fit together the two halves of the picture, the political and the military; joined, they established the dark outlines of a situation which he pondered in his mind while specious talk consumed precious minutes before the Supreme War Council. What he needed to extract from that meeting, and what he did extract, was a message of hope which he could issue to the press and proclaim in the Chamber, a message which would help to stave off the vote of lack of confidence which his political foes demanded, and which they seemed, this time, strong enough to obtain.

Ludendorff had sprung his new surprise with a crashing offensive between Rheims and Soissons, carrying the strong French segment known as the Chemin des Dames. Following the initial break-through on May 27, the German forces had rolled relentlessly southward until, on May 30, they reached the Marne. By June 1 their triangular salient extended to a depth of thirty miles between the Marne and the Aisne; they were within forty miles of Paris; and their long range cannon, as in March, had opened fire on the city. A deep mood of anger, frustration and despair welled up in French hearts, and the patience of the parliamentarians snapped. They had trusted Clemenceau too blindly. Now, even the oppressive censorship could not conceal the unpalatable truth that the French forces on the Chemin des Dames, like the British Fifth Army, had been taken unprepared. General Duchesne, the arrogant local commander of the Sixth Army, had bungled his defense; Foch and Pétain had so completely discounted the possibility of a German drive in this sector that they had sent three decimated British divisions there for a rest. When the Germans struck the Allied retreat had been so precipitate their engineers had not even paused to blow up the bridges over the Aisne across which the enemy streamed triumphantly on the first day of their attack. For the French command a final and humiliating touch was provided by the fact that the American Intelligence Service had forecast the offensive as early as May 15, and had sent repeated warnings to French headquarters where, regarded as the presumptuous product of an "amateur army," they had been almost entirely disregarded.

To many Parisians it seemed as if, despite the heroism of the poilus, despite unity of command, despite American aid, defeat not victory was the goal towards which Clemenceau had been herding an exhausted nation. "Soissons taken. Rheims no doubt. We are back where we were at the end of 1914," Aristide Briand wrote despairingly on May 30.[19] Angry demands that the Cabinet resign, that a military commission probe the evidences of neglect and incompetence, that the generals responsible confront a court martial, echoed through the press and the parliament. Clemenceau had to decide in swift order whether, to salvage his ministry, he should sacrifice Foch or Pétain, or whether he should attempt to defend them and take the risk that all might fall together. The rout on the well-fortified Chemin des Dames, considered, after Verdun, an almost impregnable corridor, had shocked French confidence, and the British and Italians, who had so recently pleaded for French divisions when their own lines collapsed, showed no eagerness to assist Pétain with reserves in his hour of need. All these facts weakened Clemenceau's position when he decided to face his critics in the Chamber of Deputies on June 4. He had made his decision, regained all his resolution and poise, and was determined to fight all critics without compromise or concession. The demand for a secret session he brushed aside brusquely as he had brushed it aside six months earlier.

> What would we achieve by an immediate discussion? Sow doubt in anxious minds. Add further misapprehensions to those already established. I cannot lend myself to this. If we should excite doubts in the minds of the soldiers regarding some of their leaders — and these perhaps the most capable — it would be a crime for which I will not assume the responsibility. . . .
>
> Our men are engaged in a battle, a terrible battle. They have been fighting, one against five, without rest, for three and four days. . . . These soldiers, these magnificent soldiers, have good leaders, great leaders, leaders worthy of them on all counts. . . .
>
> I insist, and it is my last word, that victory depends on us, provided that the civil authorities rise to the level of their responsibilities. There is no need to offer such advice to the soldiers.
>
> Dismiss me from this post if I have not served you faithfully. Expel me. Condemn me. But at least take the trouble first to formulate your charges. . . .[20]

By a vote of 377 to 110 the Chamber decided not to press for further explanations at this time. Clemenceau had triumphed again, in the face of a prepared and concerted opposition and a black array of facts. It was a triumph less of policy than of personality. Only those who heard him speak, without notes, in spurts and gushes of words, as if the phrases were torn from him, could measure the effect of his oratory. There was about him at these moments a suggestion of such controlled urgency, such pain-

[19] Georges Suarez, *Briand*, 4 vols. (Paris: Plon, 1936–40), IV, 366.

[20] *Journal Officiel: Chambre des Députés: Débats*, Session of June 4, 1918, p. 1616.

ful appraisal of tragic truths, such a heavy sense of his responsibilities and grim determination to fulfill them, that lesser minds were awed and silenced. The written records of his oratory are subdued to suave and literary rhythms which can never recapture or recreate the tempo and gusto of his spoken words. The facial expression, the gestures, above all the inflections and the emotional coloring which charged his phrases, carried them with the impact of a bullet to the heart of a hearer. Not reason and logic alone, but reason and logic stated with contagious courage and honesty, enabled him to compel assent even when he failed to convince or persuade.

The session over and the spell broken, however, his foes gathered sheepishly to explain their vote and renew their plots. Having failed to unseat the ministry in the first days of June they proposed to steal some of its authority by demanding a coalition cabinet, in which Briand might share leadership with Clemenceau. Such an attempt to "marry fire and water" as Poincaré sardonically phrased it, would have been doomed in advance.[21] But Clemenceau recognized that some method must be found to placate the impotent and exasperated parliamentarians with a little authority which would flatter their self-importance. On June 6 a joint delegation of senators and deputies descended on the Minister of War, announcing that they represented a "Committee of Defense" which would assist the Cabinet in organizing the defense of Paris. Received with flattering attention, overwhelmed with irrelevant and exhausting details, fed a diet of windy witnesses, ambiguous statistics, and interminable debates that were all bulk and no nourishment, the committee finally died of inanition. Its demise was delicately accelerated by the tactful Jeanneney and the adroit Mordacq, whose mastery of this form of euthanasia rendered them invaluable to Clemenceau during such crises.

Each day thus gained was as good as a battle won for the ministry. For German morale and German reserves were running out, and Ludendorff, for whom time was not an ally but an enemy, could muster the resources for one more major offensive at best. If this great *Friedensturm* failed to bring victory and reduce the Allies to terms the reaction in Germany would decide the war. For the population of the Central Powers could not face another turnip winter. Clemenceau's conviction that wars were won by the side which could believe in victory fifteen minutes longer than the opposing force had come to dominate Foch and Ludendorff also. If the German armies could cross the Marne, invest Rheims, and approach

[21] Suarez, *Briand*, IV, 368.

Paris, Ludendorff was confident that the Clemenceau cabinet would fall, the British would retreat to the Channel, and the Italians would appeal for a separate peace. France, by that time guided by a less resolute cabinet of the Left, would have no choice but to accept a peace without victory.

Such was the hope sustaining the German high command when it hurled the German Seventh Army across the Marne between Epernay and Château-Thierry on July 15, 1918. But this time the element of surprise was lacking. The French reacted with firmness and skill and the attack stalled. Dining with Pétain at Provins on July 16, Clemenceau pressed for a prompt counter-offensive. He knew the febrile state of Parisian nerves; some of his own ministers had lost their courage the previous day when the thunder of distant guns announced a new drive; a week of growing dread and defeatist rumors, of the type which followed the break of May 27, might well have proved too much for French will power. Fortunately, the nation was spared this final ordeal. By July 18 the Germans were on the defensive. By August 8 Ludendorff had lost hope. The expected collapse of French courage, downfall of the Clemenceau cabinet, and appeal for an armistice had failed to materialize. This time, definitely, the Germans had made their last bid in that fatal auction and they had failed to score.

CHAPTER XIII

THE TRIUMPH

August–November, 1918

Ce que j'ai fait, c'est la France qui la fait.[1]
CLEMENCEAU (November 5, 1918)

WITH the turning of the military tide in July, 1918, a new spirit came to life in France. Not all at once: a four years' nightmare is not so easily dispelled. But people began to look about them and found the horizon less black. By August a million Americans had crossed the seas and would soon be in the battle. The submarine menace had been checked and the sinkings cut in half since the previous March. Allied forces had taken the initiative and this time they kept it; the army bulletins listed daily some town or village redeemed from enemy occupation.

But this lightening of the horizon brought little respite or comfort to Clemenceau. Rather, as the possibility of victory grew more real through August and September his own spirits declined. He seemed more tense and combative than ever, more biting in debate and obstinate in argument. His irritability was a result of the friction inseparable from his role; he was the central pivot upon which the wheel of discontent revolved; and the discontent grew sharper as hope revived. The parliamentarians harassed him, the press scolded, bankers and business men deplored the government restrictions and discontented workers sabotaged production. Driven close to the limit of his physical reserves, he was compelled to drive others who were often nearer the breaking point than himself. Such a duty is likely to awaken, even in charitable souls, a rankling suspicion that somewhere slackers are not carrying a full load, that the sons of Martha are bearing too much of the burden and the sons of Mary too little. To Clemenceau, obsessed with the sacrifices which France had made and was still making, it seemed manifest that the Italian, the British and the American armies ought in justice to relieve the over-taxed French divisions. He felt that he owed it to France and to his poilus to put more pressure on the Allies.

[1] *Journal Officiel: Chambre des Députés: Débats*, Session of November 5, 1918, p. 2875.

France had set the example of unhesitating sacrifice but the limit of French manpower had been reached and passed. The Chamber of Deputies, called upon to summon the class of 1920 for service in September, 1918, revolted angrily, and fought the proposal with a bitterness which exhausted Clemenceau the more because he had to argue against his heart. For three days, July 31 to August 2, the debate flared and flickered, and truths not pleasant to hear were flung at the ministers who bore the responsibility for conditions which they could not improve or deny. To call out boys of seventeen, the opposition orators proclaimed, was inhuman even if war conditions necessitated it. But to place them in barracks where the moral and sanitary conditions were execrable, where drunkenness abounded and syphilis had increased 50 per cent in a year, was utterly indefensible.[2] Where were the unlimited drafts of American manpower which Clemenceau had promised two months earlier? If the transports were in reality landing 300,000 men a month, why put French adolescents into the firing line, schoolboys whose fathers and brothers had already been taken. Clemenceau could only reiterate that in the opinion of the ministry the new draft was necessary, that the Committee on the Army had approved it, and that if the resolution failed to pass he would resign. The chamber voted its confidence in his cabinet but postponed the application of the new draft and Clemenceau did not resign.[3]

According to their calculations, the French, in July, 1918, had 103 divisions in action or in reserve on the Western Front, the British 56, the Americans 18, and the Belgians 12. As each American division had twice the manpower of an Allied division this gave a grand total of 209 against an estimated 207 for the Germans. Many of the Allied divisions had suffered heavily, however, and the British wished to break up 10 or 12 of their hardest hit and draft the men into other units. Clemenceau insisted to Lloyd George that it would be more proper to bring these weakened divisions back to full strength; that the British conscription law had not exhausted British reserves, that it had far too many loopholes, and had never been applied to Ireland at all. To prove his case he offered to lend the British War Office the services of an expert from the French General Staff, and the latter's report, completed in August, put the British on the defensive. Foch, more tactful and more patient than Clemenceau, begged that the matter should not be pressed too strongly. The British, he pointed

[2] Léon Bernard, *La Défense de la Santé Publique pendant la guerre* (Paris: Presses Universitaires de la France, 1929), pp. 266–271.

[3] *Journal Officiel: Chambre des Députés: Débats*, Sessions of July 31 to August 2, pp. 2240–2259.

out mildly, "do not like us to meddle in their internal affairs." It was a gentle rebuke, but Clemenceau never learned to take rebukes with good grace.

Foiled in London, he turned upon the Americans. The independent American Army for which Pershing had fought so firmly was finally created at the end of July, but Clemenceau assumed that it would fight under Foch's orders. He repeatedly criticized Foch for laxity in using his new authority and would not agree to the latter's argument that it was best to "persuade" rather than to attempt to "command" the British, American and Belgian generals. After the Americans stormed the Saint-Mihiel salient, September 12, he hastened to congratulate Pershing on the achievement. But he was far from reconciled to the "autonomous" attitude preserved by the American commander. When the Americans took over the Meuse-Argonne sector on September 22, he questioned their fitness to replace the experienced units of the French Second Army. Their valiant participation in the great Allied offensive which began four days later found him still critical, and he finally decided that the failure of the Americans to advance faster, the defects manifested in their transportation and supply services, and the heavy losses which they incurred, justified his repeated judgment that they were not sufficiently organized or experienced to operate independently. On October 21 he wrote Foch a decisive letter, affirming that, as Minister of War and constitutional head of the army, he must insist upon Foch bringing Pershing under stricter orders. If Pershing would not obey, the matter must be referred to President Wilson for a final ruling.

Foch had grown more than a little weary of Clemenceau's interference in military matters, and as victory fortified his own prestige he could afford to dispense with political support. He replied calmly but firmly that he would not withdraw the authority and confidence which he had extended to Pershing in their collaborative plan of battle. Nor would he acknowledge in full the indictment of incompetence and insubordination which Clemenceau had levelled at the American general.

> It is impossible [Foch wrote] to deny the effort made by the Americans. After attacking at Saint-Mihiel the 12th September, they attacked the 26th in the Argonne. They have lost under fire, between September 26 and October 20, 54,158 men — for small gains, on a narrow front, it is true — but on a particularly difficult terrain and in the face of a serious enemy resistance.[4]

[4] Ferdinand Foch, *Mémoires pour servir à l'histoire de la guerre de 1914–1918*, 2 vols. (Paris: Plon, 1931), II, 252.

There Clemenceau had to leave the issue as more pressing problems crowded upon him. The sudden weakening of the Central Powers, creating the possibility that victory might be achieved in 1918 instead of 1919 or 1920, took the Allied generals and statesmen by surprise. Their secret war aims and territorial ambitions became matters of imminent instead of remote significance. All at once they had to evaluate their positions, their possessions, their resources, not as assets in the military sense but as vouchers to be laid on the peace table. At such moments half-realized projects may prove penalties, and possession can be nine-tenths of international law. Diplomatically, the situation had come to resemble one of those card games wherein the players draw and discard in rotation, each striving to build a hand of complete combinations, and the one whose hand is organized as a *bloc* exacts tribute from his neighbors for all the superfluous cards they have not fitted into a sequence. Clemenceau the realist comprehended the weakness of the French position in 1918. It seemed, despite the enormous sacrifices made, and in part because of them, as dubious as that of Italy. For France had suffered vast losses in life and property and held almost no conquests which could be exchanged to advantage. Indeed, the French had to incur further obligations daily and would continue to incur them until the Germans had been driven across the Rhine.

Discouraged by such thoughts he suffered a crisis of nerves in the first week of October. The Supreme War Council met at Versailles on the 7th and 8th of the month, and Lloyd George, jubilant at the collapse of Bulgaria and recent British victories in Palestine, urged the despatch of an ultimatum against Turkey. Clemenceau, to whom Germany was the great enemy, urged that the Saloniki expeditionary force should be ordered to the Danube to break Austrian resistance. But the British had other ambitions, strategic and territorial. Lloyd George proposed to despatch the British units in the Balkans, under General Milne, to seize Constantinople. The collapse of Russia, and the defeat of Germany and Austria, furnished a rare opportunity for the French and British to expand their influence in the Near East, but their mutual suspicions made effective team work impossible. "General Franchet d'Esperey," Lloyd George recorded, "now proposed to break up the British forces at Salonika under General Milne, and diverting some of them up in Bulgaria while placing a part under a French General, to march along with French troops on Constantinople. The French were very anxious to get that city into their own hands. They seem to have had a secret fear that if once the British got hold of it we might develop independent plans for its ultimate disposal. Needless to say, such an idea was completely without foundation. . . ."[5] After a tense dispute Clemenceau agreed that Milne might occupy Constantinople with a mixed Anglo-French force, but he remained far from satisfied at the drift of Near Eastern affairs.

The night of October 7 he talked later than usual with Mandel, Mordacq and Jeanneney, his monologue a pessimistic jeremiad on the dark future of France. He felt that everyone was betraying him in turn, his allies, Foch, Poincaré, his ministers, even his closest subordinates.[6] The following day, October 8, he offered Poincaré his resignation which was refused. His ostensible grievance—resentment at Poincaré's criticism of his policies and his defense of integral French interests—concealed a cabinet crisis behind the scenes. Once again, as in 1909, he had failed the expectations of a powerful group of French leaders whose aspiration was French mastery of the eastern Mediterranean through a renascent Hellas and effective intervention in Turkey. The French navy, which had installed Venizelos in power at Athens in 1917, and the French army of 200,000 men which had wasted away from malaria at Saloniki, represented an investment which should have produced dividends and had failed to do so. The British, who, with smaller forces, had fomented the Arab revolt, seized Bagdad, Jerusalem and Damascus, and now threatened an independent march on Constantinople, were depleting their contingents in France to pursue these imperial objectives. Their selfish hope, Clemenceau suspected, was to pin all French reserves to the Western Front for another winter, while British expeditions occupied vantage points in the Mediterranean and the Near East. After four years of fighting all the fronts were softening and the opportunity was at hand to garner rich rewards at the expense of defeated and disorganized powers, Russia, Turkey, Austria, Germany, Italy. But France, with her northern departments still the stage of a bitter battle, could not orient her energies towards a policy of aggression and acquisition. Clemenceau already foresaw that this would be part of the grandeur and misery of victory.

Menaced by British manoeuvres, harassed by petulant deputies, scolded by Poincaré and defied by Foch, he had reason, in those first days of October, to feel the weight of his seventy-seven years. For the crowning event of a critical week was the news that the German Chancellor, Prince Max of Baden, had addressed an appeal to President Wilson, asking for a

[5] David Lloyd George, *War Memoirs*, 6 vols. (Boston: Little Brown & Co., 1933–1937), VI, 242.

[6] Jean Jules Henri Mordacq, *Le Ministère Clemenceau*, 4 vols. (Paris: Plon, 1930–1931), II, 252–262.

general armistice. On Wilson's answer might hang not only the question of war or peace but the fate of France for a generation, and Clemenceau was powerless to influence that answer, for the American president handled the negotiations with reserve and independence. To know that momentous decisions were being made, decisions which would make or mar his ministerial record and all his labors, yet decisions in which he could, for the moment, have no share, was gall to his anxious, authoritarian spirit. He was convinced that the German overtures were a trick to gain time, a clever move intended to confuse and divide the Allied and Associated Powers on the eve of victory. He dreaded lest Wilson, by entering into a discussion, should compromise the Allied position, leaving France no choice but to accept a lenient peace which would spare Germany, or fight on alone, having forfeited American sympathy and aid. For a peace without annexations or indemnities would leave France ruined. Yet once the rumor of an imminent armistice spread among the French public they would relax their war spirit. If the promise of peace proved a mirage, the disappointment would "hamstring" the poilus and the people, whose hearts had sickened too often from such hopes deferred. Poincaré dreaded such a collapse of French morale at the eleventh hour even more keenly than Clemenceau, and he plagued the latter with daily warnings to be on guard against it.

To test the sincerity of the German peace overtures, Clemenceau suggested, it was necessary to present demands so rigorous they would amount to disarmament. He believed, and most Frenchmen shared his belief, that the German militarists were counting on a change of luck; they might even withdraw their weary divisions to the frontier but still plan to resume the offensive in the spring of 1919, or to draw upon the vast resources of Russian manpower. That Ludendorff and Hindenburg, whose legions had threatened Paris three months earlier, could so suddenly become suppliants, prepared to capitulate and disarm, was not credible. The proposal to discuss terms could only be the tricky manoeuvre of a treacherous foe and must be treated as such. To interpret in this spirit the far from transparent motives inspiring the German General Staff at this period was not magnanimous, perhaps, but it was realistic and justifiable. As late as October 25, Hindenburg assented to the continuation of the peace discussions with the excuse that "In fourteen days we can look further ahead, therefore we must gain time."[7]

[7] *Preliminary History of the Armistice: Official Documents published by the German*

From October 6 on, therefore, Clemenceau urged the Allied generals, Foch in particular, to press the retreating German armies without respite, and to draw up terms of capitulation which, once accepted, would leave the Central Powers no smallest chance of renewing the struggle. Foch needed no urging. As a professional soldier who knew his business thoroughly, he had already decided on the military stipulations which would reduce Germany to impotence. At Paris, on October 8, Clemenceau, Lloyd George and Orlando looked over suggestions for an armistice submitted to them by the military and naval advisers of the Supreme War Council. Listed under nineteen heads, the terms provided in substance that the Germans must evacuate all occupied territory (including Alsace-Lorraine) and surrender the fortresses of Metz, Thionville, Strassburg, Neu Breisach and Lille, and the Island of Helgoland. General Bliss, the American military adviser, did not assist officially in drafting the ultimatum, and it was his subsequent opinion that the Allied prime ministers, in preparing it, hoped to convey to President Wilson indirectly a broad hint of the deep distrust they felt for the Germans, especially when they tendered an olive branch.[8] Public opinion, not only in France and England but in America also, inflamed by years of propaganda, assumed that Wilson would refuse the Germans any terms short of unconditional surrender. Wilson, disposed at first to be lenient, but driven towards severity by the sentiments voiced in the Senate, the American press, and the Allied councils, raised his demands with each exchange of notes between Berlin and Washington, and gave the screw an extra turn each time the Germans weakened. When he finally turned over his correspondence with the German foreign office to the Allied Governments, on October 23, he had exacted much, learned more, and conceded nothing.

For Clemenceau these autumn weeks were more exhausting than the critical hours of spring when the German drives threatened Paris. Repeatedly he sought relief and exhilaration in action, rushing up and down the lines from one divisional headquarters to another, but he could not free his mind from the tormenting thought that the whole issue of the war was at stake, that he must secure a peace which Frenchmen would endorse, but that he remained the prisoner of alliances which he could not outwit or evade. He knew that the Germans had appealed for a peace

---

National Chancellery, edited by James Brown Scott (New York: Oxford University Press, 1924), p. 119.

[8] Tasker H. Bliss, "The Armistices," *American Journal of International Law*, XVI (1922), 515.

based upon the Fourteen Points. If Wilson was sincere in advocating such a peace and committed the United States to his program, the French would have to acquiesce, and even though they regained Alsace-Lorraine they would have no adequate guarantees for the future, and no compensations equivalent to their sacrifices. The population of the reconquered provinces would scarcely equal the war dead, and France would not profit in the same degree as Britain from captured colonies and trade, nor in annexations from Austria such as Italy claimed. He feared Anglo-American bargains at the expense of French interests. Despite the flattery of the American press, despite the warm sympathy of the American people, symbolized by nation-wide committees, campaigns, banquets, to aid "heroic France," Clemenceau believed that blood would prove thicker than champagne, and that when the emotionalism waned the Anglo-Saxon peoples would desert France and divide the world between them.

Such disillusioned thoughts were no doubt unworthy, but Clemenceau was a disillusioned man. He had seen too many hot political friendships chill to treachery to place an abiding faith in unimplemented pledges. The delays which slowed down Pershing's offensive in the Argonne in late October seemed to him evidence that at the first hint of peace even the promise to drive the Germans from France might be forgotten. The British march into Syria and negotiations with the Turks seemed to foreshadow a repudiation of French claims in the Levant. Friction between the two Powers and the two commands had helped to cripple the Dardanelles expedition and to condemn the Saloniki army to inertia. If Britain and Turkey arranged an armistice it could only mean that French claims were to be set aside. For the best part of an exhausting afternoon (October 30) Clemenceau fought Lloyd George on the issue that a French admiral and not a British general must receive the Turkish surrender. The outcome was one of those compromises proposing joint action in which, somehow, the British always seemed to emerge with the advantage.[9]

On October 26 Colonel House returned to France from the United States and the armistice discussions thereafter centred in Paris. Clemenceau studied the notes exchanged between Berlin and Washington with the avidity of a lawyer searching a contract for loopholes. At his elbow lay the conditions of surrender drawn up by the military and naval experts, stipulations designed to meet and implement Wilson's suggestion that it would be wise to "ensure to the Associated Governments the un-

[9] Charles Seymour, *American Diplomacy during the World War* (Baltimore: The Johns Hopkins University Press, 1934), pp. 341–342.

restricted power to safeguard and enforce the details of the peace." Wilson's conduct of the negotiations, it soon became clear, had left the Allies complete liberty of action. They could decline to discuss peace at all; they could open independent conversations with the Central Powers; or they could notify the American president that they accepted his mediation and ask him to inform Berlin that armistice terms were ready. If, however, they associated themselves with the German-American conversations already in progress, they would by implication be committing themselves to a peace based upon the Fourteen Points. For Wilson, in his latest note to the German Government, under date of October 23, had reiterated as a basis for negotiation "the terms of peace laid down in his address to the Congress of the United States on the eighth of January, 1918."[10]

Herein, Clemenceau recognized, lay the crux of the issue. For neither the French, the British nor the Italian leaders cared to admit publicly, or even to reveal to the representatives of the lesser powers, that they had promised themselves and one another advantages from victory which would violate the Fourteen Points. Some deft diplomatic compromises would have to be worked out, and Clemenceau welcomed the timely suggestion put forward by Colonel House that the French, British and Italian prime ministers should meet each morning informally at House's Parisian quarters, N° 78 rue de l'Université. This small steering committee, it was obvious, could debate with greater frankness and bargain with greater ease. Clemenceau improved on House's suggestion by proposing that no issue should be submitted to the Supreme War Council or the lesser powers until the steering committee had reached an agreement and sketched a solution for it. His intention was to make the political representatives of the four Great Powers the real arbiters and architects of the peace, and this was, in the fullest sense, the result of his proposal. The armistices signed with Austria on November 3 and with Germany November 11 were formulated and approved by House, Clemenceau, Lloyd George and Orlando in those morning sessions in the rue de l'Université, and the misunderstandings which multiplied so rapidly and poisoned the peace settlement date from the decisions taken in those pre-armistice days.

The question whether Austria was entitled technically to the benefit of the Fourteen Points is one historic controversy which finds an answer here. That answer seems to be no. For although the Austro-Hungarian

[10] Lansing to Solf, October 23, 1918. *Preliminary History of the Armistice: Official Documents Published by the German National Chancellery*, p. 113.

Empire, already dissolving into its national elements, had appealed to Wilson to act as intermediary in peace negotiations, the Austrians did not wait for a reply but broadcast an appeal to Italy and to the Allies for an immediate armistice. The terms granted were despatched by the Allied Powers directly, and not, as in the case of Germany, through Wilson's mediation. Lloyd George, in fact, pointed out frankly the advantage of settling the terms for Austria without waiting for Wilson's suggestions, and Clemenceau supported the proposal.

In the case of Germany the question is more complicated. When the Allied statesmen accepted the German peace overtures they acknowledged that the Fourteen Points would form the basic peace program and they authorized Wilson so to inform the German government. On only two points, freedom of the seas and reparations, did they declare an exception, and this fact has been taken to signify that they bound themselves to a strict interpretation of all the remaining terms of Wilson's humane and temperate document. Such a view is incorrect, and because it makes their later evasion of that program seem the more inexcusable, it is unjust to Clemenceau, to Lloyd George and to Orlando. For while it is true that they accepted the Wilsonian program, what they had before them was an interpretation of that program so elastic, so attenuated, it prefigured the wry compromises that were to come. Indeed it is scarcely an exaggeration to say that the betrayal of the Fourteen Points had already been half-completed, with Wilson's knowledge and House's acquiescence, before the armistice was signed.

On October 29 House cabled Wilson that he was sending an interpretation of the Fourteen Points for correction and approval. On October 30 Wilson replied:

> Analysis of fourteen points satisfactory interpretation of principles involved but details of application mentioned should be regarded as merely illustrative suggestions and reserved for peace conference.[11]

This "satisfactory interpretation," House admitted later, lay on the table throughout the subsequent discussions, and Clemenceau, Lloyd George and Orlando understood it to represent Wilson's views. Yet it was full of exceptions and evasions which vitiated or nullified most of the fourteen points as completely as did the later peace terms.

Wilson's initial point, "Open covenants of peace, openly arrived at," it

[11] Ray Stannard Baker, *Woodrow Wilson: Life and Letters*, 8 vols. (New York: Doubleday, Doran, 1927–1939), VIII, 53.

was explained, "was not meant to exclude confidential negotiations. . . ." Point V, "Impartial adjustment of colonial claims," applied only to those "created by the war." Point VI, the "evacuation of Russian territory," was indefinite because Russian territory was not "synonymous with territory belonging to the former Russian Empire." Point VII: Belgium, having been attacked illegitimately, need draw no distinction between legal and illegal destruction and could add her war debt to the bill for reparations. France, on the other hand (Point VIII), should not claim payment "for more than damage done to her north eastern *départements*." Point IX, it was admitted, allowed Italy less than the territory allotted by the Treaty of London, but "It might be provided that Italy should have her claim in the Trentino. . . ." As for her claim to a protectorate over Albania, "there is no serious objection raised to this. . . ." As for Point X, autonomous development for the peoples of Austria-Hungary, "this proposition no longer holds." Point XI, promising evacuation and restoration of Rumania, Serbia, and Montenegro, "is also altered by events." Point XII, on the disposition of the Turkish Empire, could be variously interpreted—"the same difficulty arises here concerning the word autonomous. . . ." "Syria has already been allotted to France by agreement with Great Britain. Britain is clearly the best mandatory for Palestine, Mesopotamia and Arabia."[12] It is worth noting that as these elaborations of the Fourteen Points recognize and even indicate the scope of the secret treaties binding the Allied Powers, the existence of these treaties can not have been a surprise to Wilson during the later peace discussions.

The decisions which Clemenceau, Lloyd George, House and Orlando endorsed between October 29 and November 5 determined the conditions of the armistice and the shape of things to come. They approved the occupation of the Left Bank of the Rhine and the internment of the German fleet as necessary armistice stipulations, and they were restrained from insisting upon the complete demilitarization of Germany only by the fear that such severe terms would be rejected and prolong the war, or, if accepted, would expose Germany to Bolshevism. General agreement was obtained only by compromises and concessions on the part of each member of the council. Clemenceau considered the surrender of the fleet an unwarranted humiliation. Haig and Lloyd George questioned the need for

[12] The "Interpretation" is included in *Intimate Papers of Colonel House Arranged as a Narrative by Charles Seymour*, 4 vols. (Boston: Houghton Mifflin Co., 1926–1928), IV, 192–200; and in *Papers Relating to the Foreign Relations of the United States*, Supplements: *The World War, 1918*, 2 vols. (Washington: Government Printing Office, 1933), pp. 405–413.

Foch's strict military terms, and fought the occupation of the Rhineland in particular. House, however, supported Foch's program in this and other details and it was ratified. The American delegates in general showed no tendency towards undue lenience; on the contrary, Pershing opposed any armistice at all as premature and held that the Allied governments should continue the fighting "until we force unconditional surrender from Germany."[13] Bliss, like Pershing an advocate of "unconditional surrender," advised the complete demobilization of the army and rigorous disarmament of Germany. Admiral Benson, the American naval adviser to the council, proposed that the German fleet should be sunk.

But the politicians feared that such an ignominious disposal of their battleships would prove too much for German pride and might galvanize the nation into new defiance. The naval problem was still unresolved when Lloyd George returned to London on November 3. In his absence Clemenceau submitted to the Supreme War Council a revised motion, providing that the surface craft be interned under the control of their own crews, instead of being surrendered outright. Despite the continued objection of the naval experts this solution was adopted. The concession, which reflected once more Clemenceau's indifference on naval matters, left the German sailors the opportunity to scuttle the fleet six months later at Scapa Flow.

As the terms of the armistice set the tone for the Versailles Treaty and Clemenceau has had to bear a large share of the blame for the severity of that Carthaginian peace, it is only just to note that his attitude was less draconic than that of his advisers. Where he could spare German susceptibilities without offending French sentiments, as in the disposal of the fleet, he leaned towards the more moderate solution. He believed, from the end of October on, that Germany would have to accept any terms offered, and in this conviction, as later studies reveal, he was justified. The German Chancellor, Prince Max of Baden, the secretaries of state and the army chiefs fully comprehended that the surrender of Austrian roads and railways for Allied armies to use in pressing their attack rendered the German stand almost hopeless.[14] But Clemenceau did not hold that this favorable development justified the Allies in offering any conditions they

[13] John J. Pershing, *My Experiences in the World War*, 2 vols. (New York: Stokes, 1931), II, 367.

[14] *Preliminary History of the Armistice: Official Documents Published by the German National Chancellery*, pp. 122–130.

chose. It is true that he urged the occupation of the Left Bank and bridgeheads of the Rhine: his cabinet would fall, he insisted, if this clause were omitted from the armistice; but he pledged his word of honor that the French would withdraw their forces when the peace conditions were fulfilled.[15] It should be observed, moreover, that Pershing and Bliss both approved such occupation as a *sine qua non* of surrender. Pershing would have had the German troops, disarmed, sent back to their homeland as paroled prisoners of war, while Bliss urged that the German army be disarmed and demobilized so that it could not be reassembled. In comparison, the terms Foch drew up and Clemenceau defended, which permitted the Germans to withdraw in good order, according to a prepared schedule, with a major part of their weapons, were more considerate of German pride and of the realities of the situation. The desire to humiliate the vanquished in every possible manner was very strong in French chauvinist circles and Clemenceau had to face sharp criticism for his moderation. Even Poincaré, who, as President of the Republic, was above the tides of politics and factional pressure, argued for the unconditional surrender of the German armies so that the Allies might have a clean slate on which to draw up, uninhibited by commitments to the enemy, the outlines of a victor's peace. Later he formally charged Clemenceau with the responsibility for granting the Germans an armistice when it would have been possible to compel them to unconditional surrender.[16]

Such accusations, which never failed to arouse Clemenceau's bitter resentment, prove that Foch, Poincaré and other exigent French leaders failed to appraise fairly the forces and motives which dictated his course and his decisions. German resistance, it is true, had ceased to be a factor of paramount importance after November 1. But Wilson's opposition had not. There was little enthusiasm in French or British governing circles for the Wilsonian program, even when it had been watered down by the "interpretations," but when House made it clear that unless the Fourteen Points were accepted as the nominal basis of peace Wilson would inform Congress of the fact and suggest that the United States negotiate with Germany independently, Lloyd George and Clemenceau both recognized that they must bow to the conditions formulated from Washington. Their reply, entrusted to House by the Supreme War Council, was despatched to Wilson on November 4. It accepted the Fourteen Points with two qualifications, the first, on freedom of the seas, inserted at the insistence of the

[15] Charles Seymour, *American Diplomacy during the World War*, p. 344.
[16] Pershing, *My Experiences in the World War*, II, 369.

British, the second, on reparations, raised at the demand of the French, Italian and Belgian governments, and it was worded as follows:

> The Allied Governments have given careful consideration to the correspondence which has passed between the President of the United States and the German Government. Subject to the qualifications which follow, they declare their willingness to make peace with the Government of Germany on the terms of peace laid down in the President's Address to Congress of January 8, 1918, and the principles of settlement enunciated in his subsequent Addresses.
>
> They must point out, however, that Clause 2, relating to what is usually described as the freedom of the seas, is open to various interpretations, some of which they could not accept.
>
> They must therefore reserve to themselves complete freedom on this subject when they enter the Peace Conference.
>
> Further, in the conditions of peace laid down in his Address to Congress of January 8, 1918, the President declared that the invaded territories must be restored as well as evacuated and freed, and the Allied Governments feel that no doubt ought to be allowed to exist as to what this provision implies.
>
> By it they understand that compensation will be made by Germany for all damage done to the civilian population of the Allies and their property by the aggression of Germany by land, by sea, or from the air.

In transmitting this draft to the German Government on November 5, Wilson added the information that Marshal Foch had been authorized "by the Government of the United States and the Allied Governments to receive the properly accredited representatives of the German Government, and to communicate to them the terms of an armistice." [17]

The motives which governed Clemenceau's decisions, in the first week of November, on the terms of the armistice and the interpretation of the Fourteen Points, are clearly of supreme importance in evaluating his character and his responsibility. Unfortunately motives are not easy to measure. Before October 30 he and Lloyd George displayed frank and almost contemptuous opposition to the Wilsonian program as a basis for peace. But on the morning of the 30th House held short private interviews with both prime ministers. When the steering committee assembled at 10:30 a new spirit dominated the discussions. Speed had become the order of the day. Lloyd George presented a draft reply to Wilson which embodied the British reservation on freedom of the seas and defined the question of reparations. Clemenceau promptly accepted it and he and Lloyd George then overruled Orlando's doubts and persuaded him to

[17] Harold W. Temperley, ed., *A History of the Peace Conference of Paris*, 6 vols. (London: Henry Froude, Hodder & Stoughton, 1920–1924), I, 458–459. The terms of the armistice which the Germans accepted on November 11 are given on pp. 459–476.

assent likewise. House cabled this draft to Wilson the same day, strongly urging the President to approve it "without alterations," and on October 31 he asked for a free hand in dealing with the negotiations because "It is exceedingly important that nothing be said or done at this time which may in any way halt the armistice. . . ."[18] Yet something did apparently halt the armistice. For this draft, completed and approved October 30, was not *formally* relayed to Washington for transmission to Germany until November 4.

It is possible, of course, that the Allied leaders waited deliberately, wishing to exact a capitulation from Austria before presenting terms to Germany. But if this was the case, why was House so anxious to speed the armistice with Germany on October 30, the day after Austria had flashed out an appeal for a truce? Behind the confused pattern of these crowded days it seems possible to discern the formulation of a triangular bargain, struck between October 29 and October 30, a bargain whereby House compromised on three critical issues in return for the Allies' promise of a speedy agreement which acknowledged the Fourteen Points. After those early morning conferences of October 30, Lloyd George, Clemenceau, and House each had, apparently, the assurance of what each most definitely required: Lloyd George the reservation regarding freedom of the seas, Clemenceau a suitable definition of reparations with occupation of the Rhineland, House the proclamation of an armistice based upon the Fourteen Points and inaugurated by Wilson as chief intermediary. There is no reason to doubt that the assent of Clemenceau and Lloyd George was hastened by their fear of popular criticism if they disavowed the Fourteen Points, and by alarm that the United States might make an independent settlement. But it is a little too ingenuous to suppose that fear alone caused them to accept the Wilsonian program. With Austria and Germany collapsing they could already anticipate a time when Wilson's aid would be less vital. What the British, French, and American spokesmen sought and achieved, therefore, at the close of October, was a temporary diplomatic compromise.

Of the three protagonists in that triangular contest, House, Lloyd George and Clemenceau, Clemenceau yielded least. For he obtained his definition of the reparations clause, and he obtained the march to the Rhine. On these issues, which Lloyd George had opposed, the stand which House took was decisive, and House elected to throw his support

[18] *Intimate Papers of Colonel House*, IV, 174.

to the French. It is regrettable that no minutes exist for the conversation which Clemenceau held with House on the morning of October 30.

> That conversation (Mordacq recorded) had a considerable influence on the later decisions, for the President (i.e. Clemenceau), fortified by the latest recommendations of Pershing and Bliss, succeeded in convincing his interlocutor. After the arrival of Mr. Lloyd George, when the discussions were resumed, the head of the French government, sustained this time by Colonel House, ended by obtaining the consent of the British delegate for the occupation of the Left Bank of the Rhine and the bridgeheads on the Right Bank.[19]

Perhaps Clemenceau was not alone in finding the stiffened attitude of Pershing and Bliss a diplomatic asset. The same afternoon House accepted from Pershing a written statement of the latter's arguments for continuing the war until Germany was brought to unconditional surrender. This memorandum of the American commander was furnished at such a convenient moment one cannot but wonder whether military considerations alone induced Pershing to prepare it. For it provided House with a plausible justification in yielding up the Left Bank to Allied occupation, the justification that, in military opinion, the German capacity for resistance was still serious and formidable guarantees must be exacted before terms were granted.

Of House's loyalty to Wilson and his ideals there can be no question. But he realized the urgency of incorporating the Fourteen Points into the peace terms before the rapid disintegration of Austro-German resistance left France and Britain free to dictate their own settlement. It is possible, too, that House evaluated more shrewdly than his chief the opposition arising in the United States against the president's policies. The Texan diplomat was sensitive to the drift of opinion, national and international, and to the importance of seizing the appropriate hour to force a decision. His desire for haste at Paris may have been inspired in part by the hope that news of a Wilsonian peace, if it reached America in time, would help the Democrats at the elections; but he may also have reasoned that Republican gains would weaken Wilson's prestige, and consequently his program, in Europe. When the electoral verdict of November 5 turned both houses of Congress against Wilson, statesmen as shrewd as Clemenceau and Lloyd George saw his role decline and lost some of their deference for his opinions. Or if they failed to read the signs clearly, ex-President Roosevelt enlightened them a few weeks later with his startling

[19] Jean Jules Henri Mordacq, *Le Ministère Clemenceau*, 4 vols. (Paris: Plon, 1930–1931), II, 297–298.

public announcement that "Our Allies and our enemies and Mr. Wilson himself should all understand that Mr. Wilson has no authority to speak for the American people at this time."[20]

On this same November 5, while the American voters foreshadowed at the polls their subsequent disavowal of their war president, Clemenceau enjoyed his brief hour of triumph before the French Chamber of Deputies. After reading the terms of the armistice imposed upon Austria, he promised that the capitulation of Germany would soon follow. Then his gaze passed over the heads of the cheering deputies and sought more distant scenes. He recalled another historic session. "I am the last survivor," he announced suddenly, "of those who signed the protest against the mutilation of Alsace-Lorraine." The cheers rose again, while he peered across the avenging years. He saw the buttes of Montmartre, and the flashes of the Prussian guns beyond Aubervilliers, as he had seen them in 1871. He saw the mob dancing obscenely about the bodies of General Lecomte and General Thomas in the rue des Rosiers. His voice rose again in a plea for genuine unity. "We must have national solidarity," he urged, and the Chamber grew silent while the great recalcitrant pleaded for harmony.

> We wished for the Republic and we have the Republic. We established it in peace and we have defended it in war, and it has redeemed us through conflict. . . . Let us remain united. And now let me say this: truly, it is good to be a humanitarian. But one must be a Frenchman first of all. . . . At the close of this great crusade, modifying a little the phrase of our ancestors, we will swear to be brothers in the true sense of the word. And we will swear that, if we are asked what inspired us to this ideal, we will answer France wills it! France wills it![21]

As *Père la Victoire* Clemenceau suddenly found himself the most famous, the most popular, the most adulated man in France. Telegrams of congratulation arrived by the basket load. Letters with royal crests, and letters, half-illiterate, from obscure villages, strove to inform him that France and the world would never forget what his vision, his energy, his courage had brought to faint hearts in their hour of despair. Honors were piled upon him, election to the Academy of Medicine, election to the French Academy, tributes and decorations from all the Allied governments. Greatness, like genius, is not a quality easy to define and Clemenceau's place in the halls of fame must await the verdict of history. But one great contemporary has already rendered his judgment. "Foch's rank

[20] *Intimate Papers of Colonel House*, IV, 151.

[21] *Journal Officiel: Chambre des Députés: Débats*, Session of November 5, 1918, pp. 2877–2878.

among the world's great generals may be disputed," Winston Churchill has conceded, "but it is already certain that Clemenceau was one of the World's great men." [22]

On November 7, 1918, the project of a new law was submitted to the French Senate.

> Art. 1er — Les armées et leurs chefs;
> Le Gouvernement de la République
> Le citoyen Georges Clemenceau, président du conseil, ministre de la guerre;
> Le maréchal Foch, généralissime des armées alliées;
> Ont bien mérité de la patrie.
>
> Art. 2me — Le texte de la présente loi sera gravé pour demeurer permanent dans toutes les mairies et dans toutes les écoles de la République.

The project was adopted unanimously.[23]

[22] Winston S. Churchill, *Great Contemporaries* (New York: Putnam's Sons, 1937), p. 264.
[23] *Journal Officiel: Sénat: Débats*, Session of November 7, 1918, p. 726.

CHAPTER XIV

THE PROVISIONAL PEACE

November, 1918–June, 1919

Toute l'histoire de l'homme est dans la fondamentale contradiction entre ce qu'il se propose et ce qu'il réalise.[1] CLEMENCEAU

THE sudden cessation of fighting in November, 1918, caught all the belligerents unprepared for peace. The Allies had been hoping for victory in 1919 and counting upon it by 1920. To reduce to order the momentous issues created by the revolution in Russia, the dissolution of Austria-Hungary, and the collapse of Germany, and to do so at such precipitate notice, was a task beyond the scope of existing diplomatic machinery and beyond the skill of the statesmen in power. They have been criticized for allowing two months to pass before the peace conference assembled. But some of them were clear-headed enough to recognize (as Bismarck had realized in 1871) that nations which have foundered in defeat and revolution must establish at least provisional governments before they can negotiate treaties. A period of cooling off and settling down was indispensable, for half Europe was in a state of political, economic and institutional chaos. New administrations and borders had to be laid out for the reconstituted states, old and nascent. Everything was fluid, tentative, provisory. The peace-makers of 1919 were like workmen commanded to build a tower before the bricks were baked, to consecrate with permanent diplomatic formulas a political map still unstable as the churned up Flanders mud.

Undoubtedly more adequate preparations might have been made for the organization of peace. Clemenceau's extreme tension and irritability during October and November, 1918, were an unwitting confession that events were crowding him, events which he had not foreseen promptly nor studied sufficiently in advance. All his time, thought and energy for a year had been concentrated on waging war. When questioned regarding his plans for the post-war period he had invariably replied that his duty

[1] Georges Clemenceau, *La Leçon de la Russie* (Paris: H. Floury, 1915), p. 65.

was to fight until victory was assured; he would meet the problems of peace when peace arrived. This answer had been dictated in part by a sensible desire to evade distracting arguments and premature commitments. But in diplomacy such empirical statesmanship has its defects, and he was sometimes forced to retrieve by dynamic drives positions which he might have occupied in advance by farsighted strategy. He well knew that democracies were often weak in long range planning because of a lack of continuity in policies and personnel, and this knowledge should have spurred him to appoint a group of experts to study post-war problems, and to appoint them when he first came to power in November, 1917.

His first reaction, when peace dawned upon a startled world, was the reaction of a politician. He sought to concentrate his authority and orient his reserves to meet a new crisis which might threaten his ministry. His fight, as always, would have to be waged on two fronts: against all opponents in the Chamber and the nation striving to embarrass and overthrow him, and against all diplomats, belligerent, neutral or Allied, seeking to advance their own national interests at the expense of France.

November 12, the day after the armistice was signed, he devoted exclusively to conferences with his cabinet members and his *aides*, outlining the preparations which must be completed before the peace conference assembled. To André Tardieu, in whose judgment, skill and organizing ability he had great faith, he entrusted the task of coördinating the committees already at work, under the historian Ernest Lavisse and the senator Jean Morel, on problems arising from the war. Lavisse and Morel had encouraged investigation and collected data on geographical, economic, political, historical and ethnical details which might confront the makers of a new Europe, but the labor of their committees had remained somewhat academic. In two weeks Tardieu had given a unified direction to the work, and stimulated the interchange of views and information with similar groups in Great Britain and the United States. As the conference was to meet in France and the French delegates would act somewhat in the role of hosts and organizers, Clemenceau instructed Tardieu to prepare the agenda and draw up a plan of procedure for the expected deliberations. A draft of this program, despatched to Washington, was presented to President Wilson for his criticism on November 29. To secure British approval and collaboration Clemenceau undertook a mission to London on November 30.

This French memorandum, the only logical attempt made to organize the labor of the conference in advance, sought to separate theoretical from practical problems and to prescribe a mode of procedure which would dispose of the primary and concrete issues first. It proposed (1) a timetable for general assent, with the major problems listed in the order in which they might be resolved, and it advocated (2) a preliminary treaty with Germany, and (3) a subsequent congress at which all countries, the victors, the vanquished, the new states and the neutrals, would all be represented. The Fourteen Points, as principles of public law rather than practical formulas for concrete issues, were to be relegated to later discussion. But in deference to their initial clause, prescribing open covenants openly arrived at, the French project suggested, as a preliminary step, the cancellation of all secret treaties. The cool and logical tone of the whole document nettled Wilson and he declined to approve or even to acknowledge it.[2] At London the program fared no better. If, as seems probable, Clemenceau discussed it with Lloyd George and Orlando on December 2, no agreement resulted, and the clause regarding the annulment of secret treaties may help to explain the sudden sharp antagonism towards France displayed by the Italians. This general rejection of the memorandum discouraged Clemenceau and he largely abandoned the hope of achieving any acceptable blueprint upon which the coming conference could base its deliberations.

He returned to Paris hoping against his convictions that the arrival of Wilson might help to crystallize the problems of peacemaking. Public opinion, when the armistice was renewed on December 10, was already growing querulous at the lack of progress. So far all that the diplomats had achieved was a decision to hold an Inter-Allied Conference to draft preliminaries of peace before the general congress assembled. Whatever hopes Clemenceau nursed that he and Wilson might join forces to break the deadlock and speed the discussions vanished with their first interview. Wilson's peculiar blend of vagueness and dogmatism precluded any real meeting of minds between men of such dissimilar mental quality. After a second conference Clemenceau fully appreciated the central role which the idea of a League of Nations had come to play in Wilson's thought and the deep and sincere faith he reposed in the principles which he had enunciated. With such a man it would not be easy to work out compromises or even to debate with the conviction that a mutual agreement was

[2] Harold Nicolson, *Peacemaking, 1919* (Boston: Houghton Mifflin, 1933), pp. 102, 113, 146–147. The draft of the French memorandum may be found in Ray Stannard Baker, *Woodrow Wilson and World Settlement*, 3 vols. (Garden City: Doubleday Page, 1922–1923), III, 55–63.

obtainable. "During the hour and a half we were together," House wrote in his diary after the second meeting, "the President did nearly all the talking. . . . Clemenceau expressed himself, in a mild way, in agreement with the President. He thought a League of Nations should be attempted, but he was not confident of success, either of forming it, or of its being workable after it was formed. . . ." [3]

So Wilson left to visit England and Italy, feted everywhere by the populace as the prophet of a new world order, while Clemenceau sought a mandate from the French parliament, explaining frankly the kind of treaty he would attempt to make if he represented France at the making of it. The pre-war system of alliances, national armaments, and a balance of power had fallen into disfavor for the moment, he admitted readily. But it had been the system pursued by European statesmen for centuries and no alternative plan had yet been made to work. For himself, he could not pretend to put his faith in any substitute so far proposed. He did not share Wilson's admirable faith in the efficacy of a League of Nations to preserve peace. "M. Wilson," he announced, choosing his words slowly and carefully, "did me the honor of visiting me. I had made a resolution not to cross-question him, but to let him develop his ideas and express them freely and spontaneously. . . . He is a man who inspires respect by the simplicity of his words and the noble ingenuousness of his spirit." [4] As *candeur* in French carries the implication of simple-mindedness as well as frankness some of the Socialist deputies protested against what they took to be a slight on Wilson's intelligence. But the Chamber as a whole appreciated Clemenceau's reasoning and shared his attitude. The deputies voted their confidence in his ability to conduct the peace negotiations by a vote of 398 to 93.

To maintain that Clemenceau at this stage pretended a hypocritical reverence for the Fourteen Points, while plotting a vindictive peace behind the façade of Wilsonian idealism, is untenable in the face of the record. Clemenceau did not pretend to House, to Wilson, or to the French Chamber of Deputies that he believed in the League as a prudent or practical resolution for the problem of national defense, or that he and Wilson saw matters from the same point of view or even from reconcilable points of view. "Though Clemenceau pins his faith on a System of Alliances, and Wilson places his in a League of Nations, they are in reality

[3] *Intimate Papers of Colonel House Arranged as a Narrative by Charles Seymour*, 4 vols. (Boston: Houghton Mifflin, 1926–1928), IV, 253.

[4] *Journal Officiel: Chambre des Députés: Débats*, Session of December 29, 1918, p. 3783.

the same," the *Temps* affirmed, on January 1, 1919, seeking to gloss over the conflict of ideas which Clemenceau had honestly defined. But other French journals were less hypocritical, admitting frankly that "The policies of reality and idealism are at grips."[5] House has testified to Clemenceau's undisguised honesty in expressing his convictions. "He came at problems by direct attack, there was no indirection. There he stood almost alone among the old-line diplomats and some of the fledglings, also, who sought to imitate them. His courage was too unyielding to permit of dissimulation. He was afraid of nothing, present or to come, and least of all of mere man."[6]

The vote of confidence which the Chamber passed on December 29 Clemenceau read as a mandate to make peace as seemed to him best with the aid of such men as he selected to work with him. Suggestions that he reconstruct his cabinet to meet the peace offensive influenced him not at all; he assumed the major tasks himself and prepared to preside at the Inter-Allied Conference as he had presided at the Supreme War Council. France was entitled to five delegates, and he might well have honored (and conciliated) some of his great political rivals by appointing them as plenipotentiaries: Briand, who had headed five cabinets, Ribot, patriot and war premier second only to Clemenceau himself in energy, Léon Bourgeois, who had represented France at two Hague Conferences. But he preferred to choose lesser men, Stephen Pichon, his Minister for Foreign Affairs, Louis-Lucien Klotz, his Minister of Finance, André Tardieu, War Commission head who had served so effectively at Washington, and Jules Cambon, ex-ambassador to Berlin. He wished to have subordinates to assist him with whom he could work; he wanted no undue independence, division or intrigue within his entourage while he coped with the idealism of Wilson and the wiles of Lloyd George. His popularity in France was for the moment so great that he could afford to defy the hints from the Chambers; but he would have, and did, affront them in the same defiant spirit when his popularity had waned.

But the pride, the obstinacy, the stoicism which armed him against external attacks provided no sure defense against his own self-disparagement. The honors heaped upon him at the close of 1918 brought him no elation; they were as exaggerated and undeserved, he declared wryly, as the calumnies more frequently launched at his head. Now that he could no longer

[5] George Bernard Noble, *Policies and Opinions at Paris, 1919* (New York: Macmillan, 1935), pp. 90–91.

[6] *Intimate Papers of Colonel House*, IV, 191.

recharge his energies, phoenix-like, in the sacrificial fires of the battle front, he found the poisoned air of Paris more stale and exhausting than ever. The trip to London at the opening of December fatigued him; the sessions with Wilson, ghostly wrestling in a rarefied, hypnotic atmosphere, left him with a sense of mental frustration; the duel with the parliament tasked his patience and diplomacy. On December 31 he slipped away from Paris almost furtively for a week in his Vendéean cottage. In all his ardent life he had never known an emotion more sincere and single-hearted than the quest for solitude. Alone with his thoughts and his books, with the sound of the surf at night, and the cold, wet winds sweeping in from the Bay of Biscay, he found his mind washed free of foolishness and new strength flowing through his frame. Leaving Paris on that first New Year's Eve of the peace, he had confessed to Mordacq that the desire was strongly upon him to flee to some other continent. Like Danton he knew hours of misanthropy when he was "sick of the human race." But this favored spot in the Vendée, which always seemed to him anew like the end of the world, restored his spirits, and he returned to his responsibilities refreshed and reinvigorated.

The Inter-Allied Conference was almost ready to assemble. History has chosen to forget that this assembly of the Allied and Associated Powers was intended to be a preliminary conference which would prepare the agenda for an international world congress. When the preliminary conference imperceptibly evolved into the "Peace Conference" the absence of neutral and enemy delegates was recognized as an advantage: it simplified decisions. But the limited and provisory character of the early sessions must be kept in mind if the work is to be judged fairly, for this provisory mood permitted many important issues to be settled as it were by default. The ruthless executive temper of the Supreme War Council survived and colored the sessions of the Council of Ten, which became, under Clemenceau's driving presidency, the "cabinet" of the Peace Conference. The lesser delegates formed a sort of impotent legislature which met only six times to discharge the formalities of a plenary session. No ten statesmen, however sincere and hardworking, could have reached decisions which would have solved the world's problems in the winter of 1918–1919. The harsh judgments passed on the Versailles Treaty have too often been urged by critics who fail to appreciate that the obstacles to a just settlement of international problems were as real in 1919 as they had been in 1914; that the war, which had excited such ardent idealism in millions of hearts, had also intensified old rivalries and created new hatreds; and that no arrangement which emerged from the intellectual tug-of-war that was the Paris Conference could have been wholly judicious or impartial. The "Big Four," Clemenceau, Lloyd George, Wilson and Orlando, were not judges handing down a verdict, they were politicians seeking a lowest common multiple for discordant factors, factors which sometimes changed their values almost as fast as formulas could be found for them.

From the second week of January to the end of March the key committee of the conference was the Council of Ten. This body was composed of Clemenceau and Pichon, Lloyd George and Balfour, Orlando and Sonnino, Wilson and Lansing, and Saionji and Makino, that is, the leading representative and the foreign minister of France, Britain, Italy, the United States and Japan. The spirit and direction of the meetings owed much to Clemenceau's initiative. The order of business, in general, was prepared by the French Foreign Office, and the secretarial staff, the leading members of which were M. Dutasta and M. Paul Mantoux, was largely French. But much of the actual labor was left to the various committees, sub-committees, and commissions, fifty-eight in all, and experts were available whenever testimony was needed on any point of debate. "The trouble about the Paris Conference," Harold Nicolson has pointed out, "was not that there was too little information but that there was too much. The fault was not lack of preparation but lack of coördination. It was the latter fault which vitiated the whole system from the start."[7] Clemenceau's efforts to fix upon and dispose of concrete issues first could not prevail in face of the essential dichotomy dominating a situation in which "the policies of realism and idealism were at grips." The demands of France, of Italy, of Britain, could not be met without violating Wilson's principles, and the strain to effect a compromise wearied the protagonists. In comparison with this obstructive conflict, the opposition of the lesser powers, the voice of public opinion, the resentment of the vanquished were feeble impediments. When the second Plenary Session, held January 25, criticized the Council of Ten for its secrecy, its independence and irresponsibility, Clemenceau scolded the delegates as if they had been the French Chamber of Deputies.

> Experience has proved to me that the more numerous committees are the less they are likely to accomplish. But, back of us, there is something very great, very imposing, and at times very imperious, something which is called public opinion. It will not enquire of us whether this or that state was represented on such and such a

[7] Nicolson, *Peacemaking, 1919*, p. 25.

committee. That does not interest anyone. It will ask us what we have accomplished. . . . My business is to direct the work so that we may get things finished.[8]

Unfortunately it proved impossible to get things finished although the Council of Ten met morning and afternoon week after week. Each question that emerged seemed beset with thorns; reparations, the Rhineland, the Saar, Fiume and the Trentino, the Syrian mandate, the Polish Corridor, the reorganization of Russia, the Japanese claim to Shantung. When some recommendation was submitted to the Council of Ten, debated, and not categorically opposed, Clemenceau, to speed things up, would rasp "Objections? . . . Adopté!" and another item would be struck off the agenda, dismissed as a rule in a few paragraphs prepared and submitted by one of the special committees. But the major problems which involved a clash of principles, the fate of the Rhineland, the Italian claims, the reparations controversy, consumed endless hours without result.

Some of the difficulties raised by the French, British and Italians were undoubtedly developed as bargaining points, objections which could be abandoned to advantage at the tactical moment. Wilson, however, had little to surrender except his principles, and as the days passed his opposition grew more irritating, his definitions more doctrinaire. As the American president planned to return to Washington for the opening of Congress, Clemenceau hoped for speedier progress with Lansing or House substituting for him. On February 14 he watched the presidential train depart from the Gare des Invalides with the feeling that one obstacle had been temporarily cleared from his laborious path.

The nemesis of delay was not to be so easily exorcized. On February 19, as he was leaving the rue Franklin in his car, Clemenceau saw a youth, who had haunted the neighborhood for several days, rush forward with a levelled revolver. The chauffeur speeded up the automobile, but shot after shot struck the vehicle as if careened down the street and a sudden agonizing pain in his back warned Clemenceau that he had been hit. The assailant had been seized; the car was turned around; and a few minutes later he was back in his home, stretched on the couch.

The doctors discovered that one of the bullets fired by the unbalanced youth had lodged in the shoulder and they confined their august patient to bed with strict orders against moving or talking. But nothing which failed to cripple him completely (the only fate which he genuinely feared) could chain Clemenceau's energies. The attempt at assassination restored

[8] Jean Jules Henri Mordacq, *Le Ministère Clemenceau*, 4 vols. (Paris: Plon, 1930–1931), III, 105.

some of the piquancy which life had lacked of late and he carried on his duties by dictation and telephone, with Sister Théoneste vigilant at his bedside to warn him against over-exertion. Within a week he astonished the world and his colleagues by reappearing at the ministry and the Council of Ten, sarcastic and combative as ever.

While leisure permitted he had studied the draft Covenant of the League of Nations, prepared by the League committee under the guidance of Wilson. More firmly than ever he felt convinced that it would assure 39,000,000 Frenchmen no adequate or permanent protection against 65,000,000 Germans. Foch was insisting upon a "soldier's peace" with French control of the Rhine, Poincaré, almost equally intransigent, pressed Clemenceau to work harder for reparations and guarantees. Wilson, after fighting a growing spirit of criticism and hostility in the United States, was soon on his way back to Paris, determined to see a treaty concluded as speedily as possible, a treaty which would incorporate the League Covenant and create the League itself. For the League, its advocates believed, would serve as a rectifying instrument, and whatever remained incomplete or defective in the work of the Peace Conference could be adjusted in the later League sessions.

Out of this blend of international idealism, national greed, and hard-headed political bargaining, Clemenceau was pledged to extract terms for France which would satisfy the parliamentary critics. March and April would be months of major decisions and he was determined that those decisions should embody sane and adequate guarantees for French security. With the return of Wilson on March 14 the *combat des trois* entered its final act. The Council of Ten, to promote greater speed in deliberation, was reduced to the Council of Four, then, with Orlando's departure in April, to the "Big Three." At session after session Clemenceau, Wilson and Lloyd George discussed the French demands, Clemenceau reiterating them, now with jets of eloquence, now with phlegmatic insistence. Fortified with facts, statistics and memoranda drafted by Tardieu and other *aides* he waged his battle for France, convinced that the only sure guarantee against a new German attack was to keep Germany weak and disarmed and France strong and vigilant. As a substitute for occupation of the Left Bank of the Rhine and the bridgeheads on the Right Bank, Lloyd George and Wilson finally suggested a formal treaty of alliance, whereby Great Britain and the United States would promise to come to the aid of the French if they suffered unprovoked aggression. This proposal Clemenceau accepted with thanks, but as an additional guarantee, not as a substitute for occupation. But the separation of the Rhineland from Germany, and its subordination to French control, Wilson and Lloyd George could not approve. Such a disposal, they clearly foresaw, would create a new Alsace-Lorraine. They agreed, however, to reduce Germany to impotence: to limit her army to 100,000 men, to demilitarize the Left Bank of the Rhine and extend the zone fifty kilometers beyond the Right Bank, to forbid her an air force and to keep her under strict international surveillance.

On March 31 Marshal Foch was invited to offer his views. He insisted dogmatically that permanent occupation of the Left Bank would be indispensable to French security. Without that, "no disarmament, no written clause of any kind, can prevent Germany from seizing the Rhine and debouching from it at an advantage. . . . The Rhine remains today the barrier essential to the safety of the peoples of Western Europe, and therefore of civilization."[9] Foch's insistence failed to convince Wilson or Lloyd George who had heard these arguments so often that they were weary of them. Even Henry White, former American ambassador at Paris, member of the peace commission, and a sincere friend of France, had lost patience with the uncompromising French attitude. "It is impossible," he wrote from Paris on March 19, "to comprehend the extraordinary obsession felt in this country lest Germany within the next few years repeat the actions which she took in 1914."[10] As spokesman of the French people, Clemenceau had become a Cassandra, dowered with a desperate foresight, but mocked by his more complacent allies.

The need to produce a treaty of some sort had become imperative. Yet the treaty makers were still unsure what status they should assume or how definite or permanent their decisions would prove to be. "It is to be remembered that we are not holding a Peace Conference at present," House had written Wilson as late as March 4, "but merely a conference of the Allies and ourselves for the purpose of agreeing upon terms to offer Germany at the Peace Conference to be held later."[11] But Wilson, on his return to Paris ten days later, advocated a prompt settlement which would not only establish peace with Germany but with Austria-Hungary and Bulgaria also, and include the Covenant of the League. The suspicion arises that the peacemakers sometimes chose to style their work provisory

[9] André Tardieu, *The Truth about the Treaty* (Indianapolis: Bobbs-Merrill Co., 1921), p. 185.

[10] Allan Nevins, *Henry White, Thirty Years of American Diplomacy* (New York: Harper, 1930), p. 411.

[11] *Intimate Papers of Colonel House*, IV, 356.

to soften their sense of responsibility for the flaws and compromises which it contained. The thought that the final appeal would rest with a Peace Conference which would assemble later — the Peace Conference, or rather Congress which was never called — freed them from the overwhelming burden of irrevocable decisions.

Certainly Clemenceau, apprehensive that there might be a softening of the terms at a subsequent date, steeled himself to fight for the maximum advantages at the outset, experience warning him that some at least of the guarantees would fail. His demand for the Rhine frontier remained proof against all argument, even against Wilson's threat, April 2, to return to the United States. The following week when Wilson, ill with influenza, was absent from the Council sessions, he worked upon House who took the president's place. By April 22 he had wrung from his colleagues the maximum concessions which they would yield. Without loss of time the terms were written into the draft of the almost completed treaty and preparations made to summon German delegates that the defeated nation might receive its sentence.

For fifteen years inter-Allied troops were to occupy the Left Bank and bridgeheads of the Rhine, retiring by zones every five years, provided the Germans fulfilled the stipulations of the treaty. For the additional security of France, Great Britain and the United States were to guarantee the republic against an attack by Germany. So far as it was possible to formulate a policy of security on paper Clemenceau had done so, for Articles 429–432 of the Treaty further provided that the period of occupation might be indefinitely prolonged, or renewed, if at any time the precautions against aggression by Germany were deemed insufficient, or if Germany failed to fulfill all undertakings including the payment of reparations. As the amount of the reparations bill had not been fixed, and estimates ranging from 150 to 200 billion dollars had been mentioned, this clause promised France an excuse for prolonged occupation. Furthermore, in the Saar Valley with its valuable coal mines, German sovereignty was to be "suspended" for fifteen years, at the end of which the inhabitants were to decide by ballot what political status they would permanently elect. The mines were assigned to France as compensation for French mines damaged or destroyed by the Germans during their occupation of French territory.

The *combat des trois* had reached its finale. No one was wholly satisfied and no one was wholly happy at the solutions which had been worked out. To ardent and anxious French nationalists, obsessed with the thought of the sacrifices in men and material which France had made in four years of war, the provisions that Clemenceau had extorted seemed desperately inadequate. The feeling deepened in France that Germany was likely to get off too lightly and forget her crimes too soon; that it had been a mistake to make an armistice and the peace should have been dictated in Berlin. On March 17, when the Council of Four had asked Foch to notify the Armistice Committee that German plenipotentiaries should appear before the Council by March 25, Foch refused to transmit the order. He was convinced that the fifteen-year time limit set for the occupation of the Left Bank was a betrayal of France and he did not conceal his opinion from the press. For Clemenceau the situation might have proved embarrassing, as Foch's insubordination and the mood which inspired it, spreading through military and political circles, provided a threat the government could not safely ignore. A careful censorship of the journals stifled the news of Foch's protest; Clemenceau forwarded the notice for the German delegation by another channel; and the Council of Four tactfully ignored the *contretemps* created by the attitude of the generalissimo. Few foreigners comprehended that victorious France could be threatened by an internal conflict between the civil and military powers, or appreciated the unremitting campaign which Clemenceau waged behind the scenes to retain his ascendency throughout these fretful months. One of these few was the former American ambassador, Henry White. Like Colonel House, White recognized that Clemenceau "despite his hatred of Germany and whole-souled devotion to France's interests alone, was essentially far more moderate than Foch or Poincaré." [12]

Nor were the extreme nationalists and militarists the only powerful and organized groups in France pressing Clemenceau to garner more substantial penalties from a powerless foe. As early as 1917 the *Comité des Forges*, the great French metallurgical combine, had urged the government to recognize that economic security and the promotion of heavy industry within the nation demanded:

> The re-annexation of Alsace-Lorraine
> The annexation of the Saar
> A free hand for France on the Rhine
> A free supply for France of German coal

Though himself no student of economics Clemenceau could easily obtain private information on French war needs in the economic field. His

[12] Nevins, *Henry White*, pp. 388–389.

brother Paul was a director of the *Société Centrale de Dynamite* and an administrator of the *Société pour la Fabrication des Munitions d'Artillerie*. His acquaintanceship with Basil Zaharoff, moreover, was sufficiently close that he could obtain the expert opinion of the munitions king when he desired it. These connections do not prove, as some Socialist critics have hinted, that Clemenceau in 1919 was a tool of French industrial concerns. But believing as he did that peace is but war pursued in a more orderly manner, and aware of the vital role which the heavy industries would continue to play in national defense, it was logical for him to augment the resources of the *Comité des Forges* as an indispensable article in the program of guarantees.

So jealously did the peacemakers guard the secret of their labors the lesser powers did not learn the terms of the completed draft until May. On the 7th of that month the German delegation was summoned to a plenary session of the Peace Conference to receive the treaty dictated by the victors. The representatives of the twenty-seven Allied and Associated Powers had assembled in the Trianon Palace Hotel, and the German plenipotentiaries were escorted into the hall and seated at a table directly facing Clemenceau. At his right sat Wilson and Lansing, at his left, Lloyd George and Bonar Law. As President of the Conference he set the tone of the proceedings and he conducted them as if he were presiding over a legal tribunal. His curt opening sentences sounded like the voice of doom to the representatives of the vanquished nation.

> This is neither the time nor the place for superfluous words. You have before you the accredited plenipotentiaries of the great and lesser Powers, both Allied and Associated, that for four years have carried on without respite the merciless war which has been imposed upon them. The time has now come for a heavy reckoning of the accounts. You have asked for peace. We are prepared to offer you peace.

Clemenceau then explained, in the same brusque and staccato sentences, that the Germans would be granted fifteen days to study the terms and submit any observations. The Supreme Council would reply, likewise in writing, and decide the length of time during which the discussion might continue.

In replying to Clemenceau's cold harangue Brockdorff-Rantzau committed the *faux pas* of remaining seated, inspired to this discourtesy by resentment at the formal atmosphere and his half-expectation to hear a sergeant-at-arms rasp out "The defendant will rise." His attitude and his reply were severely criticized in the Allied press.

> Gentlemen [he began], we are deeply impressed with the great mission which has brought us here to give to the world forthwith a lasting peace. We are under no illusions as to the extent of our defeat and the degree of our powerlessness. We know that the strength of the German arm is broken. We know the intensity of the hatred which meets us, and we have heard the victor's passionate demand that as the vanquished we shall be made to pay, and as the guilty we shall be punished.
>
> The demand is made that we shall acknowledge that we alone are guilty of having caused the war. Such a confession in my mouth would be a lie. . . .
>
> The measure of guilt of all those who have taken part can be established only by an impartial enquiry, a neutral commission before which all the principals in the tragedy are allowed to speak, and to which all archives are open. We have asked for such an enquiry and we ask for it once more. . . .
>
> A peace which cannot be defended before the world as a peace of justice would always evoke new resistance. No one could sign it with a clear conscience, for it could not be carried out. No one could venture to guarantee its execution, though this obligation is implied in the signing of the treaty.[13]

When Brockdorff-Rantzau ceased to speak, Clemenceau closed the session with his usual peremptory formula. "Has anyone any more observations to offer? Does no one wish to speak? If not, the meeting is closed."

The manner in which the treaty was presented to them, no less than the terms of the document itself, stamped indelibly on the mind of the German people the conviction that they had been duped into an armistice by fair promises and then compelled to accept a treaty which violated those promises. Their disarmed condition, and the maintenance of the blockade, helped to intensify this impression. It is true that as late as April Clemenceau, Wilson and Lloyd George had still debated whether to give Germany a dictated peace or to permit discussion and possible modification of the terms. Like the other compromises, their decision on this point was ambiguous. For in permitting the Germans two weeks to submit objections, and softening the territorial clauses to a small extent (a plebiscite in Upper Silesia, concessions in the area of Bromberg) the Allies justified in their own opinion their agument that the treaty was not a *Diktat* but an agreement. The opposition which the terms aroused in Germany, the consequent delay in the negotiations, and the uncertainty whether the German government would yield and sign, stimulated anew

[13] Alma Luckau, *The German Delegation at the Paris Peace Conference* (New York: Columbia University Press, 1941), pp. 220–223. For a comparative account of the session which provides slight variants in the wording of Clemenceau's address and Brockdorff-Rantzau's reply, see David Hunter Miller, *My Diary at the Conference of Paris, with Documents,* 21 vols. and atlas (New York: Printed for the Author by the Appeal Printing Co., 1924), IX, 297–301.

the fear and hatred still felt for the Germans, and the people of the Allied countries were convinced by this new display of German resistance that the terms were in no wise too severe for a treacherous foe. As President of the Conference Clemenceau carried on the correspondence which constituted the only formal attempt made by the Allies to adjust and mediate the opposing views of the conquerors and the conquered. His spirit remained unyielding; his communications grew more curt and imperative in tone as the weeks passed; and the deadline for acceptance found him fully prepared to order the French armies into Germany. By the end of June the tense contest was over. The German delegates appeared, were escorted to Versailles, and there, in the Galerie des Glaces where the German Empire had been proclaimed forty-eight years earlier, the representatives of the Third Reich acknowledged the guilt, the penalties decreed, and the probationary status of their country.

"The affair," Colonel House confided to his diary, "was elaborately staged and made as humiliating to the enemy as it well could be."[14] Lloyd George, too, felt that the vindictive procedure might have been softened by some element of chivalry, but his tentative efforts to spare the fallen had been discouraged by a powerful section of the British Parliament as well as by Clemenceau's tenacious tactics. What Clemenceau himself thought, as he left the palace of Louis XIV amid the booming of cannon to watch the fountains play in the gardens which Le Nôtre designed for the Sun King, no one can guess. He was answering congratulations with affable phrases, but there was no elation in the deep-sunk eyes of that yellowed Mongolian face. It is probable his busy brain was already coining phrases with which to defend before the Chambers his failure to obtain more adequate guarantees for the security of France.

The German estimate of the treaty, then and later, was to change little. Walter Simon, one of the calmest and most judicious of the German delegates, formulated that estimate after reading the first draft of the terms.

> The treaty which our enemies have laid before us is, so far as the French dictated it, a monument of pathological fear and pathological hatred, and in so far as the Anglo-Saxons dictated it, it is the work of a capitalist policy of the cleverest and most brutal kind. Its shamelessness does not lie in treading down a brave opponent, but in the fact that from beginning to end all these humiliating conditions are made to look like a just punishment, while in truth there is in them neither shame, nor any respect for the concept of justice.[15]

[14] *Intimate Papers of Colonel House*, IV, 487.

[15] Luckau, *The German Delegation at the Paris Peace Conference*, p. 71.

To post-war critics the architects of the Versailles Treaty appeared to be bunglers even as most of the generals had proved to be bunglers: they failed to recognize and to capitalize upon a unique opportunity. But whereas in war it was recognized that the resources entrusted to a military leader, and the chance offered him to wage a glorious and decisive campaign, might be negated by the equal and opposite intelligence and strength of the enemy, in 1919 the popular illusion reigned that at the peace conference the extraordinary powers entrusted to the plenipotentiaries could somehow be pooled for the collective benefit of mankind. This ideal vision of a new and harmonious international economy, this dream of world *solidarité*, was very real to myriads of people in 1919 and Wilson was its prophet. To Clemenceau such hopes were an illusion. He saw no sober chance of establishing a world court or a world society by international fiat. He expected to find, and perhaps for that reason he did find, national rivalries deadlocked about the peace table as inevitably as national rivalries had been deadlocked in the trenches. Every gain, every advantage, had to be purchased at a price, and the profits of victory melted in the hand that clutched them. The world which emerged from the Paris Conference proved to be, as Clemenceau never doubted it would be, the world of 1914, scarred, lame and in bandages, resembling very little and that superficially the brave new world of Wilsonian idealism.

Because he had never doubted that this must be the case, because he refused to acknowledge the possibility of creating a new and better world order, Clemenceau has been denounced as the evil genius who betrayed the great crusade. It would be more charitable and more appropriate to describe him as playing the Sancho Panza to Wilson's Don Quixote. He came to the conference, not as a knight of humanity riding forth to redress all wrong, but as a lawyer comes to a courtroom with a specific brief. His client was France; his assignment, to protect essential French interests, as he understood them, to the limit of his skill. Like most lawyers he had to fight the distrust, impulsiveness, ignorance, vindictiveness and greed of his client as firmly as he fought the cunning and coercion of opposing counsel. And like most lawyers he found his client ungrateful and dissatisfied with the inadequate settlement which he obtained. But that, too, he had anticipated.

CHAPTER XV

THE LIVING LEGEND
1919–1929

Note carefully what I tell you. In six months, a year, five years, ten years, when they wish and as they wish, the Boches will invade us.[1]

CLEMENCEAU (1927)

THE last decade of Clemenceau's life was an epilogue. With the conclusion of peace his ministry lost its *raison d'être* and the gathering forces of opposition prescribed a change. The elections in the autumn of 1919, which divided the Chamber of Deputies between the Bloc National and the Cartel des Gauches, finally destroyed his ascendency, for the Socialists assailed him for his rude repression of strikes and the Right could not pardon his moderate peace policy. *Père la Victoire* had become *Perd la Victoire*, and a febrile and disillusioned nation, convalescing slowly from the fever of war, visited its chagrin upon the physician whose rigorous regimen had carried it through the crisis.

In the circumstances, Clemenceau exposed himself to an added rebuff by allowing his friends to nominate him for the presidency of the Republic. It was the final honor which France might have bestowed upon him, but the honor was withheld. With Poincaré's retirement at the end of his septennate, the National Assembly chose to elect the relatively obscure Paul Deschanel on January 17, 1920. Clemenceau felt the slight keenly as a deliberate revenge plotted by his enemies. He immediately submitted the resignation of his cabinet and took final leave of the Supreme War Council. Lloyd George, seeking to console him for the rebuff he had received, remarked that such ingratitude was a characteristic of politics, and prophesied that the British electorate would no doubt repudiate him shortly in the same manner. But Clemenceau demurred. The British, he insisted, were a sporting race: they might dismiss but they would not humiliate a leader who had served them conscientiously.

[1] Georges Clemenceau, *Le Silence de M. Clemenceau*, ed. by Jean Martet (Paris: A. Michel, 1929), p. 34.

Thrown once again upon his own resources, with leisure for personal pursuits, he chose first of all to visit the ancient East. The impulse which had goaded him a year earlier to flee to other continents could now be gratified, and he made 1920 another *Wanderjahr*. New scenes amused and distracted him; he dined with the military governor of Cairo; shot tigers in Gwalior; watched the burning of the dead by the Ganges; and addressed a missionary school in Singapore. Then, relaxed, rested, delivered from the disgust and resentment which had driven him to leave France, he returned to the Vendée.

"I have passed almost all my life in being impatient," he confessed to the citizens of his birth-place, Mouilleron-en-Pareds. "But in proportion as life wore out I have learned patience. I think I can assure you that henceforth I shall conform to this principle of living."[2] Patience—and industry. For he still had his thoughts and his pen; and although he had sworn to avoid political controversies he had other causes to vindicate. Up at dawn, caressing his roses, or seated on his bench while the grey sea turned golden, he invited his thoughts and forged his phrases. The remainder of the morning found him writing happily, as in the old days; after lunch, served by the faithful Albert, a secretary arrived to gather and type the scattered pages. In the afternoon, as a concession to his craving for movement, he might summon his chauffeur and drive rapidly about the countryside on some manufactured errand or none, returning to browse in his study, stroll in his garden, or talk with visitors. He dined at eight or nine and retired early.

The fruit of these secluded hours, and of others almost equally tranquil spent at Giverny or the rue Franklin, was some of the most thoughtful and carefully constructed prose he had produced. It was not, perhaps, his best prose: some of the color, the glee, the wit and irony had departed, and the turns of thought, the hard outlines of his metaphors, had grown sharper but less substantial, like edges of a familiar landscape at dusk. But it had vigor and clarity and it pointed a moral. The fascination of politics he could not quite forego; it was his breath of life; and he indulged it vicariously, corresponding with André Tardieu and some younger men who organized a new journal, the *Echo National* in 1922. An American publisher offered him a fortune for his memoirs and was promptly shown the door; but the three works which he did complete in this twilight decade, and the fourth published after his death, were all autobiographical in inspiration. The human yearning, in the face of the great silence, to

[2] Georges Suarez, *Clemenceau*, 2 vols. (Paris: Les Éditions de France, 1932), II, 317.

utter some last words of self-vindication, permeated and had always permeated his writing more than the author himself realized.

Thus a casual essay on Demosthenes, inspired by his enthusiasm for classical Greece, developed into a biographical study of the life and influence of the great Athenian orator. Clemenceau felt a spiritual kinship with this elder statesman who gave his life to a defense of liberty, culture and human dignity as he understood them, in opposition to the military tyranny of Macedonia. The classical example furnished a prefigurement of the fate in store for France, for the Athens of the modern world had been depleted of its manhood and defiled by invasion. A new European order, half-spartan and half-Macedonian in spirit, was waiting to destroy the fine flower of Gallic culture because that culture had not known how to preserve and defend itself. "History," Clemenceau prophesied, "will be severe on the French people of the post-war period who have failed in action and in character to rise to the level of their proud duties and responsibilities."[3]

The second monograph which he wrote at this period, dedicated to Claude Monet, was likewise a labor of love. He revered because he understood this stubborn and self-critical painter, and he shared and sought to exorcize Monet's horror at the fear of approaching blindness which haunted his last years. As art criticism Clemenceau's appreciation is not particularly profound, but as a tribute to a deep friendship between two dark and lonely and disharmonic spirits, it remains, together with his letters to Monet, a profoundly sincere and moving document. Both men comprehended and sought to assuage in the other the occasional annihilating moods of failure that visited them. For Monet these hours were filled with a sense of abasement which recalls the "black night of the soul" described by religious mystics. Clemenceau chided and teased him out of them with the patience of an elder brother; his friendship for the painter was one of the most honest and generous emotions he had ever known; and when he followed Monet's body to the grave in December, 1926, a part of himself died also.

Fortunately he had other friends as devoted to him as Monet and more coöperative, among them the upright and unselfish Nicolas Piétri. Without Piétri's assistance it is doubtful whether he could have completed the *chef d'oeuvre* of these final years, the two volume testament of faith which he called *Au Soir de la Pensée*. There, in a thousand pages of compact and vigorous prose, he traced his intellectual autobiography. Some of the

[3] Georges Clemenceau, *Grandeur et misère d'une victoire* (Paris: Plon, 1930), p. 90.

material had been gathered fifteen years earlier when he contemplated his monumental history of democracy. But as reconsidered in these crepuscular years the project became a treatise on life and the universe as it had appeared to Georges Clemenceau, a supreme *apologia* for his activities and his allegiances. "*Au Soir de la Pensée*," he declared, "is for me the end, the ultimate achievement; if I had never written that I should feel myself uncomfortable in eternity."[4]

> What more worthy "examination of conscience" than an "examination of knowledge"? This is the superlative venture, in the widened realm of evolution, of a personality capable of observation and judgment.
>
> The psychological interest of a life is less in the external acts, the motives, the affections, than in the true or false bearings and coördinations.[5]

All his life Clemenceau had hungered after realities. In this cosmography he summarized the wisdom life had brought him, the conclusions reached and tested in hours of tumult and hours of thought, the systematized knowledge sifted and distilled in the alembic of his independent mind. Perhaps the nearest American equivalent to his philosophical survey is *The Education of Henry Adams*. But Adams felt himself an alien in the modern world of positivism where the dynamo was king, while Clemenceau's Faustian spirit rejoiced at the struggle for existence to which all creatures, all faiths and all institutions were condemned. His concept of the cosmos and of man, an epitome of nineteenth-century positivist philosophy synthesized from the conclusions of the physicists, the astronomers and the biologists, satisfied him because he had grown up in such a "climate of opinion." But his presentation of this knowledge, which seemed so profoundly convincing to his generation, lacked originality. *Au Soir de la Pensée* is not simple and lively enough to be a successful popularization, not complete and logical enough to be a text book, not profound or systematic enough to be a philosophy.

For although Clemenceau undoubtedly possessed a superior mind his mental endowment was not matchless or unique; it might have fitted him to become a successful teacher in a *lycée*. What raised him to greatness were his personal qualities, his penetrating frankness, his will power, his force of character. The courage which carried him through a hundred fights, the scorn of odds, the defiance of hypocrisy which drove him to harass the indolent, unmask the incapable, and pillory the corrupt, these made him the most bitterly hated but most salutary polemicist in French

[4] *Le Silence de M. Clemenceau*, ed. by Jean Martet (Paris: A. Michel, 1929), p. 207.

[5] Georges Clemenceau, *Au Soir de la Pensée*, 2 vols. (Paris: Plon, 1927), I, 9.

Keystone View Co. "Photo Choumoff"

Clemenceau, in his eighty-sixth year, working at his famous horseshoe desk in the study of his apartment at No. 8, rue Franklin.

public life. Every society has need of such uncomfortable catalysts to precipitate passive discontent into positive remedial legislation. Clemenceau's career, like that of Napoleon, might be summarized as *une longue impatience*. It is difficult to find a line he wrote or a phrase he uttered which did not have a didactic aim. He was the self-appointed censor of three generations of French politicians.

Challenged to define the program and the principle for which he fought he would have answered Democracy. But his standard of democratic polity was above the level of events; he demanded a society of intelligent, patriotic and responsible citizens inspired by an unfailing civic spirit and unflagging industry. The idealists of the eighteenth century, the visionaries of the French Revolution, had caught a glimpse of such a perfected society; the republicans who conspired to overthrow the Empire of Napoleon III had recaptured that vision; the Third Republic was to have been its fulfillment. But the vision failed. "The consideration, the issue, the essential thing," Charles Péguy had written, "is that, in each order, in each system, the *mystique* shall not be swallowed up by the politics to which it has given birth."[6] Clemenceau had fought to preserve the *mystique*, the vital morale, of the great experiment, but save in a few supreme moments, as the Dreyfus contest or the high points of the war, the noble and unselfish dream had faded among the soiled realities of politics. This was the consummation which, at the last, he brought himself ruefully to acknowledge.

> What angers me about France is that my whole life I have fought for what is called freedom of the press, freedom of speech and so forth. Now it seems to me that all these liberties culminate in the worst sort of slavery, which is degeneration. Before giving the French their liberty it would have been wiser to teach them what liberty is and how to use it properly. I have come to feel that the preparation was not sufficient. . . .[7]

In the same disillusioned spirit he saw the heroic sacrifices of the war as a labor of Sisyphus. Guarantees would fail, alliances disintegrate, defenses crumble. The French, he realized, had lost something in the crucible of war which could not be re-instilled. Something of fortitude, of character, of conviction had gone out of them. They needed a new *mystique* to foster and release a latent strength. But he did not expect to see it in his time.

[6] Charles Péguy, *Nôtre Jeunesse* (Paris: Éditions de la Nouvelle revue française, 1916), p. 60.

[7] *Le Silence de M. Clemenceau*, p. 97.

The resolution which Clemenceau had taken on retiring from politics, to confront all criticism thenceforth with dignified silence, helped to conserve his peace of mind and his reputation. He did not, however, keep the resolve uniformly. In 1922 he emerged from his retirement to undertake a short lecture tour in the United States, a tour which lasted four weeks and took him to New York, Boston, Chicago and Saint Louis. Everywhere he was accorded most generous ovations, but they were a tribute to the man rather than the statesman, and his eloquence did not persuade American audiences to approve the arbitrary attitude of the French government, then on the point of ordering troops into the Ruhr Valley in an effort to compel German reparations payments.

This visit to the United States was Clemenceau's last voyage. His remaining years were divided between the rue Franklin, Giverny, and the seaside cottage at Saint-Vincent-du-Jard. Years of study and writing, these were, of alert interest in many subjects, of quizzical comments on the human comedy. Years, too, the first in his life, of spacious and unurgent leisure for long unhurried thought. "With books, flowers and the sea," he wrote in 1923, "I am in a good retreat. For the past week I have not stirred from my window."[8] His health declined slowly as time took toll of that much-enduring frame. In 1927 a sharp drop in vitality, with diabetic complications, filled the journals with premature rumors of his approaching death, but he rallied and regained his strength in the Vendée.

The hard shell of assumed indifference, the scorn for the judgment of his contemporaries, to which he had so long pretended, concealed in Clemenceau a real and at times acute sensitivity. Concern for his fame, "that last infirmity of noble mind," grew keener as the days drew in. He sifted his papers, burned most of them, dispatched others to the *Quai d'Orsay*, and left a part in trust to be handed over to the government after twenty years.[9] His testament provided that he should be buried without ceremony and without a stone, in a plot of his own choosing in his native Vendée. But he requested that a book his mother had given him be placed in the coffin, and a wreath of withered flowers, relics of a bouquet some soldiers had presented to him on one of his visits to the front line.

These dispositions made, he waited for death, but waiting proved a tedious business. Attacks upon his war administration and peace negotiations, attacks which penetrated his reserve, inflamed his thoughts until

[8] *Le Silence de M. Clemenceau*, p. 38.

[9] Jean Jules Henri Mordacq, *Clemenceau au soir de sa vie, 1920–1929*, 2 vols. (Paris: Plon, 1933), II, 179–181.

the urge to answer overcame him. The result was *Grandeurs et Misères d'une Victoire*, twenty-three essays in defense of his official acts and decisions. This re-descent into the arena of active argument exhausted his spirit. The documents he needed to vindicate his position were not always available, colleagues to whom he appealed for confirmation on debated points were slow to answer. Himself "the living image of punctuality," Clemenceau fretted excessively at these delays, for his strength was gone; he was driving himself on his nerves with the desperate determination of a man who knows that once he pauses he may not find the energy to resume. "You will see, General, this book will kill him," [10] the devoted valet, Albert, prophesied to Mordacq, who visited the rue Franklin in the middle of November, 1929. But how could a Clemenceau die except in harness? Three days later, still dissatisfied with his revisions, he laid down his pen and took to his bed. Almost immediately a great lassitude enveloped him and he sank into an intermittent coma. A week later he was dead.

That which a man most loves, the Greek proverb runs, shall in the end destroy him. Clemenceau died as he had lived, in the midst of controversy, forging mordant arguments in defense of the causes he had pleaded, the decisions he had taken. He lived fighting and he died fighting, and he died still fighting himself. For the inspiration of his last articles was divided and for that reason exhausting; they were attempts to vindicate the policies of Clemenceau as an individual and at the same time to vindicate France. Love of France burned so fiercely in him that to the end he felt that he must assail her critics and upbraid her children for their failure to be more worthy of her. Such intense and jealous patriotism is not always a sound guide; it did not make Clemenceau a good European; it did not always make him a good Frenchman. Frequently it inspired him to push his course stubbornly athwart the sanest current opinion of his day. But right or wrong, with the majority of Frenchmen or against them, Clemenceau's patriotism, like his personal courage, had a touch of grandeur about it. Even in the most withering controversies it wrung the tribute of admiration from his opponents. As the tides of political antagonism recede his stature promises to rise higher in the memory of his countrymen, until the indomitable figure of the Tiger, transmuted into Père la Victoire, comes to symbolize the agonies, the ardors — and perhaps one must add the errors — which formed the spirit of France under the Third Republic.

[10] Mordacq, *Clemenceau au soir de sa vie*, II, 263.

BIBLIOGRAPHY

THE MATERIALS for an adequately documented life of Georges Clemenceau have not yet been collected. Of his personal papers the greater part were destroyed before his death; part were transferred to the Ministry of Foreign Affairs; and part left in trust to be turned over to the French Government in 1949. At his home in the rue Franklin, now the Musée Clemenceau, a devoted staff has preserved the library and furnishings as he left them, and is compiling a valuable bibliography for scholars. The Société des Amis de Clemenceau, an informal group of friends and admirers faithful to his memory, is reëditing his writings and collecting his fugitive articles and his correspondence for a complete edition of his works. This patient and important labor will undoubtedly clarify many incidents of his career which have hitherto been obscured by rumor and legend, and lay the basis for a definitive biography worthy of the leading statesman of the Third French Republic.

I

PUBLISHED OFFICIAL DOCUMENTS

AUSTRIA

Österreich-Ungarns Aussenpolitik, 1908–1914, ed. by Ludwig Bittner, Alfred Francis Pribram, Heinrich Srbik, and Hans Übersberger, 8 vols. (Vienna: Österreichischer Bundesverlag, 1930).

FRANCE

Améline, Henri, ed. *Dépositions des témoins de l'enquête parlementaire sur l'insurrection du 18 mars*, 3 vols. (Paris, 1872).

Annales de l'Assemblée nationale. Compte-rendu in extenso des séances, vols. I and II, 1870–1871 (Paris, 1871).

Bulletin des lois de la République Française, XII série. Premier semestre de 1907 (Paris: Imprimerie nationale, 1907).

Chambre des Députés. Affaire Dreyfus. Débats parlementaires, avril 6–7, 1903 (Paris, 1903).

Chambre des Députés. Commission d'enquête sur les affaires de Panama, 3 vols. (Paris, 1893).

Chambre des Députés. Rapport général fait au nom de la commission d'enquête sur les affaires de Panama (Paris, 1898).

Journal Officiel. Débats parlementaires. Sénat and *Chambre des Députés*, 1876–1920 (Paris, 1876–1921).

Ministre des Affaires Étrangères. Documents diplomatiques françaises. Affaires de Maroc, vol. V, 1908–1910 (Paris, 1910); vol. VI, 1910–1912 (Paris, 1912).

——— *Documents relatifs aux négociations concernant les garanties de sécurité contre une aggression de l'Allemagne, 10 janvier, 1919–7 décembre, 1923* (Paris: Imprimerie nationale, 1924).

GERMANY

Die grosse Politik der europäischen Kabinette, 1871–1914, ed. by Johannes Lepsius, Albrecht Mendelssohn-Bartholdy, und Friedrich Thimme, 40 vols. (Berlin: Deutsche Verlagsgesellschaft für Politik und Geschichte, 1922–1927).

Preliminary History of the Armistice. Official Documents published by the German National Chancellery, ed. by James Scott Brown (New York: Oxford University Press, 1925).

GREAT BRITAIN

British Documents on the Origins of the War, 1898–1914, ed. by G. P. Gooch and Harold Temperley, 11 vols. (London: H.M. Stationery Office, 1926–1938).

RUSSIA

Une livre noir, diplomatie d'avant guerre, d'après les documents des archives russes, 4 vols. (Paris: Librairie du travail, 1922–1934).

UNITED STATES

Department of State. Papers relating to the Foreign Relations of the United States. Supplements. The World War: 1914, 1915, 1916, 1917, 1918. Russia, 1918, ed. by Tyler Dennett and Joseph V. Fuller, 12 vols. (Washington: Government Printing Office, 1928–1935).

Army. American Expeditionary Force, 1917–1919. Final Report of General John J. Pershing (Washington: Government Printing Office, 1920).

GENERAL

Official Statements of War Aims and Peace Proposals, December, 1916 to November, 1918. Prepared under the supervision of James Brown Scott (Washington, 1921), Carnegie Endowment for International Peace.

Benno de Siebert, *Entente Diplomacy and the World Matrix of the History of Europe, 1909–1914*, edited, arranged, and annotated by George Abel Schreiner (New York: Knickerbocker Press, 1921).

II

PRINTED WORKS

Clemenceau's Writings

American Reconstruction, 1865–1870, with the Impeachment of President Johnson, edited, with introduction, by Fernand Baldensperger (New York: Lincoln MacVeagh, 1928).

Au fil des jours (Paris: Fasquelle, 1900).

A collection of Clemenceau's studies, portraits, travel scenes from various journals.

Au pied du Sinai. Illustrations de Henri de Toulouse-Lautrec (Paris: Floury, 1898).

Six narratives dealing with Jewish life and character.

At the Foot of Sinai, authorized translation by A. v. Ende (New York: Bernard C. Richards, 1922).

Au soir de la pensée, 2 vols. (Paris: Plon, 1927).

Clemenceau's intellectual testament, embodying his nineteenth century positivist philosophy.

In the Evening of My Thought, translated by Charles Miner Thompson and John Heard, Jr., 2 vols. (Boston and New York: Houghton Mifflin Company, 1929).

Aux ambuscades de la vie (Paris: Fasquelle, 1903).

Studies largely concerned with human character in conflict with itself and with society.

The Surprises of Life, translated by Grace Hall (Garden City: Doubleday, Page & Co., 1920).

Claude Monet: les nymphéas (Paris: Plon, 1928).

Claude Monet: The Water Lilies, translated by George Boas (Garden City: Doubleday Doran, 1930).

Clemenceau peint par lui-même, ed. by Jean Martet (Paris: Albin Michel, 1929).

Clemenceau: The Events of his Life as Told by Himself to his Former Secretary, Jean Martet, translated by Milton Waldman (London and New York: Longmans, Green & Co., 1930).

Contre la justice (Paris: Stock, 1900).

102 articles by Clemenceau on the Dreyfus Case, originally published in *L'Aurore* between December 12, 1898 and March 31, 1899.

Dans les champs du pouvoir (Paris: Payot, 1913).

Articles from *L'Homme libre*, issues of May 5 to July 13, 1913.

De la génération des éléments anatomiques (Paris: J. B. Baillière et fils, 1865), 2me édition, précédé d'une introduction par M. le professeur Ch. Robin, 1867.

Clemenceau's doctoral dissertation.

Démosthène (Paris: Plon, 1926).

A biographical study of the great Athenian whose role Clemenceau found analogous to his own.

Demosthenes, translated by Charles Miner Thompson (Boston and New York: Houghton Mifflin Company, 1926).

Discours de Guerre, publiés par les Amis de Clemenceau (Paris: Plon, 1934).

The most important articles and speeches of Clemenceau from May, 1913 to November, 1918.

Discours de Paix, publiés par les Amis de Clemenceau (Paris: Plon, 1938).

Speeches, debates, and correspondence, selected to cover the most important developments affecting Clemenceau's ministry, November, 1918 to October, 1919.

La France devant l'Allemagne (Paris: Payot, 1916).

France facing Germany; speeches and articles by G. Clemenceau, translated from the French by Ernest Hunter Wright (New York: E. P. Dutton & Co., 1919).

Articles from *L'Homme libre,* May 5, 1913 to September 28, 1914, and *L'Homme enchaîné,* October 9, 1914 to May 14, 1916.

Figures de Vendée (Paris: Maurice Méry, 1903).

Ten short stories or character sketches published between 1894 and 1897.

Figures de Vendée (Paris: Plon, 1930).

Twenty-four stories or studies, including the narratives which had appeared under the same title in 1903 supplemented by others from *Le Grand Pan, Au fil des jours* and *Aux ambuscades de la vie.*

Le Grand Pan (Paris: Fasquelle, 1896).

Sketches, narratives and short stories, composed by Clemenceau between 1893 and 1896. The volume reflects his self-education in literary style.

Grandeurs et misères d'une victoire (Paris: Plon, 1930).

Twenty-three articles of varying length, defending disputed points from the unity of command and appointment of Foch to the war debts controversy in 1926. Uneven, and at times splenetic, these essays still reflect the qualities of mind and heart which made Clemenceau great.

Grandeur and Misery of Victory, translated by F. M. Atkinson (New York: Harcourt Brace & Co., 1930).

Le Honte (Paris: Stock, 1903).

Sixty-five articles on the Dreyfus Affair, written by Clemenceau for *La Dépêche de Toulouse* between September, 1899 and December, 1900.

L'Iniquité (Paris: Stock, 1899).

One hundred sixty-two articles on the Dreyfus Affair, contributed by Clemenceau to *L'Aurore* and *La Justice* between December, 1894 and July, 1898.

Injustice militaire (Paris: Stock, 1902).

Seventy-eight articles contributed to *L'Aurore* between August and December, 1899.

Des juges (Paris: Stock, 1901).

Forty articles, still concerning *l'Affaire,* published in *L'Aurore* in April and May, 1899.

La Leçon de la Russie (Paris: L'Édition de l'Homme Enchaîné, 1915).

Fourteen articles on the Russian war effort written in 1914 and 1915.

La Mêlée sociale (Paris: Charpentier, 1895).

Articles contributed to *La Dépêche de Toulouse* in 1894 and to *La Justice* between 1893 and 1895.

Notes de voyage dans l'Amérique de Sud, Argentine, Uruguay, Brésil (Paris: Hachette, 1911).

The observations Clemenceau jotted down during his lecture tour in the summer of 1910.

South America Today: A Study of Conditions, social, political and commercial, in Argentine, Uruguay and Brazil (New York: G. P. Putnam's Sons, 1911).

An English translation of the *Notes de voyage*, issued by Fisher in London at the same time.

Pages françaises par Georges Clemenceau, edited with an introduction and notes by Régis Michaud (New York: Scott, Freeman and Co., 1921).

Twenty-two selections, well chosen, which afford a very good illustration of Clemenceau's literary ability.

Les Plus forts: roman contemporain (Paris: Fasquelle, 1898).

Clemenceau's single attempt at writing a novel, translated into English as *The Strongest* (Garden City: Doubleday, Page & Co., 1919).

Le Silence de M. Clemenceau (Paris: Albin Michel, 1929).

Clemenceau's conversation, in the post-war years, taken down and edited by Jean Martet. An English version is included in *Clemenceau: The Events of his Life as Told to his Former Secretary, Jean Martet*, listed above.

Sur la démocratie: Neuf conférences de Clemenceau, rapportées par Maurice Ségard (Paris: Larousse, 1930).

A lively series of notes on Clemenceau as a writer, a lecturer, and a traveller. Dr. Ségard accompanied Clemenceau on the trip to South America in 1910.

Le Tigre (Paris: Albin Michel, 1930).

More conversations with Jean Martet, included in the English translation, *Clemenceau: the Events of his Life*.

Vers la réparation (Paris: Stock, 1899).

One hundred thirty-five articles on the Dreyfus Case, published in *L'Aurore* at the height of the affair, July to December, 1898.

Le Voile de bonheur, pièce en un acte (Paris: Fasquelle, 1901).

Clemenceau's somewhat sardonic comedy, the chief character of which is happier while blind than after he gains his sight. The play was produced at the Théâtre de la Renaissance in 1901 and l'Opéra-Comique in 1911. It was republished in 1911, 1918 and 1930.

Biographical Studies of Clemenceau

This list of biographical material might easily be quadrupled. The works listed have been chosen because they are the best that have appeared to date, because they represent the type of study Clemenceau's turbulent character evoked, and because most of them are available in the United States.

Adam, George, *The Tiger: Georges Clemenceau, 1841–1929* (London: Jonathan Cape, 1930).

A journalistic biography, not very clear in organization and occasionally careless in regard to chronology.

Churchill, Winston S., *Great Contemporaries* (New York: G. P. Putnam's Sons, 1937).

Churchill writes of Clemenceau with high appreciation of his somber genius.

Daudet, Léon, *La Vie orageuse de Clemenceau* (Paris: Michel, 1938).

Lively, conversational, and at times frankly eulogistic, but it contains little new information. It has been translated into English by Elizabeth G. Echlin as *Clemenceau, a stormy Life* (London: William Hodge & Co., 1940).

Dubly, Henry Louis, *La Vie ardente de Georges Clemenceau*, 2 vols. (Lille: Mercure de Flandre, 1930).

Though open to criticism in matters of structure and detail, and too sympathetic in treatment, Dubly's study suggests Clemenceau's depths, culture, personal charm and generous enthusiasm more convincingly than more thorough and careful biographies. Impressionistic rather than factual.

Geffroy, Gustave, *Georges Clemenceau, sa vie, son oeuvre* (Paris: Larousse, 1919).

The sympathetic but not uncritical estimate of one who had known and worked with Clemenceau for many years.

Hyndman, H. M., *Clemenceau, the Man and his Time* (New York: Frederick A. Stokes, 1919, and London: Grant, 1919).

An ambitious and moderately successful biography, but uneven in execution and dependent upon secondary sources supplemented by the author's personal impressions.

Judet, Ernest, *Le Véritable Clemenceau* (Berne: F. Wyss, 1920).

Judet had fought Clemenceau and suffered from the Tiger's claws. This is the ablest and most savage of the hostile biographies, but it offers some keen and useful insight into Clemenceau's character and methods.

Michon, Georges, *Clemenceau* (Paris: G. Rivière, 1931).

Critical but penetrating. Michon understands better than most historians the political, economic, and diplomatic realities with which Clemenceau dealt. He is familiar with and utilizes primary source materials.

Mordacq, Jean Jules Henri, *Clemenceau* (Paris: Les Éditions de France, 1939).

The best of the shorter biographies, crisp, factual and sympathetic. Mordacq's close collaboration with Clemenceau during the second ministry makes his careful notes the most valuable source for the reconstruction of Clemenceau's administrative methods and the motives for many important decisions.

——— *Clemenceau au soir de sa vie, 1920–1929*, 2 vols. (Paris: Plon, 1933).

Anecdotes, conversations, clarifications on incidents from the earlier years, woven together with an episodic narrative of Clemenceau's life during the final decade.

Suarez, Georges, *Clemenceau*, 2 vols. (Paris: Les Éditions de France, 1932). A new and enlarged edition of the author's *La Vie orgueilleuse de Clemenceau* (Paris: Gallimard, 1930).

Popular in style, but carefully planned, based on a wide garnering of the most readily available sources, and rich in anecdote and drama. The main defect lies in the characterization. Suarez does not convey adequately the intense and tragic forces in Clemenceau which explain his influence. There is a useful list of Clemenceau's published volumes, and the printed sources upon which Suarez drew, in I, 11–15.

Diaries, Memoirs, Correspondence, Biographies

Baker, Ray Stannard, *Woodrow Wilson, Life and Letters*, 8 vols. (New York: Doubleday Doran, 1927–1939).

Bertie, Francis L., Viscount Bertie of Thame, *Diary, 1914–1918*, 2 vols. (London: Hodder and Stoughton, 1924).

Dawes, Charles G. D., *A Journal of the Great War*, 2 vols. (Boston: Houghton Mifflin Company, 1921).

Desachy, Paul, *Une grande figure de l'Affaire Dreyfus: Louis Leblois* (Paris: Rieder, 1934).

Dreyfus, Alfred and Pierre, *The Dreyfus Case*, translated and edited by Donald C. McKay (New Haven: Yale University Press, 1937).

Foch, Ferdinand, *Mémoires pour servir à l'histoire de la guerre de 1914–1918*, 2 vols. (Paris: Plon, 1931).

Gambetta, Léon, *Dépêches, circulaires, décrets, proclamations et discours de Léon Gambetta*, ed. by Joseph Reinach, 2 vols. (Paris: 1886–91).

Garvin, James Louis, *The Life of Joseph Chamberlain*, 3 vols. (London: Macmillan, 1932–34).

Grey, Edward, Viscount Grey of Fallodon, *Twenty-five Years*, 2 vols. (London: Hodder and Stoughton, 1925).

Haldane, Richard Burdon, Viscount Haldane, *An Autobiography* (New York: Doubleday Doran, 1929).

Hart, B. H. Liddell, *Foch, the Man of Orleans* (Boston: Little, Brown, 1932).

House, Edward Mandell, *The Intimate Papers of Colonel House arranged as a narrative by Charles Seymour*, 4 vols. (Boston: Houghton Mifflin, 1926–28).

Izvolsky, Alexander Petrovich, *Au service de la Russie: Alexandre Iswolsky, correspondance diplomatique, 1906–1911*, 2 vols. (Paris: Les Éditions Internationales, 1937–39).

Kokovtsov, Vladimir Nikolaevich, *Out of My Past: the Memoirs of Count Kokovtsov*, Hoover War Library Publication, No. 6, ed. by H. H. Fisher, translated by Laura Matveev (Stanford: Stanford University Press, 1935).

Lloyd George, David, *War Memoirs of David Lloyd George*, 6 vols. (Boston: Little, Brown, 1933–37).

——, *Memoirs of the Peace Conference*, 2 vols. (New Haven: Yale University Press, 1939).

Louis, Georges, *Les Carnets de Georges Louis* (Paris: Rieder, 1926).

Ludendorff, Erich, *My War Memories*, 2 vols. (London: Hutchinson, 1919).

Miller, David Hunter, *My Diary at the Conference of Paris, with documents*, 21 vols. and atlas (New York: printed for the author by the Appeal Printing Co., 1924).

Neumann, Robert, *Zaharoff*, translated from the German by R. T. Clark (New York: Knopf, 1935).

Nevins, Allan, *Henry White: Thirty Years of American Diplomacy* (New York: Harpers, 1930).

Pershing, John Joseph, *My Experiences in the World War* (New York: Stokes, 1931).

Poincaré, Raymond, *Au service de la France, neuf ans de souvenirs*, 10 vols. (Paris: Plon-Nourrit, 1926–33).

Porter, Charles W., *The Career of Théophile Delcassé* (Philadelphia: University of Pennsylvania Press, 1936).

Robertson, Sir William, *From Private to Field Marshal* (London: Constable, 1921).

Steed, Henry Wickham, *Through Thirty Years*, 2 vols. (Garden City: Doubleday, Page & Co., 1924).

Stock, Pierre Victor, *Mémorandum d'un éditeur. Deuxième série.* (Paris: Stock, 1936).

———, *Mémorandum d'un éditeur. Troisième série, L'Affaire Dreyfus anecdotique* (Paris: Stock, 1938).

Suarez, Georges, *Briand*, 4 vols. (Paris: Plon, 1936–38).

Witte, Sergei Yulievich, Count, *The Memoirs of Count Witte* (Garden City: Doubleday Doran, 1921).

Zuckerkandl, Berta Szeps, *My Life and History* (New York: Knopf, 1939).

General Works

Acomb, Evelyn Martha, *The French Laic Laws, 1879–1889* (New York: Columbia University Press, 1941).

Bernard, Léon, *La Défense de la Santé publique pendant la guerre* (Paris: Les Presses Universitaires de la France, 1929).

Bernheim, Pierre, *Le Conseil municipal de Paris de 1789 à nos jours* (Paris: Les Presses modernes, 1937).

Bourgeois, Léon, *Solidarité* (Paris: Armand Colin, 1912).

Bourgin, Georges, *Histoire de la Commune* (Paris: Cornély, 1907).

Brabant, Frank Herbert, *The Beginnings of the Third Republic in France, a History of the National Assembly, February–September, 1871* (London: Macmillan, 1940).

Brogan, D. W., *France under the Republic* (New York: Harpers, 1940).

Burnett, Philip M., *Reparations at the Paris Peace Conference from the Standpoint of the American Delegation* (New York: Columbia University Press, 1940).

Buthman, William Curt, *The Rise of Integral Nationalism in France with Special Reference to the Ideas and Activities of Charles Maurras* (New York: Columbia University Press, 1939).

Caillaux, Joseph, *Agadir: ma politique extérieure* (Paris: Albin Michel, 1919).

———, *Mes Prisons* (Paris: Aux éditions de la Sirène, 1921).

Chambers, Frank P., *The War behind the War, 1914–1918. A History of the Political and Civilian Fronts* (New York: Harcourt Brace, 1939).

Clémentel, Étienne, *La France et la politique économique interalliée* (Paris: Les Presses Universitaires de la France, 1931).

Combes, Marguerite, *Le Rève de la personnalité* (Paris: Bouvin et Cie, 1932).

Dahlin, Ebba, *French and German Public Opinion on Declared War Aims, 1914–1918* (Stanford: Stanford University Press, 1933).

Damé, Frédéric, *La Résistance: les maires, les députés de Paris, et la comité central du 18 au 26 mars, avec pièces officielles et documents inédits* (Paris: A. Lemerre, 1871).

Dansette, Adrien, *Le Boulangisme, 1886–1890* (Paris: Librairie Académique Perrin, 1938).

Driault, Édouard, and Lhéritier, Michel, *Histoire diplomatique de la Grèce de 1821 à nos jours*, 5 vols. (Paris: Les Presses Universitaires de la France, 1925–26).

Esmein, Adhémar, *Éléments de droit constitutionnel français et comparé*, 2 vols., 7th ed. (Paris, 1921).

Flourens, Émile, *La France conquise: Édouard VII et Clemenceau* (Paris: Garnier Frères, 1906).

Forster, Kent, *The Failures of Peace, the Search for a Negotiated Peace During the First World War* (Philadelphia: University of Pennsylvania Press, 1941).

Frank, Walter, *Nationalismus und Demokratie in Frankreich der dritten Republik, 1871–1918* (Hamburg: Hanseatische Verlaganstalt, 1933).

Gide, Charles, *La Solidarité* (Paris: Les Presses Universitaires de la France, 1932).

Gooch, R. K., *The French Parliamentary Committee System*, University of Virginia Institute for Research in the Social Sciences, Institute Monograph No. 21 (New York and London: Appleton Century Co., 1935).

Hart, B. H. Liddell, *A History of the World War, 1914–1918* (Boston: Little, Brown, 1935).

Herzog, Wilhelm, *Der Kampf einer Republik: die Affäre Dreyfus* (Munich: Europa Verlag, 1932).

Good brief biographical estimate of Clemenceau, pp. 107–38.

Hosse, Carl, *Die englisch-belgischen Aufmarschpläne gegen Deutschland vor dem Weltkriege* (Zurich: Amalthea-Verlag, 1930).

Humbert, Sylvain, *Le Mouvement syndical. Histoire des partis socialistes en France*, vol. IX. Publiée sous la direction de Alexandre Zévaès (Paris: Marcel Rivière, 1912).

Jacques, Léon, *Les Partis politiques sous la IIIe République* (Paris: Sirey, 1913).

Jellinek, Frank, *The Paris Commune of 1871* (London: V. Gollanz, 1937).

Jèze, Gaston, and Truchy, Henri, *The War Finance of France*, Economic and Social History of the World War, general editor, James T. Shotwell (New Haven: Yale University Press, 1927).

Laronze, Georges, *Histoire de la Commune de 1871* (Paris: Payot, 1928).

Leblois, Louis, *L'Affaire Dreyfus: l'iniquité, la réparation, les principaux faits et les principaux documents* (Paris: A. Quillet, 1929).

Levine, Louis (L. L. Lorwin), *Syndicalism in France*, 2nd revised edition (New York: Columbia University Press, 1914).

Lockroy, Édouard, *La Commune et l'Assemblée* (Paris, 1871).

Luckau, Alma, *The German Delegation at the Paris Peace Conference: A Documentary Study of the Treaty of Versailles* (New York: Columbia University Press, 1941).

March, Thomas, *The History of the Paris Commune of 1871* (London, 1896).

Marx, Karl, *The Civil War in France* (London: Martin Lawrence, 1933).

Mason, E. S., *The Paris Commune* (New York: Macmillan, 1930).

Menne, Bernard, *Blood and Steel: the Rise of the House of Krupp* (New York: Lee Furman, Inc., 1938).

Michon, Georges, *L'Alliance Franco-Russe, 1891–1917* (Paris: André Delpeuch, 1927).

Mordacq, Jean Jules Henri, *Le Ministère Clemenceau. Journal d'un témoin, novembre, 1917–janvier, 1920*, 4 vols. (Paris: Plon, 1930–31).

Mowat, R. B., *A History of European Diplomacy*, 3 vols. (London: Longmans Green, 1927).

Les Murailles politiques françaises, 3 vols. (Paris, 1875).

Nicolson, Harold, *Peacemaking, 1919, Being Reminiscences of the Paris Peace Conference* (Boston and New York: Houghton Mifflin Co., 1933).

Noble, George Bernard, *Policies and Opinions at Paris, 1919. Wilsonian Diplomacy, the Versailles Peace, and French Public Opinion* (New York: Macmillan, 1935).

Noel-Baker, Philip, *The Private Manufacture of Armaments* (New York: Oxford University Press, 1937).

Péguy, Charles, *Notre jeunesse* (Paris: Nouvelle Revue Française, 1917).

Pouquet, Jeanne Maurice, *Le Salon de Madame Arman de Caillavet* (Paris: Hachette, 1926).

Reinach, Joseph, *Histoire de l'Affaire Dreyfus*, 7 vols. (Paris: Éditions de la Reine blanche, 1901–1911).

Renouvin, Pierre, *The Forms of War Government in France*, Carnegie Endowment for International Peace, Division of Economics and History (New Haven: Yale University Press, 1927).

Schuman, Frederick L., *War and Diplomacy in the French Republic* (New York: McGraw Hill Book Co., 1931).

Schwartzkoppen, Maximilian W. von, *Die Wahrheit über Dreyfus; aus dem Nachlass herausgegeben, von Bernard Schwertfeger* (Berlin: Verlag für Kulturpolitik, 1930).

Seldes, George, *Iron, Blood and Profits* (New York: Harpers, 1934).

Seymour, Charles, *American Diplomacy during the World War* (Baltimore: Johns Hopkins University Press, 1934).

Shliapnikov, Aleksandr G., ed., *Les Alliés contre la Russie* (Paris: Delpeuch, 1926).

Statesman's Year Book, 1905–1910.

Stuart, Graham H., *French Foreign Policy from Fashoda to Sarajevo, 1898–1914* (New York: Century Company, 1921).

Tardieu, André, *France and America: Some Experiences in Coöperation* (Boston and New York: Houghton Mifflin Company, 1927).

———, *La Paix*, préface de Georges Clemenceau (Paris: Payot, 1921).

The American edition, translated as *The Truth about the Treaty* (Indianapolis: Bobbs Merrill, 1921), differs considerably from the French.

Temperley, Harold W., ed., *A History of the Peace Conference of Paris*, 6 vols. (London: H. Frowde, Hodder and Stoughton, 1920–24).

Terrail, Gabriel (Mermeix, pseud.), *Le Commandement unique* (Paris: Ollendorff, 1920).

———, *Les Négotiations secrètes et les quatres armistices avec pièces justificatives* (Paris: Ollendorff, 1919).

———, *Les Combat des trois, notes et documents sur la conférence de la paix* (Paris: Ollendorff, 1922).

Truchy, Henri, *Les Finances de guerre de la France* (Paris: Les Presses Universitaires de la France, 1926).

Tyler, J. E., *The British Army and the Continent, 1904–1914* (London: Edward Arnold, 1938).

Washburne, E. B., *The Franco-German War and the Insurrection of the Commune; Correspondence of E. B. Washburne* (Washington: Government Printing Office, 1878).

Weil, Bruno, *Der Prozess des Hauptmanns Dreyfus* (Berlin: W. Rothschild, 1930).

———, *Panama* (Berlin: W. Rothschild, 1933).

White, Harry D., *The French International Accounts, 1880–1913*, Harvard Economic Studies, vol. XL (Cambridge: Harvard University Press, 1933).

Zévaès, Alexandre, *Au temps du boulangisme* (Paris: Gallimard, 1930).

III

PERIODICAL MATERIAL

Articles

Abensour, Léon, editor, "Un grand projet de G. Clemenceau," *Grande revue*, CXXXI (1930), 529–550.

Baldensperger, Fernand, "L'Initiation Américaine de Georges Clemenceau," *Revue de la Littérature Comparée*, VIII (janvier–mars, 1928), 127–154.

Bliss, Tasker H., "The Evolution of the Unified Command," *Foreign Affairs*, I (December 15, 1922), 1–30.

———, "The Armistices," *American Journal of International Law*, XVI (1922), 509–522.

Brown, Alice P., "The Love Story of Georges Clemenceau," *The Mentor* (October 1928), pp. 17–19.

Delaisi, Francis, "Corruption in Armaments," *Living Age* (September 1931).

Delbrück, Hans, (Commentary on foreign affairs) *Preussische Jahrbücher* (Berlin: Verlag Georg Stilke, 1909), CXXXIV, 176–177.

Langer, William L., "The European Powers and the French Occupation of Tunis," *American Historical Review*, XXXI (October 1925), 55–79; XXXI (January 1936), 251–266.

Leaman, Bertha R., "The Influence of Domestic Policy on Foreign Affairs in France, 1898–1905," *Journal of Modern History*, XIV (Dec., 1942), 449–79.

Maurel, André, *Six écrivains de la Guerre* (Paris: Renaissance du Livre, 1917), essay on Clemenceau, pp. 1–24.

Mollin, Captain, "Who Started the Spy System in France?" *Catholic Mind* (New York), April 22, 1905, pp. 179–201.

Pratt, Julius W., "Clemenceau and Gambetta, a Study in Political Philosophy," *South Atlantic Quarterly*, XX (Durham, 1921), 95–104.

Renouvin, Pierre, "The Part Played in International Relations by the Conversations between the General Staffs on the Eve of the World War," *Studies in Anglo-French Diplomacy*, ed. by Alfred Coville and Harold Temperley (Cambridge: The University Press, 1935), pp. 159–173.

Sellas, Victor, "Nécessité d'une nouvelle adaptation sociale du service militaire," *Revue politique et parlementaire*, XIII (1906), 262–263.

Tardieu, André, "France et Allemagne, 1906–1909," *Revue des deux mondes*, XII (July 1, 1909), 65–98.

Winnacker, R. A., "The Influence of the Dreyfus Affair on the Political Development of France," *Papers of the Michigan Academy of Science, Arts and Letters*, XXI (1935), 465–478.

——, "The Délégation des Gauches," *Journal of Modern History*, IX (December 1937), 449–470.

NEWSPAPERS

A list of the principal French journals to which Clemenceau contributed, with the dates of his collaboration and the number of articles submitted, may be found in the biography by Henri Louis Dubly, *La Vie ardente de Georges Clemenceau*, 2 vols. (Lille: Mercure de Flandre, 1930), II, 461–462. The reaction of the French press, with copious illustrations, for the period of the First World War, may be followed in the interesting analytical work of Lucien Graux, *Les Fausses nouvelles de la Grande Guerre*, 6 vols. (Paris: L'Édition française illustrée, 1916–1920). Clemenceau's activity and influence as a writer are worth extensive study but the complete files of French journals, essential to such research, are not available in this country.

INDEX

INDEX